AMISTAD LITERARY SERIES

LANGSTON HUGHES

Critical Perspectives
Past and Present

Also by Henry Louis Gates, Jr.

Figures in Black: Words, Signs, and the "Racial" Self
Signifying Monkey: Toward a Theory of Afro-American Literary Criticism
Loose Canons: Notes on the Culture Wars
Black Literature and Literary Theory (editor)
The Classic Slave Narratives (editor)
Reading Black, Reading Feminist (editor)

Also by K. A. Appiah

Assertion and Conditions
For Truth in Semantics
Necessary Questions: An Introduction to Philosophy
Avenging Angel (fiction)
In My Father's House: Africa in the Philosophy of Culture
Early African-American Classics (editor)

AMISTAD LITERARY SERIES

LANGSTON HUGHES

Critical Perspectives
Past and Present

EDITED BY
Henry Louis Gates, Jr., and K. A. Appiah

Amistad

NEW YORK, NEW YORK

Critical Perspectives Past and Present

MICHAEL C. VAZQUEZ, *Project Coordinator*

WAYNE L. APONTE
LISA GATES
SONJA OKUN

Amistad Press, Inc.
1271 Avenue of the Americas
New York, NY 10020

Distributed by:
Penguin USA
375 Hudson Street
New York, NY 10014

Designed by Stanley S. Drate/Folio Graphics Company, Inc.
Produced by March Tenth, Inc.

10 9 8 7 6 5 4 3 2 1

Library of Congress Cataloging-in-Publication Data

Langston Hughes : critical perspectives past and present / edited by
   Henry Louis Gates, Jr., and K. A. Appiah.
       p.   cm. — (Amistad literary series)
    Includes bibliographical references and index.
     ISBN 1-56743-016-3 : $24.95. — ISBN 1-56743-029-5 (pbk.) : $14.95
     1. Hughes, Langston, 1902–1967—Criticism and interpretation. 2. Afro-
Americans in literature.   I. Gates, Henry Louis.
II. Appiah, Anthony.   III. Series.
PS3515.U274Z672   1993
818'.5209—dc20   92-45756
                                                                        CIP

Contents

ESSAYS

Preface

◆◆◆◆◆◆◆◆◆◆◆◆◆

Langston Hughes
(1902–1967)

With a career that spanned the Harlem Renaissance of the twenties and the Black Arts movement of the sixties, Langston Hughes was the most prolific black poet of his era. Between 1926, when he published his pioneering *The Weary Blues*, to 1967, the year of his death, when he published *The Panther and the Lash*, Hughes would write sixteen books of poems, two novels, seven collections of short stories, two autobiographies, five works of nonfiction, and nine children's books; he would edit nine anthologies of poetry, folklore, short fiction, and humor. He also translated Jacques Roumain, Nicholás Guillén, Gabriela Mistral, and Federico García Lorca, and wrote at least thirty plays. It is not surprising, then, that Hughes was known, variously, as "Shakespeare in Harlem" and as the "poet laureate of the Negro."

Langston Hughes was born in Joplin, Missouri, in 1902. His father, James Nathaniel, was a businessman, and his mother, Carrie Langston Mercer, was a teacher. Hughes attended Columbia University between 1921 and 1922, and received his A.B. from Lincoln in 1929. His dramatically unorthodox career included stints as a laundry boy, an assistant cook, and a busboy; he also served as a seaman on voyages to Europe and Africa. Fluent in French and Spanish, he lived for various periods in Mexico, France, Italy, Spain, and the Soviet Union. Among the "New Negro" writers of the Harlem Renaissance, Hughes had no peer as an internationalist, a citizen of the world. And yet his cosmopolitanism, rare for *any* American in his time, never displaced his passionate engagement with and commitment to African-American vernacular culture.

Hughes knew *everybody*, although almost no one knew him, or was able to penetrate the veils and masks that the truly vulnerable fabricate to present public personae to the world. Hughes's public faces—despite the fact that he sought and found refuge in his beloved Harlem, he was certainly our most public poet, speaking in one week alone to some ten thousand people—were crafted in such a way that his human substance could not be perceived from among his carefully manufactured shadows.

He was apparently a lonely man, and he suffered this isolation in the most private ways, almost never voicing it, despite the fact that he was such a public person. This irony did not escape him; he fondly quoted Dickinsons's famous lines

> How public—like a Frog—
> To tell your name—the livelong June—
> To an admiring Bog!

to express his own sense of his predicament. His acquaintances were a veritable "who's who" of twentieth-century art, from Stella Adler and Toshika Akiyashi, Thomas Mann and Dorothy Maynor, to Ezra Pound and Allen Tate, to Mark Van Doren, Kurt Weill, Max Yergan, and Yevgeny Yevtushenko. In so many ways and to so many people, Hughes was "the Negro," or at least "Negro literature," its public face, its spoken voice, its cocktail party embodiment as well as its printed texts. What Arnold Rampersad's definitive biography of Hughes makes clear is how deeply ingrained American Negro literature was in the larger American tradition—even if scholars, until very, very recently, had bracketed it, kept it a ghetto apart, as the Harlem of the American canon.

Hughes's books were reviewed widely in mainstream journals by mainstream writers, even if few understood his experiments with black vernacular forms, such as blues, jazz, and dialect. His concern for these forms were shared by his remarkably popular newspaper character, Jesse B. Semple (a.k.a. "Simple"), whose musings and exploits were published in the *Chicago Defender*. Simple's discussion of the nature of be-bop is an example of how rich Hughes's columns were; when juxtaposed against Hughes's comments about the ways that jazz informed his poetry, we begin to understand that we must learn to read Hughes in new ways, both "through" and "against" the African-American vernacular.

Hughes excels in the creation of "images, analogical, melodious, and rhythmical, with assonance and alliteration," Leopold Sedar Senghor remarks. "You will find this rhythm in French poetry; you will find it in Péguy, you will find it in Claudel, you will find this rhythm in St. John Perse. . . . And it is this that Langston Hughes has left us with, this model of the perfect work of art." In these and other respects, Hughes's best work was his vernacular poetry, cast in "the idiom of the black folk," and found especially in *The Weary Blues*, *Fine Clothes to the Jew*, and *Ask Your Mama*.

Hughes, well before his compeers, Sterling Brown and Zora Neale Hurston, demonstrated how to use black vernacular language and music—especially the blues and jazz—as a poetic diction, a formal language of poetry, and at a moment when other black writers thought the task fruitless at best, detrimental at worst. Indeed, so much of the best of the African-American literary tradition—Brown, Hurston, Ellison, Morrison—grows out of his transmutation of the vernacular into the very stuff of literature. Hughes, in other words, undertook the project of constructing an entire literary tradition upon the actual spoken language of the black working and rural classes—the same vernacular language that the growing and mobile black middle classes considered embarrassing and demeaning, the linguistic legacy of slavery. Ironically, we may fail to recognize the sheer boldness of his innovation, in large part because of the very success of Hughes's venture, as it has been adopted, accepted, and naturalized by his literary successors. Even aside from Hughes's range of interests, his command of so many genres, it is in virtue of this signal contribution that Hughes's place in American letters is secure.

The sequence of reviews that open this volume chronicle the development of Hughes's oeuvre, from his discovery of dialect to his forays into fiction and autobiography. The reviews, drawn from magazines, journals, and newspapers from the mainstream and African-American press, span the range of his career. Contemporary portraits of the man and his work, they provide a unique vantage point on the fortunes of an American original.

The ten critical essays that follow suggest the richness and ambition of his artistic project. In a deftly argued piece, Hughes's definitive biographer, Arnold Rampersad, suggests that *Fine Clothes to the Jew* is Hughes's greatest achievement, a near-perfect document of the ways and speech of poor black folk. Cannily reversing a truism of Hughes criticism, he argues that Hughes's black vernacular is the result of his distance from, not his intimacy with, folk culture; that his impressionistic recording of everyday life resulted from his impotence, his acknowledged sense of inferiority to the black masses from whom he took his voice.

Steven C. Tracy locates Hughes's poetry in the rich world of the blues tradition, tracing specific influences and detailing the history of the blues in Texas, Kansas, and Mississippi. In taking note of Hughes's debt to the blues, he tries to specify Hughes's *limitations* as well as his genius in translating the blues into poetry.

Exploring further the nature of Hughes's originality as well as his humanism, Richard K. Barksdale argues that Hughes broke with black literary tradition by turning to folk literature and song against the conventions of a black establishment bent on integration—and determined to suppress the history and culture of the "lower orders." He describes the struggle to document that culture, the orature, as the essence of his humanism, and details several literary techniques—poetic dialogue, dramatic monologue, impressionism, jazz cadences—employed in the course of that struggle. Focusing on one aspect of Hughes's technique, R. Baxter Miller assays his poetry for its lyric dimension in relation to the history of the lyric itself, from folk song to Walt Whitman.

Raymond Smith, in a portrait of Hughes's overall poetic development, argues that all of his poetry is animated by the DuBoisian struggle to reconcile the divided consciousness of the African-American—through art. Against the grain of much Hughes criticism, Smith envisions an essential continuity in all of Hughes's work, even after the poet turned to seek his audience from the black masses.

In a polemical essay, Onwuchekwa Jemie draws on poetry from the full range of Hughes's career to detail his celebration of the reservoirs of strength and power in the life and history of black America. In addition, Jemie adduces the pent-up anger and the radical, even revolutionary, ambitions expressed in the lynching poems of the 1930s and the militant poems of the 1960s.

In an acute and densely argued close reading of several poems, including "On the Road," "Big Meeting," "Home," and "Father and Son," the poet and critic James A. Emanuel shows how Hughes makes selective use of images of Christ to underscore the plight of the black masses in the face of violence and unremitting racial enmity.

In a partly biographical study, Leslie Catherine Sanders explores Hughes's ambivalent depiction of black religion and the "store-front churches" in his later plays, particularly *Tambourines to Glory*. Susan L. Blake's reading of the Simple tales, meanwhile, is concerned with Hughes's debt to the folk tradition. She maintains that Hughes's appropriation of folktales is imitated by Simple's attitude toward history: Both strive to make the past live in the present.

In the volume's final essay, Maryemma Graham focuses on Hughes's fiction of the 1930s in comparing him to Richard Wright, examining the tensions between the artist and the revolutionary, socialist realism and the blues. Sidestepping debates about naturalism and revolution, she argues that Hughes's adoption of folk art made for a new kind of realism, a literary communism or "social art," an authentically proletarian literature. In distinguishing "social art" from "racial art," she concludes that Hughes transcended the confines of race.

—*Henry Louis Gates, Jr.*

REVIEWS

THE WEARY BLUES (1926)

◆◆◆◆◆◆◆◆◆◆◆◆◆

COUNTEE CULLEN

Opportunity: A Journal of Negro Life, February 1926

Here is a poet with whom to reckon, to experience, and here and there, with that apologetic feeling of presumption that should companion all criticism, to quarrel.

What has always struck me most forcibly in reading Mr. Hughes' poems has been their utter spontaneity and expression of a unique personality. This feeling is intensified with the appearance of his work in concert between the covers of a book. It must be acknowledged at the outset that these poems are peculiarly Mr. Hughes' and no one's else. I cannot imagine his work as that of any other poet, not even of any poet of that particular group of which Mr. Hughes is a member. Of course, a microscopic assiduity might reveal derivation and influences, but these are weak undercurrents in the flow of Mr. Hughes' own talent. This poet represents a transcendently emancipated spirit among a class of young writers whose particular battle-cry is freedom. With the enthusiasm of a zealot, he pursues his way, scornful, in subject matter, in photography, and rhythmical treatment, of whatever obstructions time and tradition have placed before him. To him it is essential that he be himself. Essential and commendable surely; yet the thought persists that some of these poems would have been better had Mr. Hughes held himself a bit in check. In his admirable introduction to the book, Carl Van Vechten says the poems have a *highly deceptive air of spontaneous improvisation.* I do not feel that the air is deceptive.

If I have the least powers of prediction, the first section of this book, *The Weary Blues,* will be most admired, even if less from intrinsic poetic worth than because of its dissociation from the traditionally poetic. Never having been one to think all subjects and forms proper for poetic consideration, I regard these jazz poems as interlopers in the company of the truly beautiful poems in other sections of the book. They move along with the frenzy and electric heat of a Methodist or Baptist revival meeting, and affect me in much the same manner. The revival meeting excites me, cooling and flushing me with alternate chills and fevers of emotion; so do these poems. But when the storm is over, I wonder if the quiet way of communing is not more spiritual for the God-seeking heart; and in the light of reflection I wonder if jazz poems really belong to that dignified company, that select and austere circle of high literary expression which we call poetry. Surely, when in *Negro Dancers* Mr. Hughes says

> *Me an' ma baby's*
> *Got two mo' ways,*
> *Two mo' ways to do de buck!*

he voices, in lyrical, thumb-at-nose fashion the happy careless attitude, akin to poetry, that is found in certain types. And certainly he achieves one of his loveliest lyrics in *Young Singer*. Thus I find myself straddling a fence. It needs only *The Cat and The Saxaphone*, however, to knock me over completely on the side of bewilderment, and incredulity. This creation is a *tour de force* of its kind, but is it a poem:

> *EVERYBODY*
>
> *Half-pint,—*
> *Gin?*
> *No, make it*
>
> *LOVES MY BABY*
>
> *corn. You like*
> *don't you, honey?*
> *BUT MY BABY..............*

In the face of accomplished fact, I cannot say *This will never do*, but I feel that it ought never to have been done.

But Mr. Hughes can be as fine and as polished as you like, etching his work in calm, quiet lyrics that linger and repeat themselves. Witness *Sea Calm*:

> *How still,*
> *How strangely still*
> *The water is today.*
> *It is not good*
> *For water*
> *To be so still that way.*

Or take *Suicide's Note*:

> *The Calm,*
> *Cool face of the river*
> *Asked me for a kiss.*

Then crown your admiration with *Fantasy in Purple*, this imperial swan-song that sounds like the requiem of a dying people:

> *Beat the drums of tragedy for me,*
> *Beat the drums of tragedy and death.*
> *And let the choir sing a stormy song*
> *To drown the rattle of my dying breath.*
>
> *Beat the drums of tragedy for me,*
> *And let the white violins whir thin and slow,*
> *But blow one blaring trumpet note of sun*
> *To go with me to the darkness where I go.*

Mr. Hughes is a remarkable poet of the colorful; through all his verses the rainbow riots and dazzles, yet never wearies the eye, although at times it intrigues the brain into astonishment and exaggerated admiration when reading, say something like *Caribbean Sunset:*

> *God having a hemorrhage,*
> *Blood coughed across the sky,*
> *Staining the dark sea red:*
> *That is sunset in the Caribbean.*

Taken as a group the selections in this book seem one-sided to me. They tend to hurl this poet into the gaping pit that lies before all Negro writers, in the confines of which they become racial artists instead of artists pure and simple. There is too much emphasis here on strictly Negro themes; and this is probably an added reason for my coldness toward the jazz poems—they seem to set a too definite limit upon an already limited field.

Dull books cause no schisms, raise no dissensions, create no parties. Much will be said of *The Weary Blues* because it is a definite achievement, and because Mr. Hughes, in his own way, with a first book that cannot be dismissed as merely *promising*, has arrived.

◆◆◆◆◆◆◆◆◆◆◆◆◆

JESSIE FAUSET

The Crisis: A Record of the Darker Races, March 1926

Very perfect is the memory of my first literary acquaintance with Langston Hughes. In the unforgettable days when we were publishing THE BROWNIES' BOOK we had already appreciated a charming fragile conceit which read:

> *Out of the dust of dreams,*
> *Fairies weave their garments;*
> *Out of the purple and rose of old memories,*
> *They make purple wings.*
> *No wonder we find them such marvelous things.*

Then one day came "The Negro Speaks of Rivers". I took the beautiful dignified creation to Dr. Du Bois and said: "What colored person is there, do you suppose, in the United States who writes like that and yet is unknown to us?" And I wrote and found him to be a Cleveland high school graduate who had just gone to live in Mexico. Already he had begun to assume that remote, so elusive quality which permeates most of his work. Before long we had the pleasure of seeing the work of the boy, whom we had sponsored, copied and recopied in journals far and wide. "The Negro Speaks of Rivers" even appeared in translation in a paper printed in Germany.

Not very long after Hughes came to New York and not long after that he began to travel and to set down the impressions, the pictures, which his sensitive mind had registered of new forms of life and living in Holland, in France, in Spain, in Italy and in Africa.

His poems are warm, exotic and shot through with color. Never is he preoccupied with form. But this fault, if it is one, has its corresponding virtue, for it gives his verse, which almost always is imbued with the essence of poetry, the perfection of spontaneity. And one characteristic which makes for this bubbling-like charm is the remarkable objectivity which he occasionally achieves, remarkable for one so young, and a first step toward philosophy. Hughes has seen a great deal of the world, and this has taught him that nothing matters much but life. Its forms and aspects may vary, but living is the essential thing. Therefore make no bones about it,—"make the most of what you may spend".

Some consciousness of this must have been in him even before he began to wander for he sent us as far back as 1921:

> *"Shake your brown feet, honey,*
> *Shake your brown feet, chile,*

Shake your brown feet, honey,
Shake 'em swift and wil'— . . .
Sun's going down this evening—
Might never rise no mo'.
The sun's going down this very night—
Might never rise no mo'—
So dance with swift feet, honey,
(The banjo's sobbing low . . .
The sun's going down this very night—
Might never rise no mo'."

Now this is very significant, combining as it does the doctrine of the old Biblical exhortation, "eat, drink and be merry for tomorrow ye die", Horace's "Carpe diem", the German "Freut euch des Lebens" and Herrick's "Gather ye rosebuds while ye may". This is indeed a universal subject served Negro-style and though I am no great lover of any dialect I hope heartily that Mr. Hughes will give us many more such combinations.

Mr. Hughes is not always the calm philosopher; he has feeling a-plenty and is not ashamed to show it. He "loved his friend" who left him and so taken up is he with the sorrow of it all that he has no room for anger or resentment. While I do not think of him as a protagonist of color,— he is too much the citizen of the world for that—, I doubt if any one will ever write more tenderly, more understandingly, more humorously of the life of Harlem shot through as it is with mirth, abandon and pain. Hughes comprehends this life, has studied it and loved it. In one poem he has epitomized its essence:

Does a jazz-band ever sob?
They say a jazz-band's gay.
Yet as the vulgar dancers whirled
And the wan night wore away,
One said she heard the jazz-band sob
When the little dawn was grey.

Harlem is undoubtedly one of his great loves; the sea is another. Indeed all life is his love and his work a brilliant, sensitive interpretation of its numerous facets.

FINE CLOTHES TO THE JEW (1927)

◆◆◆◆◆◆◆◆◆◆◆◆◆

DUBOSE HEYWARD

The New York Herald Tribune, February 20, 1927

When Langston Hughes published his first volume less than a year ago under the title of "The Weary Blues" he sounded a new note in contemporary American poetry. Like practically all first books of lyric poetry the quality was uneven. At its worst it was interesting, because it was spontaneous and unaffected. At its best the poems contained flashes of passionate lyrical beauty that will probably stand among the finest examples of the author's work. This irregularity of quality is to be expected in a volume that is in a way a spiritual biography of the poet. Writing has been an escape; it has registered the depths, and it has caught the fire of the emotional crises through which its author has passed. Because Langston Hughes had suffered with intensity and re-joiced with abandon and managed to capture his moods in his book he sounded an authentic note.

Unfortunately, writing poetry as an escape and being a poet as a career are two different things, and the latter is fraught with dangers. In "Fine Clothes to the Jew" we are given a volume more even in quality, but because it lacks the "high spots" of "The Weary Blues" by no means as unforgettable as the first book. The outstanding contribution of the collection now under review is the portraiture of the author's own people. Langston Hughes knows his underworld. He divines the aspirations and the tragic frustrations of his own race, and the volume is a processional of his people given in brief, revealing glimpses. Here is a boy cleaning spittoons, who sings of his work: "A bright bowl of brass is beautiful to the Lord." And here is the psychology of the Negro man in a single stanza:

> I'm a bad, bad man
> I'm a bad, bad man
> 'Cause everybody tells me so.

8

I'm a bad, bad man.
Everybody tells me so.
I takes ma meanness and ma licker
Everywhere I go.

In "The Death of Do Dirty," "The New Cabaret Girl," "Prize Fighter," "Ballad of Gin Mary," "Porter," "Elevator Boy" and the several poems bearing the sadness of the Negro prostitute, we are given sharply etched impressions that linger in the memory.

The "Glory Hallelujah" section of the book contains a number of devotional songs which have the folk quality of the spiritual. A lovely example is the "Feet o' Jesus".

At de feet o' Jesus,
  Sorrow like a sea.
Lordy, let yo' mercy
  Come driftin' down on me.

At de feet o' Jesus,
  At yo' feet I stand.
Oh, ma little Jesus,
  Please reach out yo' hand.

From the section "From the Georgia Roads" tragedy emerges in the poignant, "Song for a Dark Girl."

Way down South in Dixie,
  (Break the heart of me).
They hung my black young lover
  To a cross-roads tree.

Way down South in Dixie,
  (Bruised body high in air).
I asked the white Lord Jesus
  What was the use of prayer.

Way down South in Dixie,
  (Break the heart of me).
Love is a naked shadow
  On a gnarled and naked tree.

"Fine Clothes to the Jew" contains much of beauty, and in most of the poems there is the same instinctive music and rhythm that distinguished the poet's best earlier work. Against this must be set what appears to me to be an occasional conscious striving for originality, as in the title, and the employment in one or two of the poems of a free verse that invades the territory of prose. But if this second book does not lift the art of the author to a new high level it does appreciably increase the number of first-rate poems to the credit of Langston Hughes, and it renews his high promise for the future.

◆◆◆◆◆◆◆◆◆◆◆◆◆◆

MARGARET LARKIN

Opportunity: A Journal of Negro Life, March 1927

In casting about for a precise category in which to identify the work of Langston Hughes, I find that he might be acclaimed a new prophet in several fields, and very likely he does not think of himself as belonging to any of them.

There is still a great deal of talk about "native American rhythms" in poetic circles, and the desirability of freeing poetry from the stiff conventions which Anglo Saxon prosody inflicted upon it. In turning to the rhythm pattern of the folk "blues," Langston Hughes has contributed something of great value to other poets, particularly since he uses the form with variety and grace.

> "De po' house is lonely,
> An' de grave is cold.
> O, de po' house is lonely,
> De graveyard grave is cold.
> But I'd rather be dead than
> To be ugly an' old."

This apparently simple stuff is full of delicate rhythmic variety through which the long ripple of the form flows boldly. The "blues" are charming folk ballads and in the hands of this real poet present great possibilities for beauty.

Ever since I first heard Langston Hughes read his verse, I am continually wanting to liken his poems to those of Bobby Burns. Burns caught three things in his poems: dialect, speech cadence, and character of the people, so that he seems more Scotch than all of bonnie Scotland. It is a poet's true business to distil this pure essence of life, more potent by far than life ever turns out to be, even for poets. I think that Hughes is doing for the Negro race what Burns did for the Scotch—squeezing out the beauty and rich warmth of a noble people into enduring poetry.

In hearing a group of young poets reading their new poems to each other recently, I was struck with their common tendency to intricacy, mysticism, and preoccupation with brilliant technique. Their poems are competent and beautiful, and the antithesis of simple. To any but other poets, skilled in the craft, they are probably as completely mysterious as though in a foreign tongue. The machine age and the consequent decline of the arts has driven many poets and artists into the philosophy that art is the precious possession of the few initiate. Poets now write for the appreciation of other poets, painters are scornful of all but painters, even music, most popular of all the arts, is losing the common touch. Perhaps this is an inevitable development. Yet the people perish. Beauty is not an outworn ideal, for they still search for it on Fourteenth street. While the poets and artists hoard up beauty for themselves and each other, philosophizing upon the "aristocracy of art," some few prophets are calling for art to come out of rich men's closets and become the "proletarian art" of all the people.

Perhaps Langston Hughes does not relish the title of Proletarian Poet, but he deserves it just the same. "Railroad Avenue," "Brass Spitoons," "Prize Fighter," "Elevator Boy," "Porter," "Saturday Night," and the songs from the Georgia Roads, all have their roots deep in the lives of workers. They give voice to the philosophy of men of the people, more rugged, more beautiful, better food for poetry, than the philosophy of the "middle classes."

This is a valuable example for all poets of what can be done with simple technique and "every day" subjects, but it is particularly valuable, I believe, for other Negro poets. Booker T. Washington's adjuration to "educate yourself" has sunk too deep in the Race philosophy. As in all American life, there is a strong urge to escape life's problems by reaching another station. "The life of a professional man must surely be happier than that of a factory worker," America reasons. "A teacher must surely find greater satisfaction than a farmer." Poets, influenced by this group sentiment, want to write about "nicer" emotions than those of the prize fighter who reasons

> "Only dumb guys fight.
> If I wasn't dumb
> I wouldn't be fightin'
> I could make six dollars a day
> On the docks,
> And I'd save more than I do now.
> Only dumb guys fight."

or the pondering on circumstance of the boy who cleans spitoons

> "Babies and gin and church
> and women and Sunday
> all mixed up with dimes and
> dollars and clean spitoons
> and house rent to pay.
>   Hey, boy!

A bright bowl of brass is beautiful to the Lord.
Bright polished brass like the cymbals
Of King David's dancers,
Like the wine cups of Solomon.
    Hey, boy!"

Yet this, much more than the neurotic fantasies of more sophisticated poets, is the stuff of life.

There is evidence in this book that Langston Hughes is seeking new mediums, and this is a healthy sign. If he were to remain the poet of the ubiquitous "blues" he would be much less interesting. He will find new forms for himself, and I do not believe that he will lose his hold on the simple poignancy that he will lose his hold on the simple poignancy that he put into the "blues" as he adds to his poetic stature. The strong, craftsmanlike handling of "Mulatto," one of the best poems in the book, the delicate treatment of "Prayer," the effective rhythm shifts of "Saturday Night" are promises of growing power.

Not all of the poems of *Fine Clothes to the Jew* are of equal merit. Many of them are the product of too great facility. To be able to write easily is a curse, that hangs over many a poet, tempting him to produce good verse from which the fine bead of true poetry is lacking. But even the most demanding critic cannot expect poets to publish perfect volumes. It ought to be enough to find one exquisite lyric like the "New Cabaret Girl" surcharged with an emotion kept in beautiful restraint.

NOT WITHOUT LAUGHTER (1930)

◆◆◆◆◆◆◆◆◆◆◆◆◆

V. F. CALVERTON

The Nation, August 6, 1930

Here is the Negro in his most picturesque form—the blues-loving Negro, the spiritual-singing Negro, the exuberant, the impassioned, the irresponsible Negro, the Negro of ancient folk-lore and romantic legend. "Good-natured, guitar-playing Jim Boy"; Angee Rogers loving Jim Boy no matter where he goes or whom he lives with; Aunt Hager, the old mammy of a dead generation, "whirling around in front of the altar at revival meetings . . . her face shining with light, arms outstretched as though all the cares of the world had been cast away"; Harriet, "beautiful as a jungle princess," singing and jazzing her life away, sneering at sin as a white man's bogy, and burying beneath peals of laughter "a white man's war for democracy"; and Sandy, seeing his people as a "band of black dancers captured in a white world," and resolving to free them from themselves as well as from their white dictators—these are the Negroes of this novel, these the people who make it live with that quick and intimate reality which is seldom seen in American fiction.

"Not Without Laughter" continues the healthy note began in Negro fiction by Claude McKay and Rudolph Fisher. Instead of picturing the Negro of the upper classes, the Negro who in too many instances has been converted to white norms, who even apes white manners and white morality and condemns the Negroes found in this novel as "niggers," McKay, Fisher, and Hughes have depicted the Negro in his more natural and more fascinating form. There can be no doubt that the Negro who has made great contributions to American culture is this type of Negro, the Negro who has brought us his blues, his labor songs, his spirituals, his folk-lore—and his jazz. And yet this very type of Negro is the one that has been the least exploited by contemporary Negro novelists and short-story writers. It has been white writers such as DuBose Heyward, Julia Peterkin, Howard W. Odum, and Paul Green who have turned to this Negro for the rich material of their novels, dramas, and stories.

13

These writers, however, have known this Negro only as an exterior reality, as something they could see, listen to, sympathize with, even love; they could never know him as an inner reality, as something they could live with as with themselves, their brothers, their sweethearts—something as real as flesh, as tense as pain. Langston Hughes does. As a Negro he has grown up with these realities as part of himself, as part of the very air he has breathed. Few blurs are there in these pages, and no fumbling projections, and no anxious searching for what is not. Here is this Negro, or at least one vital aspect of him, as he really is, without ornament, without pretense.

All this praise, however, must not be misconstrued. "Not Without Laughter" is not without defects of style and weaknesses of structure. The first third of the novel, in fact, arrives at its points of interest with a pedestrian slowness; after that it picks up tempo and plunges ahead. Unfortunately, there are no great situations in the novel, no high points of intensity to grip and overpower the reader. Nor is there vigor of style—that kind of vigor which could have made of Sandy's ambition to emancipate his race, for example, a more stirring motif. But "Not Without Laughter" is significant despite these weaknesses. It is significant because even where it fails, it fails beautifully, and where it succeeds—namely, in its intimate characterizations and in its local color and charm—it succeeds where almost all others have failed.

◆◆◆◆◆◆◆◆◆◆◆◆◆◆

STERLING A. BROWN

Opportunity: A Journal of Negro Life, September 1930

We have in this book, laconically, tenderly told, the story of a young boy's growing up. Let no one be deceived by the effortless ease of the telling, by the unpretentious simplicity of *Not Without Laughter*. Its simplicity is the simplicity of great art; a wide observation, a long brooding over humanity, and a feeling for beauty in unexpected, out of the way places, must have gone into its makeup. It is generously what one would expect of the author of *The Weary Blues* and *Fine Clothes to the Jew.*

Not Without Laughter tells of a poor family living in a small town in Kansas. We are shown intimately the work and play, the many sided aspects of Aunt Hager and her brood. Aunt Hager has three daughters: Tempy, Annjee and Harriett. Tempy is doing well; having joined the Episcopalian Church she has put away "niggerish" things; Annjee is married to a likeable scapegrace, Jimboy, guitar plunker and rambling man; Harriett, young, full of life and daring, is her heart's worry. She has a grandchild, Sandy, son of Anjee and Jimboy. And about him the story centers.

Sandy with his wide eyes picking up knowledge of life about the house; Sandy listening to his father's blues and ballads in the purple evenings, watching his Aunt Harriett at her dancing; Sandy at school; Sandy dreaming over his geography book; Sandy at his job in the barbershop and hotel; Sandy at his grandmother's funeral; Sandy learning respectability at Aunt Tempy's,—and learning at the same time something of the ways of women from Pansetta; Sandy in Chicago; Sandy with his books and dreams of education—so run the many neatly etched scenes.

But the story is not Sandy's alone. We see Harriett, first as a firm fleshed beautiful black girl, quick at her lessons; we see her finally a blues singer on State Street. The road she has gone has been rocky enough. She has been maid at a country club where the tired business men made advances; she has been with a carnival troupe, she has been arrested for street walking. We follow Annjee in her trials, and Jimboy, and Tempy. And we get to know the wise, tolerant Aunt Hager, beloved by whites and blacks; even by Harriett who just about breaks her heart. Lesser characters are as clearly individualized and developed. We have Willie Mae, and Jimmy Lane, and Joe Willis, "white folks nigger," and Uncle Dan, and Mingo, and Buster, who could have passed for white. The white side of town, the relationships of employers with laundresses and cooks, all these are adequately done. The book, for all of its apparent slightness, is fullbodied.

One has to respect the author's almost casual filling in of background. The details are perfectly chosen; and they make the reader *see*. How representative are his pictures of the carnival, and the dance at which "Benbow's Famous Kansas City Band" plays, and the gossip over back fences! How recognizable is Sister Johnson's "All these womens dey mammy named Jane an' Mary an' Cora, soon's dey gets a little somethin', dey changes dey names to Janette or Mariana or Corina or somethin' mo' flowery than what dey had."

As the title would suggest the book is not without laughter. Jimboy's guitar-playing, Harriett's escapades, the barber shop tall tales, the philosophizing of the old sheep "who know de road," all furnish something of this. Sandy's ingenuousness occasionally is not without laughter. But the dominant note of the book is a quiet pity. It is not sentimental; it is candid, clear eyed instead—but it is still pity. Even the abandon, the fervor of the chapter called *Dance*, closely and accurately rendered (as one would expect of Langston Hughes) does not strike the note of unclouded joy. We see these things as they are: as the pitiful refuges of poor folk against the worries of hard days. It is more the laughter of the blues line—*laughin' just to keep from cryin'*.

The difference between comedy and tragedy of course lies often in the point of view from which the story is told. Mr. Hughes' sympathetic identification with these folk is so complete that even when sly comic bits creep in (such as Madame de Carter and the Dance of the Nations) the laughter is quiet—more of a smile than a Cohen-like guffaw. But even these sly bits are few and far between. More than Sandy's throwing his boot-black box at the drunken cracker, certainly a welcome case of poetic justice, one remembers the disappointments of this lad's life. Sandy went on Children's Day to the Park. "Sorry," the man said. "This party's for white kids." In a classroom where the students are seated alphabetically, Sandy and the other three colored children sit behind Albert Zwick. Sandy, in the white folks' kitchen, hears his hardworking mother reprimanded by her sharp tempered employer. And while his mother wraps several little bundles of food to carry to Jimboy, Sandy cried. These scenes are excellently done, with restraint, with irony, and with compassion.

Sandy knows the meaning of a broken family, of poverty, of seeing those he loves go down without being able to help. Most touching, and strikingly universal, is the incident of the Xmas sled. Sandy, wishful for a Golden Flyer sled with flexible rudders! is surprised on Christmas Day by the gift of his mother and grandmother. It is a sled. They had labored and schemed and sacrificed for it in a hard winter. On the cold Christmas morning they dragged it home. It was a home-made contraption—roughly carpentered, with strips of rusty tin along the wooden runners. "It's fine," Sandy lied, as he tried to lift it.

Of a piece with this are the troubles that Annjee knows—Annjee whose husband is here today and gone tomorrow; Annjee, who grows tired of the buffeting and loses ground slowly; and the troubles of Aunt Hager who lives long enough to see her hopes fade out, and not long enough to test her final hope, Sandy. . . . Tempy, prosperous, has cold-shouldered her mother; Annjee is married to a man who frets Hager; Harriett has gone with Maudel to the sinister houses of the bottom. "One by one they leaves you," Hager said slowly. "One by one yo' chillen goes."

Unforgettable is the little drama of Harriett's rebellion. It is the universal conflict of youth and age. Mr. Hughes records it, without comment. It is the way life goes. Harriett, embittered by life, wanting her share of joy, is forbidden to leave the house. The grandmother is belligerent, authoritative, the girl rebellious. And then the grandmother breaks. . . . "Harriett, honey, I wants you to be good." But the pitiful words do not avail; Harriett, pitiless as only proud youth can be, flings out of doors—with a cry, "You old Christian Fool!" A group of giggling sheiks welcomes her.

Of all of his characters, Mr. Hughes obviously has least sympathy with Tempy. She is the *arriviste*, the worshipper of white folks' ways, the striver. "They don't 'sociate no mo' with none but de high toned colored folks." The type deserves contempt looked at in one way, certainly; looked at in another it might deserve pity. But the point of the reviewer is this: that Mr. Hughes does not make Tempy quite convincing. It is hard to believe that Tempy would be as blatantly crass as she is to her mother on Christmas Day, when she says of her church "Father Hill is so dignified, and the services are absolutely refined! *There's never anything niggerish about them—so you know, mother, they suit me.*"

But, excepting Tempy, who to the reviewer seems slightly caricatured, all of the characters are completely convincing. There is a universality about them. They have, of course, peculiar problems as Negroes. Harriett, for instance, hates all whites, with reason. But they have even more the problems that are universally human. Our author does not exploit either local color, or race. He has selected an interesting family and has told us candidly, unembitteredly, poetically of their joy lightened and sorrow laden life.

Langston Hughes presents all of this without apology. Tolerant, humane, and wise in the ways of mortals, he has revealed beauty where too many of us, dazzled by false lights, are unable to see it. He has shown us again, in this third book of his—what he has insisted all along, with quiet courage:

> *Beautiful, also, is the sun.*
> *Beautiful, also, are the souls of my people. . . .*

THE WAYS OF WHITE FOLKS (1934)

◆◆◆◆◆◆◆◆◆◆◆◆◆

SHERWOOD ANDERSON

The Nation, July 11, 1934

Carl Carmer went to Alabama a bit too anxious to please. He is so sunny and good-natured about everything from grits and collard greens to Scottsboro that it rather makes your bones ache. These Alabamans are so persistently and so confoundedly cute, even in their cruelties, the old aristocracy is so aristocratic and the niggers so niggery. Thank you kindly. Hand me the Bill Faulkner.

Sample, page ninety-three: "We had planned a few days' tour before the visit Mary Louise had planned was to begin. An hour or so after we had started we had seen the red-gold of the dust turn to white. Below that white surface black soil—the Black Belt from whose dark and fertile land rose pillared glories with names that are poems—Rosemont, Bluff Hall, Gainswood, Oakleigh, Farmdale, Snow Hill, Tulip Hill, Winsor, Chantilly, Athol, Longwood, Westwood, Waldwie."

Poems man? You do not make words poetic by asserting they are poetic. Where is your poetry?

The book promises well. There is poetry in the title and the foreword excites. And then, too, Farrar and Rinehart have made the book well. Physically it is beautiful and Mr. Cyrus LeRoy Baldridge has made some drawings that are charming, but for me the book doesn't come off. I have already seen that some critic has said that it was not made for home consumption and I think he is wrong. I think the Southerners will love it, particularly the professional Southerners of New York and Chicago. Mr. Stribling you are quite safe. This man will never steal your Alabama from you.

Nerts, say I. All this fuss because some Alabama farmer invites you to supper. It always did annoy me, this business, some Yank going South. No one shoots him. A Negro woman brings a cup of coffee to his bed in the morning. He eats hot bread. The hotel rooms are dirty. Now he is off. . . . "Oh this gorgeous land, home of old romance," etc., etc. Not that it isn't all true enough, if you could get below Alabama life, down into it. . . . Indiana life for that matter . . . what makes people what they are, the real feel of the life around you, get down into you, become a part of you and come out of you.

I don't think Mr. Carmer does it. He skirts it now and then and when he becomes what he really is, a very competent gatherer-up of names of fiddlers' tunes, collector of folk tales told by others, etc., the book begins to have real value. He should have confined himself to that work. The man is not a story teller.

And, as I have said, this other business, this damned halt apology before Southerners for being born a Northerner, this casualness about Southern cruelty. There is an innocent school teacher taken out to a tree and hanged because he had a relative who was a murderer. "Give me a cigarette. Let's go down to Mary Louise's house. These Alabamans are so cute, don't you think."

There is one favorite Southern tale I didn't find in the book. It is about the white farmer who came down to the cross-road general store. Several other white farmers lounging about. "Well," he says, "I killed me a nigger this morning." Silence. He yawns. "Boys," he says, "I bet you that nigger will go three hundred pounds." To make his book quite perfect, Mr. Carmer should have got that one in. It is so cute.

"The Ways of White Folks" is something to puzzle you. If Mr. Carmer goes one way, Mr. Langston Hughes goes another. You can't exactly blame him. Mr. Hughes is an infinitely better, more natural, story teller than Mr. Carmer. To my mind he gets the ball over the plate better, has a lot more on the ball but there is something missed. Mr. Carmer is a member of the Northern white race gone South, rather with jaws set, determined to please and be pleased, and Mr. Hughes might be taken as a member of the Southern colored race gone North, evidently not determined about anything but with a deep-seated resentment in him. It is in his blood, so deep-seated that he seems himself unconscious of it. The Negro people in these stories of his are so alive, warm, and real and the whites are all caricatures, life, love, laughter, old wisdom all to the Negroes and silly pretense, fakiness, pretty much all to the whites.

It seems to me a paying for old sins all around, reading these two books. We'll be paying for the World War for hundreds of years yet and if we ever get that out of us we may still be paying interest on slavery.

Mr. Hughes, my hat off to you in relation to your own race but not to mine.

It is difficult. The difficulties faced by Mr. Hughes, as a story teller, are infinitely greater than those faced by Mr. Carmer. Mr. Carmer has but to take the old attitude toward the American Negro. "They are amusing. They are so primitive." If you go modern you go so far as to recognize that Negro men can be manly and Negro women beautiful. It is difficult to do even that without at least appearing to be patronizing.

You begin to sound like an Englishman talking about Americans or a Virginian talking about a Texan. Even when you don't mean it you sound like that.

The truth is, I suspect, that there is, back of all this, a thing very little understood by any of us. It is an individualistic world. I may join the Socialist or the Communist Party but that doesn't let me out of my own individual struggle with myself. It may be that I can myself establish something between myself and the American Negro man or woman that is sound. Can I hold it? I am sitting in a room with such a man or woman and we are talking. Others, of my own race, come in. How can I tell what is asleep in these others? Something between the Negro man and myself gets destroyed . . . it is the thing D. H. Lawrence was always speaking of as "the flow." My neighbor, the white man, coming in to me as I sit with my Negro friend, may have qualities I value highly but he may also stink with old prejudice. "What, you have a damn nigger in here?" In the mind of the Negro: "Damn the whites. You can't trust them." That, fed constantly by pretense of understanding where there is no understanding. Myself and Mr. Carmer paying constantly for the prejudices of a whole race. Mr. Hughes paying too. Don't think he doesn't pay.

But story telling is something else, or should be. It too seldom is. There are always too many story tellers using their talents to get even with life. There is a plane to be got on—the impersonal. Mr. Hughes gets on it perfectly with his Negro men and women. He has a fine talent. I do not see how anyone can blame him for his hatreds. I think Red-Headed Baby is a bum story. The figure of Oceola Jones in the story, The Blues I'm Playing, is the most finely drawn in the book. The book is a good book.

THE BIG SEA (1940)

RICHARD WRIGHT

A Journal of Opinion, October 28, 1940

The double role that Langston Hughes has played in the rise of a realistic literature among the Negro people resembles in one phase the role that Theodore Dreiser played in freeing American literary expression from the restrictions of Puritanism. Not that Negro literature was ever Puritanical, but it was timid and vaguely lyrical and folkish. Hughes's early poems, "The Weary Blues" and "Fine Clothes to the Jew," full of irony and urban imagery, were greeted by a large section of the Negro reading public with suspicion and shock when they first appeared in the middle twenties. Since then the realistic position assumed by Hughes has become the dominant outlook of all those Negro writers who have something to say.

The other phase of Hughes's role has been, for the lack of a better term, that of a cultural ambassador. Performing his task quietly and almost casually, he has represented the Negroes' case, in his poems, plays, short stories and novels, at the court of world opinion. On the other hand he has brought the experiences of other nations within the orbit of the Negro writer by his translations from the French, Russian and Spanish.

How Hughes became this forerunner and ambassador can best be understood in the cameo sequences of his own life that he gives us in his sixth and latest book, "The Big Sea." Out of his experiences as a seaman, cook, laundry worker, farm helper, bus boy, doorman, unemployed worker, have come his writings dealing with black gals who wore red stockings and black men who sang the blues all night and slept like rocks all day.

Unlike the sons and daughters of Negro "society," Hughes was not ashamed of those of his race who had to scuffle for their bread. The jerky transitions of his own life did not admit of his remaining in one place long enough to become a slave of prevailing Negro middle-class prejudices. So beneficial does this ceaseless movement seem to Hughes that he has

made it one of his life principles: six months in one place, he says, is long enough to make one's life complicated. The result has been a range of artistic interest and expression possessed by no other Negro writer of his time.

Born in Joplin, Missouri, in 1902, Hughes lived in half a dozen Midwestern towns until he entered high school in Cleveland, Ohio, where he began to write poetry. His father, succumbing to that fit of disgust which overtakes so many self-willed Negroes in the face of American restrictions, went off to Mexico to make money and proceeded to treat the Mexicans just as the whites in America had treated him. The father yearned to educate Hughes and establish him in business. His favorite phrase was "hurry up," and it irritated Hughes so much that he fled his father's home.

Later he entered Columbia University, only to find it dull. He got a job on a merchant ship, threw his books into the sea and sailed for Africa. But for all his work, he arrived home with only a monkey and a few dollars, much to his mother's bewilderment. Again he sailed, this time for Rotterdam, where he left the ship and made his way to Paris. After an interval of hunger he found a job as a doorman, then as second cook in a night club, which closed later because of bad business. He went to Italy to visit friends and had his passport stolen. Jobless in an alien land, he became a beachcomber until he found a ship on which he could work his way back to New York.

The poems he had written off and on had attracted the attention of some of his relatives in Washington and, at their invitation, he went to live with them. What Hughes has to say about Negro "society" in Washington, relatives and hunger are bitter poems in themselves. While living in Washington, he won his first poetry prize; shortly afterwards Carl Van Vechten submitted a batch of his poems to a publisher.

The rest of "The Big Sea" is literary history, most of it dealing with the Negro renaissance, that astonishing period of prolific productivity among Negro artists that coincided with America's "golden age" of prosperity. Hughes writes of it with humor, urbanity and objectivity; one has the feeling that never for a moment was his sense of solidarity with those who had known hunger shaken by it. Even when a Park Avenue patron was having him driven about the streets of New York in her town car, he "felt bad because he could not share his new-found comfort with his mother and relatives." When the bubble burst in 1929, Hughes returned to the mood that seems to fit him best. He wrote of the opening of the Waldorf-Astoria:

> Now, won't that be charming when the last flophouse
> has turned you down this winter?

Hughes is tough; he bends but he never breaks, and he has carried

on a manly tradition in literary expression when many of his fellow writers have gone to sleep at their posts.

◆◆◆◆◆◆◆◆◆◆◆◆◆

KATHERINE WOODS

The New York Times Book Review, August 25, 1940

It is fifteen years since Vachel Lindsay brought a new item of literary interest to the public in the discovery of a poet who was a colored bus boy in a Washington hotel. Or had he been, some asked each other, an elevator operator? As a matter of fact, he had been a great many things, in twenty-three years of a remarkably eventful history. And neither then nor in these years since, as Langston Hughes has continued to produce sensitive and thoughtful work in prose and verse, has the full course of his extraordinary career been generally guessed. Now that it is here before us, the noteworthy quality of the poet's latest book passes well beyond the content of remarkable situation and incident. Langston Hughes's autobiography is the product and portrait of a very unusual spirit, in its narrative of crowded happenings and contrasts and the envisioning of a strange and significant time.

"The Big Sea" is the story of a Negro who began life as the child of a poor family in the Midwest in the first decade of this century, and who after that was a successful business man's son and also a teacher of English in Mexico, a night-club cook and waiter in Paris, a mess boy on freighters halfway around the world, a starving beachcomber in Genoa, a laundry hand in Washington, a student at Columbia and Lincoln Universities, and at once a participant in and a clear-eyed observer of Harlem's "Black Renaissance." The book can be followed through with fascination as a success story and chronicle of adventure, full of living individuals and colorful scenes. It can be remembered more thoughtfully as a personal re-creation of Negro life from pre-war days, through war and post-war conditions and fevers, against backgrounds of contrast both in place and time. But its profound quality and lasting worth are to be found in the fact that from first to last, through all these and other experiences and observations, it remains both sensitive and poised, candid and reticent, realistic and unembittered. "Life is a big sea full of many fish. I let down my nets and pull." It is a poet who is the fisher, and the poet's miracle of combining subjectivity with detachment is in the gathering of the nets.

When Langston Hughes made himself known to Vachel Lindsay at the Wardman Park Hotel he was poor and unhappy and almost hopeless of completing his college education, but he was by no means unlearned; his life had certainly not been tethered to monotony; he was not wholly obscure. He had been writing poetry since he left grammar school (the beginning is an amusing little tale); Carl Sandburg became his literary idol when he was in high school in Cleveland, and for four years his poems had been appearing in the Negro magazine Crisis. He was reading French before he was 17, and he wanted to write about his own people, and make them live, in stories as realistic as Maupassant's. He knew a good deal of Spanish and German, too, before he was 20, and he had had a year at Columbia. "Books happened to me," he says; and from childhood he read voraciously. Then at 21 he had a sharp reaction: he was going to see life, on his own; when he got a menial job on a freighter bound for Africa he took his books to the ship and threw them into the sea; he wanted to throw his memories out, too.

But the memories clung. And although the experiences in Paris and New York will probably catch a more general attention, some of the best writing and the most lasting interest of this autobiography are in the personal record of childhood and early youth. They were just a poor Negro family in Lawrence, Kansas, so harried by dread of "the mortgage man" that they didn't always have enough to eat. But there were memories of John Brown's raid and a grandfather with a passion for freedom and justice; there was an uncle who had been United States Minister to Haiti and dean of the first Law School at Howard University; Langston's mother drifted into domestic service (there were so few opportunities for a Negro girl), but she had gone to college, and at first she was a stenographer; and existence at home was dominated by a real personality in the grandmother, whose blood was partly Negro, partly French and partly Cherokee Indian. The boy's father, however, had left them and gone to Mexico, where a Negro had as much chance as any one to make good in business. He did make good in business; when Langston joined him, at seventeen, he was the first person the boy had ever known who cared about money for its own sake. Langston was wretched in Mexico. He hated his father. He fell ill from sheer revulsion and misery. But in wretchedness he began to write his best poems: "my best poems were all written when I felt the worst."

These chapters tell the story of a sensitive youth, and tell it memorably. The episode of the child's pseudoconversion is a little masterpiece of poignant simplicity, far removed from the bitterness or the flippancy with which the same kind of story has sometimes been treated, in other memoirs. There is a passionate sincerity here which expresses itself in unstrained directness. Whether scenes and incidents are beautiful or ugly they are set down in quiet candor, without exhibitionism or apology; and only when one looks back does one realize how much reserve there is also, and how much one has read, even in this straightforwardness, by a glimpse here and there, a curtain drawn for a moment, a suggestion.

After Mexico, and Columbia, and a Winter of reading and writing on an old hulk in the Hudson, the book's "adventure" begins: the African voyage, and then Paris. . . .

Paris in the February cold, and a Negro boy arriving with $7 to find the fulfillment of a dream. He found it, even when he was all but starving; and when he got a job in the kitchen of a famous night club he had a grand time. This was the period of the transatlantic pleasure-seekers, rushing with full purses to Montmartre; and the singer Florence from Harlem could attract hordes of rich American patrons by a simple technique of insulting them. Such bizarre people, such fantastic episodes (and a charming, sad little idyl, too), such fights! And then Italy, to become the center of attention in a kindly village that had never seen a Negro, to go through the museums of Venice with the scholar Alain Locke, to set out to visit Claude McKay at Toulon—and to wake up at Genoa penniless, purse and passport stolen on the train. So the interlude of beachcombing, with companions in similar straits, and at last a "work-away" passage home and a new period of contrast and adventure.

Among the intellectuals of his own race Langston Hughes had some reputation as a writer now, and he got $20 from Crisis for an article just as he arrived in America ("so I went to see Jeanne Eagels in 'Rain' and then 'What Price Glory' before I went home"). But in Washington, where his mother was then living, it was not easy for a Negro to find good work; the well-to-do colored people were themselves snobbish beyond belief; the laundry was disgusting; the hotel job was better (he liked to work among things to eat), but he was trying to save enough to go back to college, and he was discouraged and lonely. He used to find a refuge in the poor Negro quarter, where the people were simple and courageous; and he would try, he says, to write as they sang. Some of his best-known poems are in this book.

And after he had been "discovered" there was a university scholarship, and friendliness that conquered his shyness and plenty of intellectual companionship, and a period of strange opulence. He was sensible enough to know that New York's craze for everything Negro wouldn't last. But he was in the midst of that "Renaissance" which ranged from genuine Negro thought and activity at one extreme to the fads of white tourism to Harlem at the other; and his comprehensive picture is studded with individual portrait sketches and informed with lively thought.

In 1931, after winning several other honors, Langston Hughes received the Harmon award of $400. He had never in his life had so much money of his own. But he made up his mind now to support himself by writing. And his book ends there. Literature, too, was a big sea where one put down one's nets and pulled: "I'm still pulling," he says.

The reference to literature strikes the right note for the autobiography's climax. Engrossing as the book is in event and illuminating as commentary, "The Big Sea" is essentially an individual evocation of life, in sentiment response and penetrating clarity; and it is as literature, thus, that it is to be read, in all its vivid complexity of situation and simplicity of phrase.

SHAKESPEARE IN HARLEM (1942)

◆◆◆◆◆◆◆◆◆◆◆◆◆

OWEN DODSON

Phylon: The Atlanta University Review of Race and Culture,
Fall 1942

This Shakespeare still rolls dice in Harlem, grabs a wishbone, makes a wish for his sweet mamma, long gone, long lost; still lies in bed in the noon of the day. This Shakespeare is lazy, unpoetic, common and vulgar. In short Mr. Langston Shakespeare Hughes is still holding his mirror up to a gold-toothed, flashy nature. It is the same mirror he has held up before but somehow the glass is cracked and his deep insight and discipline has dimmed. There is no getting away from the fact that this book, superior in format, is a careless surface job and unworthy of the author Mr. Van Vechten calls the "Negro Poet Laureate," who loves his race and reports and interprets it feelingly and understandingly to itself and other races. His verse resounds with the exultant throb of Negro pain and gladness.

Once Mr. Hughes wrote

> Because my mouth
> Is wide with laughter
> You do not hear
> My inner cry;
> Because my feet
> Are gay with dancing
> You do not know
> I die.

In this volume we merely hear the laughter: loud, lewd, unwholesome and degenerate. We see and hear a cartoon doing a black-face, white-lip number, trying terribly to please the populace. None of the inner struggle is revealed, no bitter cries, no protests, no gentleness, no ladders of hope being climbed. These things are hard to say about a poet I very much admire. But they must be said.

Mr. Hughes states at the beginning of the book that this is "light

verse. Afro-Americana in the blues mood. Poems syncopated and varie-
gated in the colors of Harlem, Beal Street, West Dallas, and Chicago's
South Side. Blues, ballads and reels to be read aloud, crooned, shouted,
recited and sung. Some with gestures, some not—as you like. None with
a far-away voice." This statement screens a thousand sins. Because verse
is "light" it doesn't therefore follow that anything goes. The technique
of light verse is as exacting as that of serious verse, almost more so.

If this were Mr. Hughes' first book we would say, here is some promise but in a few years he will deepen this stream, he will broaden this
stream. But as this is his fourth volume of verse all I can say is that he
is "backing into the future looking at the past" to say nothing of the
present.

Eight sections make up the book: "Seven Moments of Love", "Declarations", "Blues for Men", "Death in Harlem", "Mammy Songs", "Ballads", "Blues for Ladies", "Lenox Avenue".

The section called "Death in Harlem" has, perhaps, some of his better
work.

> They done took Cordelia
> Out to stony lonesome ground.
> Done took Cordelia
> To stony lonesome,
> Laid her down.

Another poem in this section that has a haunting and poetic shine is
"Crossing".

The real "nitty gritty" is a poem in the "Lenox Avenue" section called
"Shakespeare in Harlem"

> Hey ninny neigh!
> And a hey nonny no!
> Where, oh, where
> Did my sweet mama go?

> Hey ninny neigh!
> With a tra-la-la-la!
> They say your sweet mama
> Went home to her ma.

But the "cup" is poems like "Hey-Hey Blues", and "Little Lyric".
Whoever drinks will choke on these.

After hearing some of these poems read aloud a fellow who hadn't
heard of Mr. Hughes said: "that Langston Hughes must be a cracker."
Lord have mercy!

FIELDS OF WONDER (1947)

◆◆◆◆◆◆◆◆◆◆◆◆

HUBERT CREEKMORE

The New York Times Book Review, May 4, 1947

This fifth book of poems by Langston Hughes is notable for the brevity and leanness of its lyrics. Many are only four to six lines long, and others would be, if the regular lines were not broken up. For instance, the last stanza of "Snail":

> *Weather and rose*
> *Is all you see,*
> *Drinking*
> *The dewdrop's*
> *Mystery.*

However, the physical appearance of a poem has little to do with its effect or its value. In most cases, the effect here is of a sudden, sensitive gasp of feeling. Often the poems project a sketchiness of image, a questionable logic (as in the lines quoted above), or a suspicion in the reader that the emotional climate has not been rendered fully.

Since the poems are so stripped, so direct, except in the abundance of repetition and abstract or general terms, their brevity allows for little expansion within the reader. Among the successful ones, "Snake," "Songs" and "Personal" have the hardness of Greek epigrams. But others—poems of nature, longing, love or "dreamdust," as one is called— are frugally romantic in treatment. Little in the book is regionally or racially inspired, and much of the latter seems strained and lacking in the easy power of Mr. Hughes' earlier poems. However, after a trite beginning, "Trumpet Player: 52nd Street" shows fine penetration in its last page.

For all its variety of subject matter, the collection seems monotonous in treatment. In spite of a certain individuality in Mr. Hughes' approach, there are such strong echoes of other poets that the names of Emily Dickinson, Stephen Crane, and a whisper of E. A. Robinson and Ernest Dowson (there are even two Pierrots and a Pierrette) keep coming to mind. "Montmartre" is pure Imagism:

Pigalle:
A neon rose
In a champagne bottle.
At dawn
The petals
Fall.

This matter of influences or resemblances is, of course, unavoidable and no censure of Mr. Hughes' work. His poems have their own qualities of delicate lyricism and honesty of vision, and undoubtedly many of them will appeal to the great audience now crying for verse that appeals to their emotions without being stereotypes of the Victorian models.

ONE-WAY TICKET (1949)

◆◆◆◆◆◆◆◆◆◆◆◆◆

J. SAUNDERS REDDING

The Saturday Review, January 22, 1949

It is a tribute to Langston Hughes's earlier accomplishments that his reputation continues undimmed by verse which of late is often jejune and iterative. Intellectual recognition of the thinning out of his creativeness is inescapable, but emotional acceptance of the fact comes hard. An old loving admiration simply will not die. It is not easy to say that a favorite poet's latest book is a sorry falling off. It is not easy to declare that "One-Way Ticket" is stale, flat, and spiritless.

The reason for this dull level of lifelessness has a simple explanation: Hughes harks back to a youthfulness that is no longer green. He has long since matured beyond the limited expressive capacity of the idiom he uses in "One-Way Ticket." It is many a year since he was the naive and elemental lyrist of "The Weary Blues" and the folklike story-teller of "The Ways of White Folks." In mind, emotion, and spirit (and in time, space, and event as well) he has traveled a "far piece," and he has not traveled in circles. The old forms, the old rhythms, the old moods cannot encompass the things he sees and understands and loves and hates now.

While Hughes's rejection of his own growth shows an admirable loyalty to his self-commitment as the poet of the "simple, Negro commonfolk"—the peasant, the laborer, the city slum-dweller—, it does a disservice to his art. And of course the fact is that Langston Hughes is not now, nor ever truly was one of the simple, common people. Back in the Twenties and Thirties, his sympathy for them had the blunt, passionate forthrightness of all youthful outpourings of emotion, but lately that sympathy seems a bit disingenuous and a bit strained, like a conversation between old acquaintances who have had no mutual points of reference in a dozen years.

As an example of the artful use of folk idiom and folk rhythm, "One-Way Ticket" will interest those who know only this volume of the author's work, but it will disappoint those who remember the beauty and brilliance of "The Dream Keeper" and "Fields of Wonder."

MONTAGE OF A DREAM DEFERRED
(1951)

◆◆◆◆◆◆◆◆◆◆◆◆◆

BABETTE DEUTSCH

The New York Times Book Review, May 6, 1951

The title of this little book of verse tells a good deal about it. The language is that of the work-a-day urban world whose pleasures are sometimes drearier than its pains. The scene is the particular part of the Waste Land that belongs to Harlem. The singer is steeped in the bitter knowledge that fills the blues. Sometimes his verse invites approval, but again it lapses into a facile sentimentality that stifles real feeling as with cheap scent. As he bandies about the word "dream," he introduces a whiff of the nineteenth century that casts a slight mustiness on the liveliest context.

Langston Hughes can write pages that throb with the abrupt rhythms of popular music. He can draw thumbnail sketches of Harlem lives and deaths that etch themselves harshly in the memory. Yet the book as a whole leaves one less responsive to the poet's achievement than conscious of the limitations of folk art. These limitations are particularly plain in the work of a man who is a popular singer because he has elected to remain one. His verse suffers from a kind of contrived naiveté, or from a will to shock the reader, who is apt to respond coldly to such obvious devices.

It is a pity that a poet of undeniable gifts has not been more rigorous in his use of them. There are several contemporaries, especially among the French, whose subject matter and whose method are not too different from his, but who, being more sensitive artists, are also more powerful. Mr. Hughes would do well to emulate them.

SIMPLE TAKES A WIFE (1953)

◆◆◆◆◆◆◆◆◆◆◆◆◆

CARL VAN VECHTEN

The New York Times Book Review, May 31, 1953

It is not as generally known as it should be that Langston Hughes laughes with, cries with, and speaks for, the Negro (in all classes) more understandingly, perhaps, than any other writer. Harlem is his own habitat, his workshop and his playground, his forte and his dish of tea. He is so completely at home when he writes about Harlem that he can afford to be both careless and sloppy. In his Simple books he is seldom either, and "Simple Takes a Wife" is a superior achievement to the first of the series, "Simple Speaks His Mind." The new book is more of a piece, the material is more carefully and competently arranged, more unexpectedly presented; it is more brilliant, more skillfully written, funnier, and perhaps just a shade more tragic than its predecessor.

The genre has been employed extensively by other writers: by Finley Peter Dunne in "Mr. Dooley," by A. Neil Lyons in "Arthurs" and by Joel Chandler Harris in "Uncle Remus"; it is not too far, indeed, from the scheme of Gorky's "The Lower Depths." The locale, however, is original, the taste truly Harlem, the matters discussed pertinent to the inhabitants, and the effect prevailingly evocative. The question and answer formula is used throughout the book, but frequently Simple's replies are somewhat protracted. The views expressed for the most part have a sane basis, and it is probable that at least a modicum of these are the beliefs of Mr. Hughes himself, although they find expression on Simple's tongue.

It would be easy to refer to the author as the Molière of Harlem who has just got around to writing his "School for Wives" (or is it his "School for Husbands"?) At any rate, Mr. Hughes (himself a bachelor) seems to be as cynical in his viewpoint as Colette, when he deals with the war between the sexes. Here and there he suggests that he is writing the Harlem version of Colette's "Cheri."

There are several women in this book. The first is Mabel, "the woman like water." "'Do you want me to tell you what that woman was like? Boy, I don't know. She was like some kind of ocean, I guess, some kind of great big old sea, like the water at Coney Island on a real hot day, cool and warm all at once—and company like a big crowd of people—also like some woman you like to be alone with, if you dig my meaning. Yet and still, I wasn't in love with that woman.'" Simple passes on to other conquests and to discussions of other ideas. For instance, in chapter seven there is a long and cheerful lesson in English grammar and usage. Chapter two is an addition to the folklore of Harlem, in which Simple describes the custom under which each roomer in a house is allotted a different ring.

"'Joyce's landlady objects to my ringing her bell late. Seven rings is a lot for ten or eleven o'clock at night. So I go at six-thirty or seven. Then, I have only to ring once, which is seven times. If I go later, and nobody hears me, I have to ring twice, which is fourteen times. And, if I ring three times, which is three times seven, twenty-one times is too much for the landlady's nerves.

"'Colored rooming houses certainly have a lot of different bell signals,' I commented.

"'You told that right,' said Simple. 'I lived in a house once that had up to twenty-one rings, it were so full of roomers. Mine was twelve. I often used to miss count when somebody would ring. One time I let in another boy's best girl friend—she were ringing eleven. He had his second best girl friend in the room.'"

Somewhat further on, there is a learned discussion of Bebop, which Simple declares has its origin in the police habit of beating up Negroes' heads. "'Every time a cop hits a Negro with his billy club that old club says Bop! Bop! . . . BE-BOP! . . . MOP! . . . BOP!'"

In chapter sixteen, Simple and Joyce, his lady friend, warmly discuss the disturbing subject of miscegenation. There is a touch of Mr. Hughes' special kind of poetry in his description of night: "'Night, you walk easy, sit on a stoop and talk, stand on a corner, shoot the bull, lean on a bar, ring a bell and say "Baby, here I am."'" In chapter fifty-seven, Simple dilates on the unpleasant connotations of the word black. "'What I want to know,' asks Simple, 'is where white folks gets off calling everything bad *black?* If it is a dark night, they say it's *black* as hell. If you are mean and evil, they say you got a *BLACK* heart. I would like to change all that around and say that the people who Jim Crow me have a WHITE heart. People who sell dope to children have got a WHITE mark against them. And all the gamblers who were behind the basketball fix are the WHITE sheep of the sports world.'"

This is true humor with a bite to it, spoken in the authentic language of 135th Street and set down good-naturedly in a book which tells us more about the common Negro than a dozen solemn treatises on the "race question."

I WONDER AS I WANDER (1956)

◆◆◆◆◆◆◆◆◆◆◆◆◆

J. SAUNDERS REDDING

The New York Herald Tribune, December 23, 1956

Traveling is a sort of disease that seems to strike writers with a particular virulence—and again and again. One good bout of it immunizes most people, but not writers: they never seem able to build up a natural resistance, and probably would not if they could, for it appears that most of today's writers are convinced that travel fertilizes talent and that great sieges of it, endured periodically, are a guarantee against sterility. Considering the dozens of writers of another time who almost literally never left their own back yards, the proposition that travel is especially good for writers is debatable.

On the other hand, Langston Hughes seems to prove that it is not particularly harmful either. He started early enough. When his first book was published in 1926 he had already traveled across the northern continent through most of the United States and, as a merchant seaman barely out of knickers, to a great deal of the Western World. At a tender age he knew Mexico, where he went to live for a time with his father, and practically all of the Americas south from Toluca to Tierra del Feugo. What he saw he recorded in "The Big Sea," a book which one supposes stands as the first volume of his "autobiographical journey."

"I Wonder as I Wander" is the second volume. Here he takes us first to the eastern half of the world—from Moscow to Ashkhabad, to Tashkent, to Samarkand to Shanghai—and eventually to Spain.

At the height of the depression, with twenty-one other American Negroes, Hughes went to Russia, at that country's invitation, to make an American Negro film. Hughes' job was to write the scenario, but when he got there all of it had been written "by a famous Russian writer who had never been to America," but written so badly that the most drastic surgery of revision could not save it. The film was never made, but Hughes stayed in the U.S.S.R. a year, traveling the length and breadth of that vast land and writing for Soviet publications. Coming

35

home by way of China, he had scarcely reached California before he was off again to Spain.

The adventures Hughes had move through a scale from the bathetic to the bizarre and involve not only such an incredible character as Emma Harris, an American Negro woman who, stranded in Czarist Russia forty years ago, was known to the Soviets as the "Mammy of Moscow," but Arthur Koestler, Ivy Litvinoff, Ernest Hemingway, Karl Radek and Leland Stowe. Such names of course have special attraction—and so, it might be said, does the personality of the author.

"I Wonder as I Wander" is frank and charming, though neither events nor people are seen in depth. Mr. Hughes, it seems, did more wandering than wondering.

SELECTED POEMS (1959)

◆◆◆◆◆◆◆◆◆◆◆◆

JAMES BALDWIN

The New York Times Book Review, March 29, 1959

Every time I read Langston Hughes I am amazed all over again by his genuine gifts and depressed that he has done so little with them. A real discussion of his work demands more space than I have here, but this book contains a great deal which a more disciplined poet would have thrown into the waste-basket (almost all of the last section, for example).

There are the poems which almost succeed but which do not succeed, poems which take refuge, finally, in a fake simplicity in order to avoid the very difficult simplicity of the experience! And one sometimes has the impression, as in a poem like "Third Degree"—which is about the beating up of a Negro boy in a police station—that Hughes has had to hold the experience outside him in order to be able to write at all. And certainly this is understandable. Nevertheless, the poetic trick, so to speak, is to be within the experience and outside it at the same time— and the poem fails.

Mr. Hughes is at his best in brief, sardonic asides, or in lyrics like "Mother to Son," and "The Negro Speaks of Rivers." Or "Dream Variations":

> *To fling my arms wide*
> *In some place of the sun,*
> *To whirl and to dance*
> *Till the white day is done.*
> *Then rest at cool evening*
> *Beneath a tall tree*
> *While night comes on gently,*
>   *Dark like me—*
> *That is my dream!*
>
> *To fling my arms wide*
> *In the face of the sun.*
> *Dance! Whirl! Whirl!*

> *Till the quick day is done.*
> *Rest at pale evening . . .*
> *A tall, slim tree . . .*
> *Night coming tenderly*
>   *Black like me.*

I do not like all of "The Weary Blues," which copies, rather than exploits, the cadence of the blues, but it comes to a remarkable end. And I am also very fond of "Island," which begins "Waves of sorrow / Do not drown me now."

Hughes, in his sermons, blues and prayers, has working for him the power and the beat of Negro speech and Negro music. Negro speech is vivid largely because it is private. It is a kind of emotional shorthand— or sleight-of-hand—by means of which Negroes express, not only their relationship to each other, but their judgment of the white world. And as the white world takes over this vocabulary—without the faintest notion of what it really means—the vocabulary is forced to change. The same thing is true of Negro music which has had to become more and more complex in order to continue to express any of the private or collective experience.

Hughes knows the bitter truth behind these hieroglyphics, what they are designed to protect, what they are designed to convey. But he has not forced them into the realm of art where their meaning would become clear and overwhelming. "Hey, pop!/ Re-bop!/ Mop!" conveys much more on Lenox Avenue than it does in this book, which is not the way it ought to be.

Hughes is an American Negro poet and has no choice but to be acutely aware of it. He is not the first American Negro to find the war between his social and artistic responsibilities all but irreconcilable.

TAMBOURINES TO GLORY (1959)

GILBERT MILLSTEIN

The New York Times Book Review, November 23, 1958

About the most convenient capsule description of this short novel by Langston Hughes is to call it a sort of Negro "Elmer Gantry," mildly sardonic where Sinclair Lewis' gaudy assault on evangelism was savage, and gently funny where the other was undeviatingly and harshly satirical. As a literary work, "Tambourines to Glory," is skillful and engaging—the consistently high quality of Hughes' production over the years is, considering its great quantity, a remarkable phenomenon and the mark of an exuberant professionalism. Yet in the end, the book is a minor effort, a side glance at a major phenomenon, with an industriously contrived climax.

The phenomenon Hughes has chosen to examine here is the rise (over the last couple of decades) of a vagrant type of church in Harlem—the sidewalk, storefront, basement, apartment, abandoned-theatre church. It is fervently Christian, of course, in its origins; it is carefully non-denominational. Sometimes it is used, with equal fervor, by hustlers out for an easy buck. In his two protagonists—the stolid Essie Belle Johnson, and the free-and-easy Laura Wright Reed—Hughes offers the reader an example, respectively, of the honest Christian and the cynical operator in search of a Cadillac.

Essie Belle and Laura team up with nothing much more between them than a tambourine; an $18.50 installment-plan Bible and a street corner. From there, they progress to an apartment and from there to an aged theatre. Along the way Essie Belle piles up riches in Heaven and enough money to bring her pretty teen-age daughter, Marietta, up North to live with her. Sister Laura acquires her Cadillac and her fancy man. This character, Big-Eyed Buddy Lomax, has a connection downtown with the numbers people. He first persuades Laura to bottle tap-water and sell it as consecrated essence of Jordan. Later, she gives out "lucky texts" from the Bible at prayer meetings to increase his numbers take.

The odd partnership between Essie Belle and Laura is ended violently when Buddy tries to move in on Marietta and is stabbed to death by Laura. Laura tries to pin the killing on Essie Belle but is first turned in by another member of the congregation who witnessed it. She repents behind bars. Essie Belle praises the Lord and goes on to greater glory.

What has happened here, in the reviewer's opinion, is that the author elected to avoid the serious implications of his thesis. He has done it gracefully, it is true, but he *has* avoided it. The technique of using humor to make a point in deadly earnest is as old as mankind—Hughes has done it innumerable times and with great success in his "Simple" stories. In "Tambourines to Glory," it has fogged up the things he clearly meant to say.

ASK YOUR MAMA (1961)

RUDI BLESH

The New York Herald Tribune, November 26, 1961

Jazz and the blues have been with us all the years of this century; Langston Hughes not quite that long—"jazz poetry" began in 1926 with his well-remembered volume, "The Weary Blues." Now, with "Ask Your Mama," it begins to appear that perhaps we have as little understood the poet as the music. For, though jazz is "good time" music, within it has always been something else, something dark yet shining, harsh yet gentle, bitter yet jubilant—a Freedom Song sung in our midst unrecognized all these years. Just so, opening the covers of this gaily-designed book is to find poetry whose jazz rhythms hide the same fire and steel.

Langston Hughes is no mere observer of Africa's stormy, shuddering rise and the awakening of dark-skinned peoples all over the world. They are his people; he sings their marching Jubilees. But Langston Hughes is also an American; he sings to all of us, of the freedom that must go to all before it can be freedom for any.

"Go ask your Mama" is the retort—half-derisive, half-angry—to the smug, the stupid, the bigoted, the selfish, the cruel, and the blind among us, all those to whom these truths that America was built upon, are, even today, not yet self-evident.

With this great theme, a talented poet finds a universal voice. Like Satchmo's golden trumpet and Yardbird's blues-haunted alto, the poetry of Langston Hughes sings for—and to—all of us.

THE PANTHER AND THE LASH (1967)

◆◆◆◆◆◆◆◆◆◆◆◆◆

W. EDWARD FARRISON

College Language Association Journal, March 1968

This collection of poems was prepared for publication by the author himself and was in press when he died. Its title was derived from two recent outgrowths of matters racial in America—the Black Panthers and the white backlash. The work is dedicated to Mrs. Rosa Parks of Montgomery, Alabama, who refused to move to the back of a bus, "thus setting off in 1955 the boycotts, the sit-ins, the Freedom Rides, the petitions, the marches, the voter registration drives, and *I Shall Not Be Moved*." Twenty-six of the seventy poems in the collection were selected from Hughes's previously published volumes of verse. The other forty-four are herein first published in one volume, seventeen of them having formerly appeared in periodicals, and twenty-seven now appearing in print for the first time. All of them are indeed poems of our times, for all of them pertain directly or indirectly to the Negro's continuing struggle to achieve first-class citizenship in America. The poems are written in short-line free verse or in occasional rhymes, by both of which Hughes's poetic work has long been distinguished.

The selections are grouped under seven headings, the first of these being "Words on Fire." In this group is "The Backlash Blues," one of the two title poems in the collection. Not only is this one of the new poems but also it has been said to have been the last poem that Hughes submitted for publication before he died. It is an emphatic expression of determined aggressiveness against the opponents of civil rights for Negroes. Also in the first group and new is "Black Panther," the other title poem. Avowedly militant, like Claude McKay's "If We Must Die," this poem has for its theme the determination of black men to give no further ground to oppressors but to stand and fight back desperately, like a panther when cornered.

More ironical than militant is the group called "American Heartbreak," in whose initial poem with the same title a Negro declares generically that "I am the American heartbreak— / The rock on which

Freedom / Stumped its toe—" Still more ironical as a whole is the group called "The Bible Belt"—a group in which life principally in Alabama and Mississippi is portrayed at its non-Biblical worst. Singularly memorable as well as new is the poem in this group entitled "Birmingham Sunday," which consists of reflections on the deaths of four little Negro Sunday-school girls who were victims of the bombing of a church in Birmingham on September 15, 1963.

Especially noteworthy at present because of prevailing international affairs is the small group entitled "The Face of War." Two provocative poems in this group are "Mother in Wartime" and "Without Benefit of Declaration," both of which deal with the common failure to understand the wherefores and the futility of war. The mother, "Believing everything she read / In the daily news," was quite unaware that both sides "Might lose." Meanwhile the draftee must go "Out there where / The rain is lead," but is told "Don't ask me why. / Just go ahead and die." What simple, convincing explanatory declaration is there to give him? Alas one is reminded of John Dewey's all but forgotten observations that "The more horrible a depersonalized scientific mass war becomes, the more necessary it is to find universal ideal motives to justify it"; and "The more prosaic the actual causes, the more necessary is it to find glowingly sublime motives."

The group puckishly entitled "Dinner Guest: Me" satirizes a variety of things. Its title poem, which is based on a personal experience, ridicules white quasi-liberalism. "Un-American Investigators" coarsely twits a Congressional committee for its arbitrary methods of dealing with persons summoned before it. "Cultural Exchange," the longest poem in the volume, envisions a radical change in Southern culture in the sociological sense—an inversion of the positions of Negroes and white people in the South with Negroes living "In white pillared mansions," white sharecroppers working on black plantations, and Negro children attended by "white mammies." The *bouleversement* imagined in this poem, which was published in *Ask Your Mama* in 1961, is more ingeniously recounted in "Rude Awakening" in *Simple's Uncle Sam*, which was published in 1965.

Finally there is the group called "Daybreak in Alabama"—a title in which there is a ray of hope for the optimistic, among whom Hughes belonged. As should now be evident, two of the poems in this group rang with prophetic tones when they were published in *One-way Ticket* in 1949. Observing that first-class citizenship would never come "Through compromise and fear," "Democracy," now entitled "Freedom," left no doubt that other means of achieving it must be employed. And admonishing America to "Beware the day" when Negroes, "Meek, humble, and kind," changed their minds, "Roland Hayes Beaten," now entitled "Warning," foreshadowed at least implicitly the various freedom movements mentioned in the dedication of *The Panther and the Lash*. From the beginning of his career as an author, Hughes was articulate in the Negro's struggle for first-class citizenship. It is indeed fitting that this volume with which his career ended is a vital contribution to that struggle as well as to American poetry.

◆◆◆◆◆◆◆◆◆◆◆◆◆

LAURENCE LIEBERMAN

Poetry, August 1968

A leaning to classicism in American poetry, after fifty years of dominant modernism, will elicit cheers in some quarters; but a handful of terse epigrams, in flawlessly wrought couplets and quatrains, cannot seriously rival, much less supplant, the ascendancy of the avant garde, however poisonous the latter may have become in its persistent anti-formalism:

> "A dead tradition! Hollow shell!
> Outworn, outmoded—time it fell.
> Let's make it new. Rebel! Rebel!"
> Said cancer-cell to cancer-cell.

A number of John Nims's punctiliously charming new poems achieve perfection of a kind—my favorites are the confessions of an aging, but perseverant, lover ("The soul can cope. The trick's keep flesh alive"). *Of Flesh and Bone* is an entertaining, unpretentious book—but it is very short, under 300 lines in all.

What is most lacking in Nim's book is the full human personality that streams through Paul Goodman's *Hawkweed:*

> Indeed, these days my contempt
> for the misrulers of my country
> is icy and my indignation raucous.
> Once American faces
> were beautiful to me,
> I was their loyal lover,
> but now they look cruel
> and as if they had narrow thoughts.
> Their photographs in *Life*
> devastate my soul
> as their gasoline denudes
> the woods of Indochina.
> Let me go into exile

> —a poet needs to praise.
> It is wicked to live
> where I do not care for the people.

The quality I find most refreshing in Goodman's poetry is his constant bearing down on the diamond-bright bedrock of experience, and his ability to transmit those rare invigorating moments of beauty of personal revelation from the wide stretch of his years of intense productivity. Much of *Hawkweed* reads like a diary or journal. The many poems entitled *Long Lines* recall to mind, but only as a device, Norman Mailer's *Short Hairs*. While Mailer's marginal poetry is merely a slick medium for incidentals, Goodman's marginal poems are telling, often painful-to-read, footnotes to his public life. I'm constantly reminded of this, even as I chide at the evident scrappiness of so many of the poems. They are a vital testament of one of the most interesting minds of our time.

Goodman's uncompromising judgments of American society and politics are delivered with thunderous honesty and clarity in his prose. In the poems, he vacillates between raw self-exposure and bewilderment at his failure to set things right for himself, his family, or his country, despite his incredible creative energy and output, as well as his genius for getting across to the younger generation:

> Three years I made a thousand pages
> And a hundred flights across America
> And kept an ill-starred love affair alive.

It is his lover's quarrel with the country that I'm grateful to find he's keeping alive in the poems, and that is what gives his poetry a kind of superabundant life that is rare today. Goodman is constantly spilling over in his art, as in his love life: "Oh the beauty and the madness and the strangeness / of my six lovers astonishes me", but we can allow his excesses if we view them as a necessary surfeit of his Elizabethan dynamism.

Langston Hughes's new poems, written shortly before his death last summer, catch fire from the Negro American's changing face. To a degree I would never have expected from his earlier work, his sensibility has kept pace with the times, and the intensity of his new concerns—helping him to shake loose old crippling mannerisms, the trade marks of his art—comes to fruition in many of the best poems of his career: *Northern Liberal, Dinner Guest: Me, Crowns and Garlands*, to name a few.

Regrettably, in different poems, he is fatally prone to sympathize with starkly antithetical politics of race. A reader can appreciate his catholicity, his tolerance of all the rival—and mutually hostile—views of his outspoken compatriots, from Martin Luther King to Stokely Carmichael, but we are tempted to ask, what are Hughes's politics? And if he has none, why not? The age demands intellectual commitment from its spokesmen. A poetry whose chief claim on our attention is moral, rather than aesthetic, must take sides politically. His impartiality is supportable in *Black Panther*, a central thematic poem of *The Panther and the Lash*. The panther, a symbol of the new Negro militancy, dramatizes the shift in politics from non-violence to Black Power, from a defensive to an offensive stance: Hughes stresses the essential underlying will to survival—against brutal odds—of either position. He is less concerned with approving or disapproving of Black Power than with demonstrating the necessity and inevitability of the shift, in today's racial crisis.

Justice, an early poem that teaches the aesthetic value of rage, exhibits Hughes's knack for investing metaphor with a fierce potency that is as satisfying poetically as it is politically tumultous:

> That justice is a blind goddess
> Is a thing to which we black are wise:
> Her bandage hides two festering sores
> That once perhaps were eyes.

But this skill is all but asphyxiated in many of the new poems by an ungovernable weakness for essayistic polemicizing that distracts the poet from the more serious demands of his art, and frequently undermines his poetics. Another technique that Hughes often employs successfully in the new poems is the chanting of names of key figures in the Negro Revolution. This primitive device has often been employed as a staple ingredient in good political poetry, as in Yeats's *Easter 1916*. But when the poem relies too exclusively on this heroic cataloguing—whether of persons or events—for its structural mainstay, as in *Final Call*, it sinks under the freight of self-conscious historicity.

A virtuoso of many talents, George Garrett vivifies the interior life of a gallery of offbeat characters in his dramatic monologues. In *Ventriloquist's Dummy*, one of the slower-paced short pieces, nearly every line contains firecrackery images, flashing and spitting a trail of sparks:

> *He* with a tongue of raw meat,
> teeth like tombstones, joints as free
> and supple as rawhide, catgut,
> what does *he* know?
>
> I sing you a wooden verse.
> I clack and crack my jokes. . . .

But in longer poems like *Salome*, his style varies from a memorable and distinctive language ("my mouth, my lips, / a red yawn, a taut shriek, my tongue / fluttered like a dead leaf . . .") to the language of journalistic blandness; from a scissoring just out-of-balance rhythm to rhythms that

all seem to run one way, all at the same speed, and often—for my ear—
too fast for the pace of his thought. I get the impression that the slack
passages were composed with haste by a fast typist at one sitting. At
such times, I'd like to confine Garrett to a locked cell with a scratchy
old-fashioned quill pen.

His vivid characterization and talent for satire, strengths evidently
acquired in the development of his fiction, carry over best into two story-
telling poems, *Excursion* and *Egyptian Gold*. Garrett is most brilliant
when he sets himself to many tasks at once. Since his style is usually
clean and fluent, a complex poem can carry much thematic baggage, and
perform on many levels, without growing prolix or heavy-handed. He
has mastered, in these poems, that art of oddly opposed juxtapositions:
the clash of contrary personalities, divergent societies, and historically
irreconcilable ideas. All are geared to a common scale by the poet's
comprehensive wit.

Carl Rakosi's chief strength is the constant surgical purposefulness
in the management of his line—each line is an incision, adroitly executed
with care for tone and measure. Only rarely does a reader sense a lapse
in the controlling hand behind the line. But the surprises of the line-to-
line ingenuity are not enough to sustain the structure. In the best poems,
imagistic adventurousness—alluring to the ear and eye—saves the arbitrary framework, a verbal necessity inhering in the poem's music, as in
Equipoise:

> This commanding
> young head
> which outshines
> its antecedents,
>   magnificent
> and mortal
> compound on a tower,
> burns
>   with the cautery
> of affection.
>
> Therefore, flash
> and magnify
> the canons of perfection
>   in an ankle,
> in the waistline,
>   in the private
> morals of this lady.

In most poems, however, the enticing sequence of images is interrupted
by turn of wit, the voice skipping from imagism to clever fancifulness.

Usually, the formal observation and wry extraneous remarks don't mix well, causing a disjunction in the poem's structure. A studied lightness—the insistent illogic of associations—is pursued programmatically as a technique; it becomes, finally, as predictable and unvivacious as ordinary discursive prose.

Ideas in Rakosi's poems are usually delivered obliquely, weaving, at odd angles, through a field of essentially "unconnected images". A few lines of personal discovery seem in deadly earnest, but they are quickly resorbed in the poem's prevailing timbre of whimsy and archness. All parts of the poem's content are reduced to inert components of an over-tenacious line movement. Due to this quality of reductiveness, a single aspect of style—the line-weave—dominates all other quantities in the poems. This disturbing mannerism often leaves me feeling as though I'm reading the same poem over and over as I move through the book, despite a resourceful variety of subjects.

The career in poetry of Peter Viereck, perhaps more than that of any other writer of our time, can be viewed as an experiment in the symbiosis of poetry and politics. *The New Cultural Blues*, his best satire, draws on a complex linguistic and sociological intelligence. I can't recall when, if ever, these two cultures (language and social science) have been embraced by a more consolidating sensibility. His best satires are memorable events in the history of ideas, without loss of art.

Viereck's earliest poetry served him as an extension of political consciousness into a medium in which paramount ideas of our era could be abstracted from their worrisome contexts in international affairs and viewed freshly and intrinsically through the symbolic machinery of art. Poetry later became for Viereck a mind-style for escaping the risks of socio-political consciousness in playful, if ingenious, literary word puzzles. But in his most recent work, in going still further beyond literal reality, Viereck returns to full human force and wholeness. Enacted before our eyes in *Five Walks on the Edge* is the drama of aspiring spirit in search of the mindlessness of supra-being, the poet attaining a larger totality of mind than ever before in *Counter-Walk, Reversals*, the superb poem that ends the book. Foregoing his former escape of spiritual transcendence, there is a new toughness in immanence, identification with the indwelling natural forces in rivers, trees, cliffs, rock, mud. In *River*, a voyage of man's spirit is symbolized, but an equal interest is generated in the sheer fun of letting the river be itself, speak its being, act out its life of surfaces, appearances: nothing *is* but what can be seen, touched, poured. If the poet's mental life, a see-sawing fluid motion, is particularized and embodied in the river's cycles, his fascination with the actual properties of the river is so intense it threatens to steal attention away from its symbolic value. It is a vision in which we feel "body is not bruised to pleasure soul", nor ideas lost to things. No portion of sensibility is sacrificed or compromised to any other. The political man is perfecting his anti-self in apolitical forms and spirits in nature.

I'm particularly struck with the original design of this book, the organization taking account of Viereck's development as a cyclic eternal return to key themes, an ascent along many separate spirals: not a mere chronology. This method of arrangement befits Viereck's work more than it would the work of most other poets, but all can profit by the example— especially in what it tells of a man's style of guiding the growth of his art over a thirty-year period.

ESSAYS

◆◆◆◆◆◆◆◆◆◆◆◆◆

Hughes's *Fine Clothes to the Jew*

ARNOLD RAMPERSAD

As prolific as Langston Hughes strove to be in a variety of genres—poetry, fiction, drama, and essays notably—he saw himself from first to last primarily as a poet. Of his many collections of verse, nine must be considered major in his career by almost any accounting: *The Weary Blues* (1926); *Fine Clothes to the Jew* (1927); *Shakespeare in Harlem* (1942); *Fields of Wonder* (1947); *One-Way Ticket* (1949); *Montage of a Dream Deferred* (1951); *Ask Your Mama* (1961); and *The Panther and the Lash* (posthumously in 1967, the year of his death). To these efforts might be added the volume published by the leftist International Workers Order, *A New Song* (1938); although it contained no new poems, the verse in that slender pamphlet was unusually radical and had not been collected previously.

Of these volumes, the least successful both in terms of sales and of critical reception, at least among black reviewers, was unquestionably *Fine Clothes to the Jew*. I would like to argue that, paradoxically, this volume was by far Hughes's greatest collection of verse, that the collection marked the height of his creative originality as a poet, and that it remains one of the most significant single volumes of poetry ever published in the United States. In fact, despite its failure to gain recognition, *Fine Clothes to the Jew* may stand in relationship to black American poetry in a way not unlike Walt Whitman's 1855 edition of *Leaves of Grass* stands in relationship to white American poetry, or to the poetry of the nation as a whole.

Fine Clothes to the Jew appeared almost ten years after Hughes first began to write poetry. While his work in Lincoln, Illinois (where by his own account he wrote his first poem, in 1916), is lost, almost all of his poems written in high school in Cleveland and thereafter are available to scholars. They may be found in the *Central High School Monthly*, *Crisis*, *Opportunity*, and other magazines published largely by blacks, as well as in white magazines that cover the broad ideological spectrum from *Vanity Fair*, on one hand, to the communist *New Masses*, on the other. The work of these first years culminated in the appearance from Knopf of Hughes's first book of any kind, *The Weary Blues*. *Fine Clothes to the Jew*, the next, built on elements found in the previous volume and in the magazines, but with such emphases and revisions that it marked, in effect, an unparalleled rethinking by Hughes about poetry in the context of black America.

Once Hughes shed his most youthful approaches to poetry and felt the stirring influence of Walt Whitman, whose lines he echoed unmistakably in his first published free verse poem, "A Song of the Soul of Central" (*Central High School Monthly*, January 1919) and Carl Sandburg ("my guiding star"), his poetry fell almost inevitably into three distinct areas.[1] The first area found Hughes dwelling on isolation, despair, suicide, and the like—conventional themes for a young, romantic poet, to be sure, but notions strongly felt by Hughes personally as he struggled to overcome the effects of his father's desertion and his mother's flighty compromise of her relationship with her son. A poem such as "Suicide's Note" ("The calm / Cool face of the river / Asked me for a kiss") exemplifies this mode.[2] The second area, also present virtually from the start of Hughes's career as a poet and fiction writer, reveals an aggressive socialist, non-racial intelligence, as for example in the very titles of two poems written later, in 1932: "Good Morning Revolution" and "Goodbye Christ." The third area, for which Hughes is almost certainly best known, finds him creating in direct response to the needs of black people—epitomized by "The Negro Speaks of Rivers," published in 1921.

Whatever distinction as a poet Hughes possesses almost certainly derives from his work in this last, racial vein. In his poetry of race, one again notes relatively clear subdivisions. Some poems protest the social conditions of blacks specifically; some are boldly declarative of the beauty and dignity of the race; still others—perhaps the most revered—transcend both angry protest and bold declaration to affirm quietly the dignity and historicity of blacks. Hughes's best known poems, such as "The Negro," "Dream Variations," and "When Sue Wears Red," almost all fall into one or another of these categories.

In its most representative work, however, *Fine Clothes to the Jew* falls outside of these categories. Although all of the poems in the various categories naturally involve a poetic concern with the manipulation of form, *Fine Clothes to the Jew* is based in essence on what one might acknowledge as a separate aesthetic, a different approach to poetic art. In the other work, Hughes writes—in spite of his concern with race—as a poet impelled by the literary tradition as defined by certain major poets of the language—in particular, Walt Whitman and his epigones, notably Carl Sandburg and Vachel Lindsay. But in *Fine Clothes* Hughes attempted to work in a way no black or white poet had ever attempted to work: deliberately defining poetic tradition according to the standards of a group often seen as sub-poetic—the black masses.

In the interest of accuracy, it must be noted that although the two approaches are presented here as contradictory, Hughes would probably never have attempted the latter if he had not found the encouragement and the signs to do so in the former, especially in Whitman's historic vision of democratic voices and his primary search for an authentic, American language of poetry. On the other hand, in his dignifying of certain Afro-American forms, Hughes explored areas which Whitman had not conceived, and of which Whitman, with his documented biases against blacks in spite of his attractive portraits of them in a few places in *Leaves of Grass*, probably would not have approved.

Hughes himself did not suddenly become enlightened by his finest insights into Afro-American form. Until 1923, perhaps the closest he had come to letting the black masses speak through his art was in "Mother to Son." This apparently simple poem amounted to nothing less than a personal reclamation of black dialect (Dunbar's "jingle in a broken tongue") for the black poet; surely "Mother to Son" takes us beyond the poles of low comedy and pathos identified by William Dean Howells (in praising Dunbar's use of dialect) as the range of the black race.[3] In Hughes's poem, black speech is invoked in the context of the race's courage, endurance, and sense of duty. But dialect would be only incidental to the major initiative of Hughes in the question of poetic form; at the center of his effort would be the recognition of a link between poetry and black music, and in particular the music not of the dignified and Europeanized spirituals, so often lauded, but of the earthy, almost "unspeakable" blues.

For his first few years as a poet, even as he grew technically proficient, Hughes had no idea what to do with a form he had heard first as a child in Lawrence, Kansas, and in Kansas City, Missouri. Even then he had responded emotionally, as he would assert, to the deep, piercing sadness of the music; later, no doubt, he began to marvel at its curious, accompanying impulse toward laughter. But how was he to effect a link between his learned standards of formal poetry and songs created by the artist among the masses? This question masquerades as one simply of technique; however, it concerns not only the realities of political power—the social powerlessness of blacks translated into the declassification of their art—but the ability of the individual to attain a sufficiently deep identification with his people and their modes of utterance so that, on an individual initiative, he is able to affect a dignified fusion of learned poetic values with those of the despised masses.

When Hughes opened his greatest essay, "The Negro Artist and the Racial Mountain" (1926) by equating the desire of a certain young black poet to be seen as nothing but a poet with the desire to be white, he was (perhaps reductively) stating his understanding of the most complex problem facing the young black writer. Hughes and, no doubt, some other young black writers had no literal desire to be white. Nevertheless, the domination of white poetic standards through the many unquestionably alluring volumes of white verse, backed ultimately by the domina-

tion of white culture, effectively made their dilemma forbiddingly close
to that of a racial death-wish described by Hughes at the start of the
essay. Because his will to solve this conundrum was so strong, however,
Langston Hughes progressed where others stagnated. But he progressed only in stages.

Not long after "The Negro Speaks of Rivers," Hughes began to offer,
as poetry, the barely mediated recording of the sounds and sights of
black life, notably in religion. One poem, "Prayer Meeting" (1922–1923),
may stand here as an example.

> Glory! Hallelujah!
> The dawn's a-comin'!
> Glory! Hallelujah!
> The dawn's a-comin'!
> A black old woman croons
> In the amen-corner of the
> Ebecaneezer Baptist Church—
> A black old woman croons—
> The dawn's a-comin'![4]

In his willingness to stand back and record, with minimal intervention,
aspects of the drama of black religion (and, later, of music and dance),
Hughes clearly showed that he had begun to see his own learned poetic
art, even with his individual talent, as inferior to that of "ordinary"
blacks—inferior, for example, to an old black woman in the amen corner
who cries to Jesus, "Glory! Hallelujah!" At the heart of his sense of
inferiority—which empowered rather than debilitated Hughes—was the
knowledge that he (and other would-be poets) stood to a great extent
outside the culture he worshipped. Perhaps Hughes stood at a greater
distance from the masses than did most other black poets. Raised in
relative isolation and with a haunting sense of parental abandonment, he
stood outside because much of his life had been spent away from consistent involvement with the very people whose affection and regard he
craved.

A more fateful step came one night in March, 1923, after a visit to a
cabaret in Harlem, when he finally wrote himself and his awkward position *vis à vis* his race accurately into a poem, "The Weary Blues."

> Droning a drowsy syncopated tune,
> Rocking back and forth to a mellow croon,
>   I heard a Negro play.
> Down on Lenox Avenue the other night
> By the pale dull pallor of an old gas light
>   He did a lazy sway . . . .
>   He did a lazy sway . . . .
> To the tune o' those Weary Blues . . .

The distance between the persona or narrator of the poem (what is his race, for example, if he hears "a Negro" play and for whom is he writing?) and the black bluesman is the distance between the would-be black poet and his people. The poem has sprung equally from the poet's isolation and his will to admire. But Hughes, in an unprecedented step, also allowed the black bluesman a chance to sing his song, with minimal interference from conventional white poetic values.

> "Ain't got nobody in all this world,
> Ain't got nobody but ma self.
> I's gwine to quit ma frownin'
> And put ma troubles on the shelf."
> Thump, thump, thump, went his foot on the floor.
> He played a few chords then he sang some more . . .[5]

Within a poem based in conventional form, Hughes sets blues lyrics he had heard as a child in Kansas. The result is that, in one and the same work, the poet honors both the tradition of Europe (out of necessity, since he is writing in English) and the tradition of black America (achieved *in spite* of the English language). The latter tradition, in fact, invades the former; one must measure the opening lines of the poem against the cadences of urban black speech, derived from the South. This invasion was so unprecedented that the persona (and the poet, of course) does not know what to make of it. By his own admission, Hughes had a hard time ending the poem. For two years, he kept the poem, "whose ending I had never been able to get quite right," unpublished—at a time when he was trying to publish almost everything he wrote.[6] Rather than share this "beauty of a cabaret poem" with anyone, Hughes kept it from sight.[7] Meanwhile, he struggled to shape its ending—"I could not achieve an ending I liked, although I worked and worked on it."[8] Finally, the end confirms the persona's bewilderment and the bluesman's mystery:

> And far into the night he crooned that tune.
> The stars went out and so did the moon.
> The singer stopped playing and went to bed
> While the Weary Blues echoed through his head
> He slept like a rock or a man that's dead.

Hughes was for two years indecisive about how to end the poem. During that period, he spent a few months in a Paris nightclub in 1924, where the entertainers were black American jazz singers and musicians. He then became bolder in his incorporations of black music and dance into his poetry. One poem frames the cry of an exuberant black dancer: "Me an' ma baby's / Got two mo' ways, / Two mo' ways to do de buck!"[9] In "To A Negro Jazz Band in a Parisian Cabaret," he urges the black musicians to "Play that thing" for the white lords and ladies, "whores and gigolos," and "the school teachers out on a spree. Play it!"

> May I?
> *Mais oui.*
> *Mein Gott!*
> *Parece una rumba.*
> *!Que rumba!*
> Play it, jazz band!
> You've got seven languages to speak in
> And then some.
> Can I?
> Sure.[10]

A year in Washington, D.C., 1925, away from Parisian nightclub glitter but closer to the more elemental art forms of the black masses, only deepened his respect for the power of black music and its "lowly" source. "Like the waves of the sea coming one after another," he would write, "like the earth moving around the sun, night, day—night, day—forever, so is the undertow of black music with its rhythm that never betrays you, its strength like the beat of the human heart, its humor, and its rooted power." More and more he let the common people, and not the poets deemed great by the master culture, guide him. "I tried to write poems like the songs they sang on Seventh Street—gay songs, because you had to be gay or die; sad songs, because you couldn't help being sad sometimes. But gay or sad, you kept on living and you kept on going."[11]

The publication of *The Weary Blues* (January, 1926) did not entirely reflect this commitment; the manuscript was accepted in May of the previous year, and mainly comprised poems written much earlier. Apart from the quotation of blues in the title poem, and even briefer quotations in "Blues Fantasy" (Hey! Hey! / That's what the / Blues singers say . . ."), the blues is not present in the book—in spite of its sonorous title.[12] For every "race poem," another exists that has nothing to do with black culture. The result is a mulatto-like text. This should not be surprising since the mulatto theme—and its transcendence—is one of the most prominent in Hughes's work. But to many readers *The Weary Blues* had gone much too far toward the black masses. Countee Cullen questioned in print whether the jazz poems were poems at all, and Hughes received a frightening reminder of black snobbishness when the veteran poet George M. McClellan wrote to tell him that while he liked the poems in *The Weary Blues*, he had scissored from the dustjacket (designed by Covarrubias) "that hideous black 'nigger' playing the piano."[13]

While *The Weary Blues* was in press and in the months following its appearance, Hughes went through certain experiences that revolutionized his aesthetic. First was his sojourn, already mentioned, among the black poor in Washington. Second was his entry into black Lincoln University a few days after *The Weary Blues* appeared, when for the first time since he was nine or ten, Hughes went to school with a majority of blacks (and all male)—an experience of incalculable effect on his sense of race. Third was the impact of the brilliant circle of young stars—the key members of the Harlem Renaissance—in Harlem at the same time: Aaron Douglass, Arna Bontemps, Wallace Thurman, Bruce Nugent, and Zora Neale Hurston, for whom Hughes's *Nation* essay of June 1926, "The Negro Artist and the Racial Mountain," was manifesto; to these should be added the names of musicians Hall Johnson, Paul Robeson, Clarence Cameron White, and W. C. Handy (often called the father of the blues), with whom Hughes either worked or consulted in the summer of 1926, especially in connection with a musical, to star Robeson, called "O Blues!" (from "The Weary Blues"). The fourth experience was the reaction of the black press to Carl Van Vechten's Harlem novel, *Nigger Heaven*, and to the appearance of *Fire!!* magazine.

The younger writers in general enthusiastically approved of *Nigger Heaven* ("Colored people can't help but like it," Hughes had predicted; the novel read as if it were written by "an N.A.A.C.P. official or Jessie Fauset. But it's good").[14] To almost all the young black writers, Van Vechten's troubles were their own. The attack on him was an attack on what they themselves, or most of them, stood for—artistic and sexual freedom, a love of the black masses, a refusal to idealize black life, and a revolt against bourgeois hypocrisy. They decided to publish their own magazine, instead of relying on the staid *Crisis* and the like. For their pains, *Fire!!* received a withering reception in the black press. "I have just tossed the first issue of *Fire* into the fire," the reviewer in the *Baltimore Afro-American* fumed; Aaron Douglass had ruined "three perfectly good pages and a cover" with his drawings, while Langston Hughes displayed "his usual ability to say nothing in many words."[15]

These experiences prompted Hughes to go where no poet had gone before; in the summer of 1926 he wrote poems that differed sharply from the spirit of *The Weary Blues* and that contested the right of the middle class to criticize the mores and manners of the black masses. (The rebellious campaign continued into the fall, when Hughes wrote his first short stories since high school, the "West Illana" sequence of stories set on a ship much like the one on which he had sailed to Africa in 1923. Hughes's fiction navigated more sensual waters than ever before; whatever their limitations as art, the stories that resulted steam suggestively of miscegenation, adultery, promiscuity, and the turmoil of sexual repression— subjects all taboo to the critics who hated *Fire!!*.) During the summer he wrote almost feverishly; back in Lincoln for the fall term, he soon gathered his new poems into what he hoped would be his second book.

On Sunday, October 3, he visited New York and delivered the manuscript to Carl Van Vechten, to whom the collection was dedicated. As with Hughes's first book, they went over each of the poems; exactly what part Van Vechten played now is unclear. Three weeks later, Langston presented the revised collection to him to take to Knopf. By this time it had a name: "Fine Clothes to the Jew," after a line from Hughes's "Hard Luck":

> When hard luck overtakes you
> Nothin' for you to do
> Gather up yo' fine clothes
> An' sell 'em to de Jew . . .[16]

Knopf accepted "Fine Clothes to the Jew," but not without balking at the title (the firm had published *Nigger Heaven* apparently without difficulty). After Van Vechten personally defended the name, as he recorded in his journal, it was allowed to stand. Van Vechten perhaps had also chosen it, as he had chosen "The Weary Blues." Certainly, Hughes had been thinking of using "Brass Spitoons," from one of his poems. The choice was unfortunate. Apparently no one alerted Hughes to the effect his title would have on sales, which proved to be opposite to the result of Van Vechten's own crudeness. But he later regarded the title as one of the main reasons for the failure of the book: it was "a bad title, because it was confusing and many Jewish people did not like it."[17]

By mid-January, 1927, Hughes had copies of *Fine Clothes to the Jew.* The first reports were encouraging. Far from objecting to the title, his friend and supporter, Amy Spingarn, liked the book even more than *The Weary Blues*, because it seemed "more out of the core of life."[18] Her brother-in-law, Arthur Spingarn, who was also Jewish, noted the title but found the book a "splendid" work, in which "Jacob and the Negro come into their own."[19] The black conservative George Schuyler praised Hughes as "the poet of the modern Negro proletariat."[20] But after the attacks on *Nigger Heaven* and *Fire!!*, Hughes was nervous. "It's harder and more cynical," he explained defensively to Dewey Jones of the Chicago *Defender*, and "limited to an interpretation of the 'lower classes,' the ones to whom life is least kind. I try to catch the hurt of their lives, the monotony of their 'jobs,' and the veiled weariness of their songs. They are the people I know best."[21]

On February 5, just as he prepared to set out on a tour for Negro History Week, the black critics opened fire. Under a headline proclaiming Hughes a "SEWER DWELLER," William M. Kelley of the New York *Amsterdam News*, denounced *Fine Clothes to the Jew* as "about 100 pages of trash. . . . It reeks of the gutter and sewer." The regular reviewer of the *Philadelphia Tribune* adamantly refused to publicize it; Eustance Gay confessed that *Fine Clothes to the Jew* "disgusts me." In the *Pittsburgh Courier*, historian J. A. Rogers called it "piffling trash" that left him "positively sick." The Chicago *Whip* sneered at the dedication to Van Vechten, "a literary gutter-rat" who perhaps alone "will revel in the lecherous, lust-reeking characters that Hughes finds time to poeticize about. . . . These poems are unsanitary, insipid and repulsing." Hughes was the "poet 'low-rate' of Harlem." The following week, refining its position, the *Tribune* lamented Hughes's "obsession for the more degenerate elements" of black life; the book was "a study in the perversions of the Negro." It is questionable whether any book of American poetry, other than *Leaves of Grass*, had ever been greeted so contemptuously.[22]

To these and other black critics, Hughes had allowed the "secret" shame of their culture, especially its apparently unspeakable or unprintable sexual mores, to be bruited by thick-lipped black whores and roustabouts. How could he have dared to publish "Red Silk Stockings"?

> Put on yo' red silk stockings,
> Black gal.
> Go out an' let de white boys
> Look at yo' legs.
>
> Ain't nothin' to do for you, nohow,
> Round this town,—
> You's too pretty.
> Put on yo' red silk stockings, gal,
> An' tomorrow's chile'll
> Be a high yaller.
> Go out an' let de white boys
> Look at yo' legs.

Or "Beale Street Love"?

> Love
> Is a brown man's fist
> With hard knuckles
> Crushing the lips,
> Blackening the eyes,—
> Hit me again
> Says Clorinda.

By pandering to the taste of whites for the sensational (the critics ignored their own sensationalism, demonstrable in the scandal-ridden sheets of most black weeklies), Hughes had betrayed his race.[23]

In spite of this hostility, *Fine Clothes to the Jew* marked Hughes's maturity as a poet after a decade of writing, and his most radical achievement in language. While *The Weary Blues* had opened with references to the blues and poems written in dialect, before presenting the sweeter, more traditional lyrics, a prefatory note ("the mood of the *Blues* is almost always despondency, but when they are sung people laugh") now indicated the far greater extent to which *Fine Clothes to the Jew* falls deliber-

ately within the range of authentic blues emotion and blues culture. Gone
are the conventional lyrics about nature and loneliness, or poems in which
the experience of the common black folk is framed by conventional poetic
language and a superior, sometimes ironic poetic diction. Here few poems
are beyond range of utterance of common black folk, except in so far as
any formal poetry by definition belongs to a more privileged world. *Fine
Clothes to the Jew* was the perfect companion piece to Hughes's manifesto, "The Negro Artist and the Racial Mountain."

As a measure of his deeper penetration of the culture and his increased confidence as a poet, three kinds of poems are barely present in
Fine Clothes to the Jew—those that praise black people and culture directly, those that directly protest their condition, and those that reflect
his own personal sense of desolation. For example: "Laughers," which
celebrates blacks as "Loud laughers in the hands of Fate," is also probably the earliest piece in the book, having been published first as "My
People" in June, 1922. "Mulatto" lodges perhaps the strongest protest,
but is staged dramatically:

> . . . The Southern night is full of stars,
> Great big yellow stars.
> > O, sweet as earth,
> > Dusk dark bodies
> > Give sweet birth
> To little yellow bastard boys.
>
> > *Git on back there in the night.*
> > *You aint white.*
>
> The bright stars scatter everywhere.
> Pine wood scent in the evening air.
> > A nigger night,
> > A nigger joy.
>
> *I am your son, white man!*
>
> > A little yellow
> > Bastard boy.

Only one poem, "Sport," proposes life as an empty nothingness—as "the
shivering of a great drum / Beaten with swift sticks."

Sorrow and despair dominate *Fine Clothes to the Jew*, but mainly
through the expressive medium of the blues and its place in the lives of
poor black men and women. In "Hey!" the blues is mysterious: "I feels
de blues a comin', / Wonder what de blues'll bring?" It is also, as in
"Misery," soothing, or even cathartic:

> Play de blues for me.
> Play de blues for me.

> No other music
> 'Ll ease ma misery . . .

Although the blues drifts in most often on the heels of lost love, the feeling can come for other reasons and still have poetic power. "Homesick Blues":

> De railroad bridge's
> A sad song in de air.
> De railroad bridge's
> A sad song in de air.
> Ever time de trains pass
> I wants to go somewhere . . .

In *Fine Clothes to the Jew*, the singers and mourners are mainly women. By comparison, men are almost shallow; one man ("Bad Man") beats his wife and "ma side gal too": "Don't know why I do it but / It keeps me from feelin' blue." Men may be hurt in love, like the fellow in "Po' Boy Blues" who met "a gal I thought was kind. / She made me lose ma money / An' almost lose ma mind." But the blues are sung most often, and most brilliantly, by black women. Sometimes they sing to warn their sisters ("Listen Here Blues"):

> Sweet girls, sweet girls,
> Listen here to me.
> All you sweet girls,
> Gin an' whiskey
> Kin make you lose yo' 'ginity . . .

Or, as in "Lament Over Love," their daughters:

> I hope ma chile'll
> Never love a man.
> I say I hope ma chile'll
> Never love a man.
> Cause love can hurt you
> Mo'n anything else can.

Women lament being cheated, for having been done wrong by "a yellow papa," who "took ma last thin dime" ("Gypsy Man"); or, as in "Hard Daddy," they grieve over male coldness:

> I cried on his shoulder but
> He turned his back on me.
> Cried on his shoulder but
> He turned his back on me.
> He said a woman's cryin's
> Never gonna bother me.

Sometimes the sorrow is greater when loss or the prospect of loss is mixed with profound self-abnegation and despair. "Gal's Cry For A Dying Lover":

> . . . Hound dawg's barkin'
> Means he's gonna leave this world.
> Hound dawg's barkin'
> Means he's gonna leave this world.
> O, Lawd have mercy
> On a po' black girl.
>
> Black an' ugly
> But he sho do treat me kind.
> I'm black an' ugly
> But he sho do treat me kind.
> High-in-heaben Jesus,
> Please don't take this man o' mine.

But the blues can reflect great joy as well as sorrow, as in "Ma Man," where a black woman's emotional and sexual ecstasy is so overpowering it drives her into song:

> When ma man looks at me
> He knocks me off ma feet.
> When ma man looks at me
> He knocks me off ma feet
> He's got those 'lectric-shockin' eyes an'
> De way he shocks me sho is sweet.
>
> He kin play a banjo.
> Lordy, he kin plunk, plunk, plunk.
> He kin play a banjo.
> I mean plunk, plunk . . . plunk, plunk.
> He plays good when he's sober
> An' better, better, better when he's drunk.
>
> Eagle-rockin'
> Daddy, eagle-rock with me.
> Eagle-rockin',
> Come and eagle-rock with me.
> Honey baby,
> Eagle-rockish as I kin be!

The last stanza of this poem, the second to last in the book (as if Hughes tried to hide it), was among the most sexually teasing in American poetry—to those who understood that "eagle-rocking" was possibly more than a popular dance step.

His critics had not howled without cause, but Hughes did not retreat. First at a Baptist church and then before an African Methodist Episcopal congregation in Philadelphia, he fulfilled engagements to read his poems. Then he coolly faced Floyd Calvin of the *Pittsburgh Courier* at the Knopf office on Fifth Avenue. In spite of the reviews, Hughes said, he declined to write about Vanderbilts and Goulds. At least two-thirds of all blacks were lower-class—"even I myself, belong to that class." In any event, "I have a right to portray any side of Negro life I wish to." He defended the blues singers Bessie Smith and Clara Smith as equal to the best of European folk singers, who were honored in America; and he declared that Carl Van Vechten had done more than anyone else for black artists.[24] To the white Cleveland *Plain Dealer*, curious about the hubbub in the black press over poetry, he explained that the black reviewers still thought that "we should display our 'higher selves—whatever they are," missing the point "that every 'ugly' poem I write is a protest against the ugliness it pictures."[25]

When the *Pittsburgh Courier* invited Hughes to defend himself against his critics, he did not hesitate. In "These Bad New Negroes: A Critique on Critics," he identified four reasons for the attacks: the low self-esteem of the "best" blacks; their obsession with white opinion; their *nouveau riche* snobbery; and their lack of artistic and cultural training "from which to view either their own or the white man's books or pictures. As for the "ill-mannered onslaught" on Van Vechten: the man's "sincere, friendly, and helpful interest in things Negro" should have brought "serious, rather than vulgar, reviews of his book." A nine-point defense of his own views and practices ended in praise of the young writers, including Toomer, Fisher, Thurman, Cullen, Hurston, and the Lincoln poet Edward Silvera. And Hughes himself: "My poems are indelicate. But so is life," he pointed out. He wrote about "harlots and gin-bibers. But they are human. Solomon, Homer, Shakespeare, and Walt Whitman were not afraid or ashamed to include them."[26] (Van Vechten thought the situation easy to explain; "you and I," he joked to Hughes while making an important distinction, "are the only colored people who really love *niggers*."[27]

Hughes was not without friends in the black press. The *New York Age* found the book evocative of the joy and pathos, beauty and ugliness of black Americans, if of the more primitive type. The poet Alice Dunbar-Nelson, once married to Paul Laurence Dunbar, compared the book to Wordsworth and Coleridge's once maligned yet celebrated venture, *Lyrical Ballads*, which used the lives and speech of the common people; Hughes was "a rare poet."[28] Theophilus Lewis praised the book in the *Messenger*, and in the *Saturday Review of Literature* Alain Locke was deft about *Fine Clothes to the Jew*: "Its open frankness will be a shock and a snare for the critic and moralist who cannot distinguish clay from mire."[29] And Claude McKay wrote privately to congratulate Hughes on having written a book superior to his first.

Among white reviewers, perhaps the most perceptive evaluation came from the young cultural historian Howard Mumford Jones. Using black dialect austerely, Hughes had scraped the blues form down to the bone, and raised the folk form to literary art. "In a sense," Jones concluded, "He has contributed a really new verse form to the English language." Although, like Wordsworth, he sometimes lapsed into "vapid simplicity." But if Hughes continued to grow, he was "dangerously near becoming a major Americam poet."[30] V. F. Calverton, Margaret Larkin, Arthur Davison Ficke, Hunter Stagg, Abbe Niles, Babette Deutsch, Julia Peterkin, and a wide range of reviewers praised the stark lyrical simplicity and beauty of most of the verse. More than once he was compared to Coleridge and Wordsworth's *Lyrical Ballads;* the critics understood that Hughes was trying to effect a historic change in poetry by compelling both blacks and whites to admit the power of black language. Other critics were not so sympathetic. The Boston *Transcript* flatly preferred Countee Cullen's work and called some of the Hughes verse "tawdry"; the *Nation* reviewer thought that Hughes was merely transcribing folklore, not writing poetry; the *New York Times* judged the volume "uneven and flawed."[31]

The ignorant blasts of the black press were nicely offset when Hughes accepted an invitation ("a great honor for me") from the Walt Whitman foundation to speak at the poet's home on Mickle Street in Camden, New Jersey. Stressing Whitman's humane depictions of blacks in his poetry, Hughes when [went] on to claim that modern free verse, and his own work, descended from Whitman's great example. "I believe," Langston told the little gathering, "that poetry should be direct, comprehensible and the epitome of simplicity."[32] Suspicious of theory, Hughes had nevertheless identified one of the main ideas behind his theory of composition—the notion of an aesthetic of simplicity, sanctioned finally by democratic culture but having a discipline and standards just as the baroque or the rococo, for example, had their own. That simplicity had its dangers both extended its challenge and increased its rewards. The visit to Whitman's home left Hughes elated; to Van Vechten he mailed a postcard imprinted with an excerpt from Whitman's "Song of the Open Road": "All seems beautiful to me."[33]

Although Hughes would place the emphasis in his poetry in a different direction in the 1930s, when he wrote his most politically radical verse, he continued to write the blues even during this period. After the Depression, when Knopf published his *Shakespeare in Harlem*, the blues dominated the volume. When in the late 1940s and 1950s he allowed first be-bop (as in *Montage of a Dream Deferred*) and then increasingly "progressive" jazz (as in *Ask Your Mama*) also to shape his poetry, he was applying a basic principle he had first learned in the context of the blues. He never abandoned the form, because the blues continued as perhaps the most fertile form of black expressivity; *Ask Your Mama*, for example, is explicitly based on the "Hesitation Blues."

His initiative in the blues remains the only genuinely original achievement in form by any black American poet—notwithstanding the excellence of much of the work of writers such as Countee Cullen, Melvin Tolson, Gwendolyn Brooks, Robert Hayden, and even the rebel Amiri Baraka (surely the greatest names in modern black poetry). Their art is largely derivative by comparison. Afro-American poets did not rush to build on Hughes's foundation; most remained black poets who wished to be known simply as poets. But some poets followed the lead. Sterling Brown's *Southern Roads*, the most distinguished book of verse by an Afro-American in the 1930s, was certainly indebted to Hughes, although Alain Locke—anxious to be seen by Mrs. R. Osgood Mason ("Godmother") as opposed to Hughes after the "Mule Bone" controversy involving Hughes and Zora Hurston—used a review of *Southern Roads* to dismiss Hughes's blues and jazz writing as faddish, and to hail Brown as the authentic master of black folk poetry—a judgement without merit in spite of Brown's brilliance. Richard Wright, initially a poet, tried to write the blues, and even published one poem in collaboration with Hughes. Among whites, Elizabeth Bishop tried her hand at the form, with results certainly no worse than Wright's—the blues, they learned, is not as simple as it seems.

Black poetry, however, had to wait until the late 1960s and 1970s, with the emergence of writers such as Sherley Anne Williams, Michael S. Harper, and Raymond Patterson, to capitalize fully on Hughes's historic achievement. Ironically, because of the obscurity in which *Fine Clothes to the Jew* remains, and because the full extent of Hughes's artistic revolution has not been appreciated, many young black poets are unaware of the history of the form that they nevertheless understand as providing the only indisputably honorable link between their literary and cultural ambitions as blacks and the language compelled on them by history.

Notes

1. Langston Hughes, *The Big Sea* (New York; Knopf, 1940).
2. "Suicide's Note." *The Weary Blues* (New York: Knopf, 1926) 87.
3. Paul Laurence Dunbar, "The Poet," *Complete Poems* (New York: Dodd, Mead, 1913) 191.
4. Hughes, "Prayer Meeting," *Fine Clothes to the Jew* (New York: Knopf, 1927) 46.
5. "The Weary Blues," *Weary Blues*, 23–24.
6. *Big Sea*, 215.

7. LH to Countee Cullen, 7 April 1923; Countee Cullen Papers, Amistad Research Center, New Orleans.
8. *Big Sea*, 92.
9. "Negro Dancers," *Crisis* 29 (1925): 221.
10. "To a Negro Jazz Band in a Parisian Cabaret," *Crisis* 31 (1925): 67.
11. *Big Sea*, 209.
12. "Blues Fantasy," *Weary Blues*, 37.
13. George M. McClellan to LH, 14 July 1926; Langston Hughes Papers, Beinecke Rare Books and Manuscript Library, Yale University.
14. Langston Hughes to Alain Locke, 12 August [1926]; Alain Locke Papers, Moorland-Spingarn Research Center, Howard University.
15. *Big Sea*, 237.
16. "Hard Luck," *Fine Clothes to the Jew*, 18.
17. *Big Sea*, 264.
18. Amy Spingarn to Langston Hughes, ;[n.d.]; Langston Hughes Papers.
19. Arthur Spingarn to Langston Hughes, 3 February 1927; Langston Hughes Papers.
20. George Schuyler to Langston Hughes, 27 January 1927; Langston Hughes Papers.
21. James A. Emanuel, *Langston Hughes* (New York: Twayne, 1967), 31–32.
22. *New York Amsterdam News*, February 5, 1927; *Philadelphia Tribune*, February 5, 1927; *Pittsburgh Courier*, February 5, 1927; *Chicago Whip*, February 26, 1927; *Philadelphia Tribune*, February 12, 1927.
23. "Red Silk Stockings," *Fine Clothes to the Jew*, 73; "Beale Street Love," 57; "Laughers," 77–78; "Mulatto," 71; "Sport," 40; "Hey!" 17; "Homesick Blues," 24; "Bad Man," 21; "Po' Boy Blues," 23; "Listen Here Blues," 85; "Lament Over Love," 81; "Gypsy Man," 22; "Hard Daddy," 86; "Gal's Cry For A Dying Lover," 82; "Ma Man," 88.
24. *Pittsburgh Courier*, February 26, 1927.
25. *Cleveland Plain Dealer*, March 27, 1927.
26. "Those Bad New Negroes," *Pittsburgh Courier*, April 16, 1927.
27. Carl Van Vechten to Langston Hughes, March 25 (1927); Papers.
28. *Washington Eagle*, March 11, 1927.
29. *Saturday Review of Literature* 3 (April 9, 1927): 712.
30. *Chicago Daily News*, June 29, 1927.
31. *Boston Transcript*, March 2, 1927; *New York Times Book Review*, March 27, 1927.
32. *Camden Evening Courier*, March 3, 1927.
33. Langston Hughes to Carl Van Vechten, March 1, 1927.

◆◆◆◆◆◆◆◆◆◆◆◆◆◆

To the Tune of Those Weary Blues

STEVEN C. TRACY

Most readers of Black American literature recognize that Langston Hughes drew upon jazz and blues as resources for much of his work, particularly his poetry. In the case of the blues, however, critics often demonstrate an incomplete knowledge of the field, an inability or lack of desire to explore the blues influence, or they assume that the reader has an in-depth knowledge of the field already. What emerges from these studies is an incomplete understanding of Hughes's knowledge of the blues and of its influence on his work. By first exploring the sources for his knowledge and his attitudes toward his folk sources and their creations, a clearer picture of the way Hughes makes use of blues structure, themes, and imagery will emerge. What becomes evident is that although Hughes takes a multiplicity of traditional and literary approaches to blues in his own poems, his use of blues is limited in expression by some dominant influences.

There are many different types of blues styles, often subcategorized by blues researchers in terms of geographical location and historical time period. For example, the early Texas blues style—from about the 1880s to the 1920s—differed from the Mississippi blues style of the same era. Blues researcher Sam Charters has attributed the difference in style to the difference in environments that caused a variance in interaction of similar events.

> There was little of the oppressive plantation life of the Mississippi delta to shape the Texas blues. . . . In some Mississippi counties the Negro population is more than eighty percent of the people living in the county. . . . At its highest point, just after the Civil War, the colored population of Texas was less than thirty percent of the state's still sparse growth. . . . This has not meant that life has been easier for colored men and women in Texas. . . . But it has meant a less isolated, less confined life than the brutal colored society of Mississippi.[1]

As Charters points out, this less crowded environment produced less local competition, therefore traditional elements like slave and work songs were not displaced but were carried over wholesale into the blues performed by early Texas blues performers like Henry Thomas, "Ram-blin'" Thomas, and Texas Alexander. As time went on, brilliant original performers like Blind Lemon Jefferson cast the material in a more per-sonal style, a style less crowded, insistent, and rhythmic than the heavy Mississippi blues. In the late 1930s and early 1940s the rural style identi-fied with Jefferson—the dominant figure of the Texas blues of the 1920s—with its single-string figures set off against a regular bass beat, combined with the recorded styles of Lonnie Johnson, Scrapper Black-well, and some jazz guitarists. At that point Texas T-Bone Walker cre-ated his own style of playing, a more urban style performed in the company of a larger ensemble, a style today largely identified with B. B. King. Therefore, a blues style is based on the time, location, environment and the interaction of elements in that environment, the rise of a domi-nant local figure, and, after blues were recorded, the introduction of elements not normally associated with that area via the phonograph. As we examine the influence of the blues tradition on Langston Hughes, then, we must consider the type of blues Hughes encountered in the various environments in which he lived, keeping in mind that none of the blues environments had absolutely and exclusively one style, and that the styles were often dynamic and in transitional phases.

In his autobiography *The Big Sea*[2] Hughes discusses his birth in 1902 in Joplin, Missouri, and his childhood in Lawrence, Kansas, recounting the fact that he heard the blues in the area where he grew up until about 1915. According to Hughes, the first blues song he heard was used in his poem "The Weary Blues," written about a piano player he heard in Harlem:

> I got de weary blues
> And I can't be satisfied.
> Got de weary blues
> And can't be satisfied.
> I ain't happy no mo'
> And I wish that I had died.

The lyric, of course, is formulaic: the formula is repeated with many minor variations in the oral blues tradition, as by Texas songster Henry Thomas whose "Texas Worried Blues" makes the common substitution of "worried" for "weary";

> The worried blues
> God, I'm feelin' bad.
> I've got the worried blues
> God, I'm feelin' bad.
> I've got the worried blues
> God, I'm feelin' bad.[3]

Thomas, who was around fifty-three years old when he first recorded in 1927, represents a link to pre-war blues music, and his blues were often primitive. Hence he characteristically repeats the same three line three times, as opposed to creating a third-line resolution, as younger bluesmen have done.

The ballads, reels and crude blues of an older man like Henry Thomas, that Hughes first heard in his Lawrence childhood from 1902–15, were his earliest musical influence; therefore it is important to place that tradition in order to discern the type of the music. Lawrence is in northeast Kansas on the Kansas River, approximately sixty miles west of Kansas City, connected by highways 69 and 70 and the Santa Fe, Rock Island, and Missouri-Kansas-Texas railways to Oklahoma, Missouri, Kansas and Texas. Indeed Henry Thomas, at a 1929 recording session, recounted his experience hopping the Texas and Pacific and "Katy" (MKT) lines in his "Railroading Some," going from Texas through Kansas City and on through to Chicago, following a route that had been open to passengers, migrants and hoboes for years.[4] The blues were indeed no newcomer to the area: it was in Kansas City in 1902 (the date of Hughes's birth) that blues singer Gertrude "Ma" Rainey reportedly first heard blues music, and Kansas City blues shouter Big Joe Turner, roughly a contemporary of Hughes, recalled leading around blues singers on the streets in the late teens and early twenties, and hearing the crude banjos, gas pipes, and water jugs that were used as instruments.[5] These early blues, often sung unaccompanied, or accompanied by a guitar, piano, or crude home instruments were, in Kansas City, set in a milieu of varied musical idioms—ragtime, jazz, orchestral music—which produced the "loose, lithe, resilient orchestral jazz style to which the city gives its name." This orchestral-type blues were emerging in the teens, flowering in the era of 1925–1942, when larger ensembles touring the southwest played blues in arranged form.[6] Thus, during his childhood and visits back home, Hughes was hearing not only "pure" loosely arranged, spontaneous early blues, but most likely these other idioms and various combinations of a more arranged and sophisticated nature. What ultimately emerged in 1925–42 was the ensemble Kansas City blues style, "big city blues, but with a country, earthy feeling,"[7] that helped produce or catapult to success Big Joe Turner, Peter Johnson, Jay McShann, Mary Lou Williams, and Count Basie, among others.

But it was the early blues of itinerant musicians of the first two decades of the 20th century that influenced Hughes in his Lawrence, Kansas, days and the blues of that area were strongly influenced by slave and work songs. The Texas blues scene is more readily identifiable than that of Kansas, Missouri, or other surrounding states because more record companies held sessions in Texas,[8] whereas only the Okeh Record Company recorded sessions in Kansas City. However, the highways and train lines provided easily accessible connections to Kansas, so it is not hard to imagine someone like Texan Willard "Ramblin'" Thomas rambling in Kansas singing:

> Poor Boy
> Poor Boy
> Poor Boy long ways from home.[9]

There is a loose-formed quality to the Texas bluesman's music, due to a reduced rhythmic emphasis, a beat that is "diffuse and idiosyncratic"[10] and the influence of the extended phrases characteristic of workshops. Even so, there was a variety of approaches, exemplified by the recordings of such Texas blues greats as Blind Lemon Jefferson, Little Hat Jones, Willie Reed, Funny Papa Smith, and "Texas" Alexander—all of whom recorded in the 1920s and '30s. These bluesmen played in the area for some time before recording: Texas Alexander, whose field holler-like qualities produced a clear link between Texas blues and work songs, was born in 1880, and performed in the region for years before recording. This type of music provided Hughes's earliest source of the blues tradition, and the strong links to slave songs and field hollers present in the performances of Henry Thomas, Texas Alexander, and others, coupled with the diversity of musical styles present in the area, were to influence the diversity of presentation in his later blues poems, particularly his old, rural-type moaning blues like "Bound No'th Blues."

The next clearly discernible blues influence occurred during his year in Harlem in 1922–23. This was two years after black singer Mamie Smith opened up the market for black singers through the success of her Okeh label releases, "That Thing Called Love," "You Can't Keep A Good Man Down," and "Crazy Blues." In *The Big Sea*, Hughes describes the 1920s Harlem music scene by recounting the big name, popular performers: Hall Johnson, William Brant Still, Eubie Blake, Noble Sissle, Duke Ellington, Florence Mills, Josephine Baker, Ethel Waters, Gladys Bentley, Trixie Smith, Clara Smith, Bessie Smith, and other cabaret theatre performers offered a somewhat more sophisticated style of performing. Those among this group who sang blues, particularly the last three named, often had a marked vaudeville edge to their musical performances, although they also often derived their music from the more archaic styles prevalent in rural areas. This "classic" blues style, as it is called, was established on record by Mamie Smith, and other record companies rushed to record female blues singers in this "classic" style. Indeed this more highly arranged, dramatic, stage-influenced vaudeville style made it on phonograph recordings before the older, rural blues that preceded it in development. Hughes was drawn strongly towards these vaudeville blues singers and their performances. While these vaudeville singers usually had a more sophisticated approach, delivery, and accompaniment than performers like Henry Thomas, Texas Alexander, and Blind Lemon Jefferson, they were not necessarily the slick professionals remote from the roots of the blues that folklorist Sam Charters and Leroi Jones have claimed they were. As ethnomusicologist Jeff Titon states, "the matter needs reexamination."[11] Undoubtedly some were slick professionals; others might have substituted the more sophisticated lyrics of Andry Razaf, Clarence Williams, and W. C. Handy for the lyrics of the oral tradition they knew better. Nonetheless, their performances were often smoother and less traditional than those of their rural blues counterparts. Hughes demonstrates his preference for singers of the vaudeville-type blues by naming Bessie, Clara, and Mamie Smith and Midge Williams as the finest blues singers, along with other polished but non-vaudeville blues performers like Lonnie Johnson and Jimmy Rushing, adding barrel-house pianist-vocalist Georgia White and folk-song performer Leadbelly; in the same essay he expresses a wish that Paul Robeson and Marian Anderson would have used blues in their performances.[12] This preference for a more sophisticated vaudeville-type approach fostered by the prevalence of that style in Harlem is markedly noticeable in the form and content of many of Hughes's blues poems.

Hughes also recounts in *The Big Sea* other sources for his knowledge of the blues: the singing of George from Kentucky aboard the *S.S. Malone* in 1923; pianist Palmer Jones in Paris, who sang "Old blues and folksongs . . . inserting off-color lyrics if the crowd was that kind of crowd;"[13] all night jam sessions in 1924 that produced earthy ensemble blues, featuring trumpet, violin, piano, clarinet, drums and vocals by blacks escaping back into the most traditional blues lyrics they could remember; folks on the streets, in pool halls and barrelhouses of Washington's Seventh Street in 1925; blues singers like Memphis Minnie, whose music he reviewed in 1943 in *The Defender;*[14] Josh White, who performed some of Hughes's lyrics; Brownie McGhee, who played Gitfiddle in "Simple Heavenly" in 1952; and many other blues performers like Meade Lux Lewis, Leadbelly, and Ray Charles, both in person and on record. The sources were diverse: rural and urban, lowdown and sophisticated, male and female.

Folklorists and aficionados were also an important source for collected material, and Hughes either knew many experts personally or could draw upon their works. Sterling Brown and Zora Neale Hurston were probably the closest to Hughes: both very likely had a broader knowledge of black folklore than Hughes, both published folklore articles. Hughes felt that Hurston was the most amusing of all Harlem Renaissance artists, due probably in no small part to her folk-knowledge and mother-wit. The close contact with these people and the knowledge of the work of the Lomaxes and John Work provided additional blues material for Hughes.[15]

An artist's exposure to black folk culture does not automatically guarantee work of the calibre of Hughes's; a certain attitude towards the people and their creations is required to produce fine poetry. As early as 1925 in his "The Negro Artist and the Racial Mountain," Hughes demonstrated an admiration for the ethnic distinctiveness of the "low down folks" with their heritage of rhythm and warmth, incongruous humor that so often, as in the blues, becomes ironic laughter mixed with tears."[16] As Onwuchekwa Jemie points out, the artist who wishes to express his blackness

> . . . will find a sturdy ally in the Black masses . . . with their confident humanity, their indifference to white opinion, their joie de vivre amidst depressing circumstances . . . they are the uncontaminated reservoir of the strength of the race, the body and vehicle of its traditions.[17]

Ultimately in this essay Hughes argues that black writers, sculptors, painters, and dramatists should use folklore and folk life as professional musicians have used black folk music. He is apparently thinking of more polished musicians like the "classic" blues singers or lyricist/arrangers like Razaf, Williams and Handy, who drew upon their black folk roots but had a somewhat more distanced perspective on those roots. In 1926 and the years to follow, there were many folk musicians recorded by recording companies; indeed the peak years of the "classic" blues singers (1923–26) gave over to the peak prewar years of blues recording (1927–30), when more folk artists than ever were recording—averaging nearly 500 blues and gospel records per year.[18] Thus one can speculate that, while Hughes held great admiration for the "low down folks," his artistic strategy was to attempt to impose a more sophisticated and literary scheme on the material.

Hughes's attitude toward the material itself is evident: "The real Negro blues are as fine as any folk music we have."[19] He feels that blues and spirituals are "the two great Negro gifts to American music." Generally Hughes is accurate in his statements about the oral blues tradition: the blues are, under normal circumstances, "usually sung by one man or woman alone"; they are "songs folks make up when their hearts hurt . . . sad funny songs. Too sad to be funny, and too funny to be sad;"[20] there are, in fact, "many kinds of blues . . . family blues . . . loveless blues . . . left lonesome blues . . . broke and hungry blues . . . desperate going-to-the-war blues."[21] However, the blues are to Hughes like the old hat he described finding in *The Big Sea:* ". . . so valuable . . . quaint and folk-like . . ."[22] Since Hughes didn't intend his poetry to be simply unusual or an old-fashioned curiosity, his artistic attitude seems to revolve around the blues as a central resource for his literary art as opposed to finely wrought literary art in themselves. Hughes was much better at using the blues as a resource for his art than he was at producing a poem attempting to approximate authentic folk blues lyrics, because he tried to make those poems of his generally representative and quaintly humorous in a sad way, whereas there are startlingly original folk blues performers whose lyrics are either all sad or all funny. After all, if the blues are cathartic, and the audience laughs in response to a particularly sad lyric or experience with which they can identify, the song itself is still sad. Hughes knew that there are many different kinds of blues; thus when he calls blues "city songs rising from the crowded streets of big towns"[23] he indicates a preference for the types of blues closest to his artistic temperament: the composed, arranged, sophisticated blues of the "classic" blues singers he heard in Harlem, and of composers like W. C. Handy.

Handy, widely acclaimed "Father of the Blues," consciously took the songs of rural black musicians and worked them up into published material. Titon reports that Handy "believed he had refined black folk music by 'polishing' and publishing compositions based on the blues songs he had heard as a boy."[24] Hughes admired Handy for his part in helping disseminate and "legitimize" the blues through publishing efforts, particularly "Memphis Blues," and Handy's most famous composition, "St. Louis Blues." Hughes called the latter "one of America's best-known popular songs all over the world."[25] His letters to and from Arna Bontemps are peppered with references to Handy, especially regarding the use of "St. Louis Blues" in the play "St. Louis Woman,"[26] and as Jemie points out, Handy commented that Hughes's poem "Hope" said in four lines "what it would have taken Shakespeare two acts and three scenes to say."[27] Although the relationship between the two men needs to be further illuminated, it is apparent that both were concerned with "championing" the blues and with imposing some of their own ideas on the authentic folk material as well, Handy as a publishing musician/arranger and Hughes as a publishing poet.

Out of these varied sources and attitudes Hughes created his own blues-influenced poems, drawing heavily on oral tradition for his own literary ends in terms of structure, themes, and imagery. Hughes's poems, being written and not sung to accompaniment, obviously rely on carefully plotted attempts to render them in such a way as to capture the rhythm and spirit of performance on the page. Structurally, the traditional blues form is stanzaic, developing from the AAA pattern (the same thought repeated three times, as in Henry Thomas's "Texas Worried Blues") to the more common standard AAB pattern (the first thought repeated twice, the last word of which rhymes with the final word of the last line, which is a resolution). The chord structure of a standard blues, which characteristically lasts twelve bars, performed in the key of C involves three chords: C, F and G. Using numbers to indicate the beats (four beats to a bar) as the words are sung and placing the chord changes above the word where the chord changes, "Texas Worried Blues" is annotated thus:

```
          C
          1      2  3 4
          The worried blues
          1  23 4      1  234   123
          God I'm feelin' bad.
                        F
          4          1  2   3 4
          I've got the worried blues
                            C
          1   2   3   4  1   234    123
          God, I'm feelin' bad.
                            G
          4             1  2 3  4
          I've got the worried blues
                            C
          1   2   3   4  1   234    1234
          God, I'm feelin' bad.
```

As shown, each bar does not begin or end with the first or last word of a line: here the first five words of lines 1, 3 and 5 are sung on pick up beats—the last beat of a bar—and the last words of lines 2, 3 and 6 end almost two bars before the words of the next line. Hughes was trying to capture the beat and rhythm of blues songs like this in his poetry, so if we were to annotate a part of his "The Weary Blues" like the blues lyric—not suggesting that Hughes's poems were sung or accompanied but simply that they were attempting to capture the spirit and structure of performance, the annotation would look like this:

```
          C
          1  2  3
    I got de weary blues
          4      2   34 1  234   123
    And I can't be satisfied.
          F
    4   1  2   3
    Got de weary blues
```

```
                    C
    4   1    2  3  4  1   2 3 4   1 2 3
    And can't be satisfied.
            G
    4      1   2  3
    I ain't happy no mo'
                        C
    4    1   2   3   4   1   2 3 4   1 2 3 4
    And I wish that I had died.
```

A comparison of the two shows a remarkable similarity—basically it is Hughes's use of "and I" in lines 2 and 4 and 6 that accounts for the only substantial beat difference between the two.

Hughes, then, shows a strong ability to capture the beat and phrasing of blues songs. He also demonstrates a remarkable success with manipulating the formulaic quality of blues lyrics. Phrases like "I'm goin' away, babe" or "my gal mistreats me" recur frequently, but the formulas are not so fixed as to be merely memorized. They are part of a generating system that produces "a variety of rhythmic combinations that may be accommodated to a given tune."[28] Thus Hughes's

> I woke up this mornin'
> 'Bout half past three[29]

and bluesman Furry Lewis's

> Woke up this mornin'
> Looked up against the wall[30]

are generated from the same song formula. Hughes generated many of his blues poems from these formulas, as a comparison between several of his blues poems and the lyrics of bluesmen reveals. Hughes's

> I went down to the river
> Sat down on the bank
> I tried to think but couldn't
> So I jumped in and sank. ("Life is Fine")

parallels bluesman Peg Leg Howell's "Rock and Gravel Blues:"

> Honey, let's go to the
> River and sit down
> Honey, let's go to the
> River and sit down
> If the blues overtakes us
> Jump overboard and drown.[31]

Hughes's

> I wish I had wings to
> Fly like the eagle flies
> Wish I had wings to
> Fly like the eagle flies
> I'd fly on ma man an'
> I'd scratch out both his eyes. ("Hard Daddy")

is generated from the same formula as Peg Leg Howell's "Turtle Dove Blues:"

> If I had wings like
> Noah's turtle dove
> If I had wings like
> Noah's turtle dove
> If I had wings like
> Noah's turtle dove
> I would rise and fly and
> Light on the one I love.[32]

and Hughes's

> I got de weary blues
> And I can't be satisfied ("The Weary Blues")

derives from the same formula as Henry Thomas's "Texas Worried Blues" and Mississippi John Hurt's

> Got the blues
> Can't be satisfied[33]

Not only does Hughes draw upon song formulas for his lyrics, but he also presents his blues-influenced poems on the page in a manner approximating the blues singer's methods of singing his lines. Blues singers most often sing relatively short bursts of text, the pause sometimes located in off-beat places, as in Hughes's

> I wish I had wings to

and Howell's

> Honey, let's go to the

Thus when one transcribes these lines using Charles Olson's idea of Projective Verse, the single line of the blues singer can often be halved, creating two lines such as Hughes used in much of his twelve-bar blues poems. Therefore it is Hughes's knowledge of the blues tradition, not typographical accommodation nor the maintenance of a closer semblance to poetic form, that causes him to divide the lines as he does, rather than to render the stanza into a three-line AAB pattern. "Hard Daddy" (above), then, is in actuality a twelve-bar AAB stanza poem accommodated to the blues singer's way of rendering his material orally.

While poems like "Morning After," "Widow Women," "Young Gal's Blues," "Midwinter Blues," "Lament Over Love," and "Bound No'th Blues" use this traditional twelve-bar AAB stanza form, other Hughes blues poems drawn on the traditional eight-bar ABCB pattern for their form. When Willie McTell sang,

<pre>
        C   G
       1 2 3 4   1   2 3
You may search the ocean
            F
     4   1 2   3   4   1 2 3
You might go 'cross the deep blue sea
            C
     4   1 2   3   4
Honey you'll never find
                   C
   1   2 3 4   1   2 3 4   1 2 3 4
Another hot shot like me.[34]
</pre>

to an eight-bar musical pattern, he was thinking in the same musical terms as Hughes in writing "Sylvester's Dyin' Bed:"

<pre>
        C   G   F
       123 4   1   2 3 4 1
I woke up this mornin'
       2   3   4   1   2 3 4
'Bout half past three.
              C
      4   1   2 3
All the womens in town
     G   C
     4 1   2   3   4   1 2 3 4   1 2 3 4
Was gathered 'round me.
</pre>

"Could Be," "Bad Luck Card," "Reverie on Harlem River," and "As Befits A Man" also follow the same pattern:

<pre>
        C   G
       1 23 4   1   2 3
I don't mind dyin'—
</pre>

```
          F
   4      1    2 3 4    1    2 3
But I'd hate to die all alone!
              C
   4      1    2      3
I want a dozen pretty women
   G              C
   4  1 2   3    4    1    2 3 4   1 2 3 4
To holler, cry and moan. ("As Befits A Man")
```

Thus these poems should not be seen as twelve-bar blues; the first thought is not repeated for typographical accommodation. Hughes is conceiving the above-mentioned poems in the same way as the blues singers conceived their eight-bar lyrics, as demonstrated by placing the chord changes and 32 beats applicable to the blues singers' performed eight-bar blues on Hughes's literary efforts.

"Reverie on Harlem River" is one of these eight-bar poems that uses typography for dramatic effect in its last stanza:

> Down on Harlem River
>   Two A.M.
>   Midnight
>   By yourself
> Lawd, I wish I could die—
> But who would miss me if I left?

Here the second, third, and fourth lines are dramatically emphasized by division into three lines of material which actually lasts the same amount of beats as lines one, five, or six. Thus, we have here a kind of literary use of typography in a traditional blues stanza, indicating Hughes's willingness to use the resources of both the oral and written tradition to successfully deliver his work.

This is not the only eight-bar pattern in blues, and Hughes makes use of another eight-bar blues pattern, employed, for example, in Peetie Wheatstraw's "Ice and Snow Blues:"

```
              C
              1 2 3
I did more for you
       4          1    2 3
Than you understand
                  F
       4          1      2   3
You can tell by the bullet holes
```

```
          4           1    2 3
    Mama, now, here in my hand
                    C
        4                 1      2   3
    Baby, now, you got to reap, baby
          G
        4   1   2 3
    Just what,
            C
        4       1    2 3 4   1 2 3 4
    what you sow.35
```

Hughes uses the same pattern in "Southern Mammy Sings:"

```
                        C
                        1        2 3
        Miss Gardner's in her garden
            4                    1  2 3
        Miss Yardman's in her yard
                                F
            4                  1    2 3
        Miss Michaelmas is at de mass
            4          1      2 3 4
        And I'm getting tired.
          C         G
          1234   123
            Lawd!
          C
          4        1      2 3 4   1 2 3 4
        I'm gettin' tired!
```

In both the blues lyrics and the poems the first four lines are completed by the end of sixteen beats or four bars, and the last four bars comprise a kind of refrain that recurs in each stanza of both works. The last two lines of Hughes's poem replace the final three in Wheatstraw's stanza, which are admittedly protracted. The exclamation "Lawd" is stretched, for dramatic effect, to cover several beats—a common enough occurrence in blues music. Within this standard pattern Hughes presents a world in which people's names describe their activities or occupations, much more like a medieval order than a democracy. Once each person is "in his place," typed, defined and/or limited by it, the Southern mammy—white folks' symbol of the beneficient, kind, happy, mother figure—protests her weariness of the situation. The poem goes on to complain about white folks in an unmasked way not common to traditional blues—at least as far as reflected by commercial releases, though there are black blues and non-blues traditional songs with direct anti-white statements.

Hughes's "Same in Blues" follows this same pattern, as demonstrated here with a comparison to Tampa Red's "It Hurts Me Too":

> I said to my baby
> Baby take it slow
> I can't she said, I can't
> I got to go!
>> There's a certain
>> amount of travelling
>> in a dream deferred. ("Same in Blues")

> I can't be happy, mama
> For bein' so blue
> When you keep on worryin'
> The way you do
> When things go wrong
> Go wrong with you
> It hurts me too.[36]

In "Same in Blues," however, Hughes's modulation of the last three lines in each stanza—the refrain—creates a masterful effect quite unlike anything in traditional blues, as "travelling," "nothing," "importance," and "confusion" are identified as aspects of a dream deferred.

Poems like "Life is Fine" could fit into either one of the eight-bar patterns: the first if we consider the italicized words as interjections, the second if we consider them as a refrain:

> I came up once and hollered!
> I came up once and cried!
> If that water hadn't a-been so cold
> I might've sunk and died.
>
>> *But it was*
>> *Cold in that water!*
>> *It was cold!*

The former is much more likely, since Hughes doesn't use the words regularly as a refrain, and since he has used interjections in "Ballad of the Gypsy," "Stony Lonesome," and his "boogie poems" in *Montage of a Dream Deferred.*

The influences of twelve- and eight-bar stanzas are not always mutually exclusive in Hughes's poetry or traditional blues songs. Critic George Kent, in discussing "Early Evening Quarrel" and "Lover's Return," states that "Hughes is at his best when he attempts to capture the blues spirit and varied forms of response to existence in a poem that uses non-blues devices."[37] He goes on to list free verse, free dramatizing of concrete situations, and the formal resources of literary technique as those non-blues devices applied in these poems. But these poems both use standard blues forms, not free verse, and the dramatizing in "Early Evening Quarrel" is not unlike the comedy-blues dialogues by such duos as Butterbeans and Susie, Grant and Wilson, Billy and Mary Mack, and Johy Byrd and Mae Glover. In "Early Evening Quarrel" the speaker alternates between male and female partners, each having one twelve-bar stanza apiece; as the poem continues, however, the stanzas switch to four lines apiece, and we need to confront the question of whether the stanza influence is eight-bar or something else. Something else seems more likely: Hughes may be resorting to a common device of comedy dialogue blues. These lines may be spoken lines, each lasting one bar, the whole three stanzas lasting twelve, but merely drawing upon a common popular device of comedy-blues dialogues.

"Lover's Return" may depend on a similar pattern, only this time the one-bar lines open the poem, which finishes with a traditional twelve-bar stanza. On the other hand, there is the possibility that the structure of the poem is based on four-line eight-bar stanzas for the first three stanzas of Hughes's poem, ending with a twelve-bar stanza. There are precedents for this mixture of stanzas in traditional blues, as in King Solomon Hill's "That Gone Dead Train:"

> And I'm goin' way down
> Lord, I'm gonna try to leave here today
> Tell me that's a mean old fireman
> And that train is just that way.
>
> Get on that train
> I said I'd even brought my trunk
> Boys if you had been running around this world
> This train will wreck your mind.
>
> Lord I once was a hobo
> I crossed many points
> But I decided I'd pull down for a fast life
> And take it as it comes.
>
> There's so many people
> Have gone down today
> And these fast trains north and south
> Settled in . . [?] . . and Clay.
>
> Mm Mm
> I want to ride your train
> I said look here engineer

> Can I ride your train
> He said look you ought to know this train ain't mine
> And you asking me in vain.[38]

These eight-bar stanzas are in actuality twelve-bar stanzas with the middle four bars removed, and from the twelve-bar stanza the song continues with two more twelve-bar stanzas, ending finally with a four-bar stanza. This modulation of stanza length is used elsewhere in traditional blues: Tommy Johnson's "Canned Heat Blues" and Furry Lewis's "Big Chief Blues" both employ twelve-bar stanzas throughout the performances, changing in the last verse to eight-bar stanzas, and Sunny Boy and His Pals in "France Blues" use all twelve-bar stanzas save for the second last verse.[39] While this practice on modulation of stanza length is not all that common, there is a precedent for Hughes to follow in his blues-influenced poems.

> My old time daddy
> Came back home last night.
> His face was pale and
> His eyes didn't look just right.
> He says, "Mary, I'm
> Comin' home to you—
> So sick and lonesome
> I don't know what to do!
>
> *Oh, men treats women*
> *Just like a pair o' shoes—*
> *You kicks 'em round and*
> *Does like you choose.*
>
> I looked at my daddy—
> Lawd! And I wanted to cry.
> He looked so thin—
> Lawd! That I wanted to cry.
> But the devil told me:
>
> *Damn a lover*
> *Come home to die!*

In this poem the first two stanzas set up the situation that causes the blues, while the third stanza, italicized, presents the woman's direct statement of her troubles. When in the last stanza the speaker reports that the devil said, "Damn a lover / come home to die!" and the words are italicized, one can identify the earlier stanza with the devil's words and motives, and realize that the female speaker is battling with herself from two points of view, personifying her bitterness and her rejection of her lover in the form of the devil, and identifying her true self with the compassion expressed in her description of his pitiful appearance and in the first four lines of the final stanza. The final stanza is lengthened to a twelve-bar stanza for an important purpose: stanza one sets the stage; stanza two gives the man's point of view; stanza three gives the "devil's"/ hard line point of view; and the last stanza, the most lengthy one, combines the woman's/compassionate point of view with the devil/hard line approach. Thus Hughes uses traditional forms and typographical effect to build to his dramatic conclusion and indicate the psychological complexity of the situation.

From this more sophisticated use of the twelve- and eight-bar forms one can move to the slicker, vaudeville-type blues that seemed to attract Hughes so much. Vaudeville or "classic" blues singers often had a background in vaudeville or musical stage shows, as opposed to the traditional wandering blues singers who often played for small groups of friends or neighbors or at country dances or small, crowded bars. "Classic" blues singers were predominantly female, and were often billed as "queens" as they rather flamboyantly burlesqued opera prima donnas. As Titon points out, vaudeville blues "ordinarily began with a sung introduction, variable in form, in which the singer explained why she was blue," followed by the standard twelve-bar blues stanza, although the introduction could be, and was often, omitted. This structure owed a great deal to W. C. Handy.[40] While this is standard structure, the Tin Pan Alley tunesmiths, the often jazz or ragtime accompanists, and the "classic" blues singers often took liberties with the blues stanzas, and Hughes demonstrates a broad knowledge of those liberties.

"The Weary Blues" is a Hughes poem that seems influenced by vaudeville blues structures. Here Hughes narrates the story of a Harlem pianist, with an introduction that leads into standard twelve-bar blues stanzas and lyrics, and closes once again on the narrative role. The repeated use of rhymed couplets separated by refrains—lines 3, 6, 7, 8, 11, 14, 15, 16—lends heightened dramatization to the words after the manner of the vaudeville blues singers, and phrases like "mellow croon" and "crooned that tune" evoke a vaudeville-stage aura identifiable with the heightened drama and stagey romanticism of the vaudeville stage. However, here it is not the singer describing why he or she is blue, but the experience of a poet hearing a blues singer and understanding at bottom what the weary blues are and what they mean. While Hughes draws on the "classic" blues format, he is not a performer but an analytical, detached voice striving to identify with the "Sweet Blues!/Coming back from a black man's soul!"

"Blue Monday" is another type of vaudeville blues stanza, a sixteen-bar stanza:

```
      1  2   3   4
No use in my going
    1    2    3    4    1 2 3 4   1 2 3
Downtown to work today,
    4   1
     It's eight
    2    3  4 1
     I'm late
    2        3            4     1   2 3 4   1 2 3 4
And it's marked down that-a-way
    1    2        3
Saturday's and Sunday's
    4    1   2   3 4
Fun to sport around
      1  2   3
But no use denying—
    4       1  2   3
Monday'll get you down
    4            1  2  3 4
That old blue Monday
    1    2    3    4  1    2 3 4   1 2 3 4
Will surely get you down.
```

"Classic" blues singer Margaret Carter's "I Want Plenty Grease In My Frying Pan" has a similar structure:

```
    1   2      3    4      1 2 3
I need plenty grease in my frying pan
    4    1   2        3   4   1 2 3 4
'Cause I don't want my meat to burn
    1       2        3  4 1    2        3
You know I asked you first to get me some lard
    4  1      2    3  4   1   2 3 4
But it seems that you cannot learn.
       1  2   3      4    1
You know I use plenty grease
    2    3
Everyday
    4  1      2   3      4
But I ain't did no frying while
    1       2  3  4
You was away.
       1    2    3    4    1 2  3
I need plenty grease in my frying pan
    4   1       2     3  4 1      2 3 4
Cause I don't want my meat to burn.[41]
```

Basically the two works divide into three sections: the first five lines of the poem and the first four lines of the blues lyrics; the next four lines of each; and final two lines of each. While Carter's lyric is framed with the same two lines, and Hughes's builds to the conclusion, the two have a fairly similar vaudeville blues structure, and it is not hard to imagine a "red hot mama" singing Hughes's poem, complete with jazz-blues accompaniment and stop-time musical accompaniment to lines 6–9.

Other Hughes poems like "Missing," "Cora," "Blues at Dawn," "Miss Blues'es Child," and "Down and Out" also draw on vaudeville blues influences, and since the vast majority of vaudeville blues singers were female, it is not surprising to find that the blues influences on Hughes's poems extend to the characterizations in that Hughes often uses female speakers in both his vaudeville and traditional blues poems. Clearly this is an influence of the Harlem environment and the prevalence of vaudeville blues singers in that locale. Hughes's blues-influenced poems "Misery," "Cora," "Down and Out," "Widow Woman," "Young Gal Blues," "Hard Daddy," "Midwinter Blues," "Lament Over Love," "Lover's Return," and "Southern Mammy Sings" all utilize female speakers, indicating an interest not only in female vaudeville blues attitudes but also in the female point of view, as opposed to a strictly personal male point of view, as one would expect from a male traditional blues performer.

Therefore we can see in Hughes's work an attempt to represent both male and female speakers, portraying a broader spectrum of attitudes and experience. This is demonstrated clearly in Hughes's play "Don't You Want To Be Free?" which dramatizes a series of situations by illuminating them with blues lyrics appropriate to the situation. While Hughes's blues-influenced poems often indicate the sex of the speaker, "Blue Monday," "The Weary Blues," "Blues at Dawn," "Miss Blues'es Child," "Bound No'th Blues" and others sung in the play by a young man could be just as easily appropriate for a female. We cannot therefore automatically assume that a vaudeville blues poem necessarily has a female speaker, although within the blues tradition the female singer would be much more likely.

The female "blues-singers" of Hughes's blues poems are in direct contrast to the young female cabaret girls of some of his non-blues poems. Edward Waldron contends that the "blues women" are older and wiser than some of the sweet, young cabaret girls [Hughes] has whirling around much of his non-blues poetry."[42] The women of the blues poems are indeed world-wise and world-weary, alternately resolved and resigned, sometimes protesting, but these characteristics are meant to indicate advanced age. Those whirling cabaret girls function as exotic illusions to be played off against the reality of growing up fast in an overcrowded ghetto where the blues are never far off, where, as the poem goes, it "seems like trouble gonna drive me to my grave."[43] In other words, the difference in "age" is not so much chronological as it is experiential. Still, there is a poem like "Young Gal's Blues" that deals with the fear of the losses of looks and companionship that accompany the aging process. Ultimately, though, the vaudeville blues singers were not necessarily old women—in fact they were often young, vivacious, and extravagant—and the difference between them and the females in the non-blues poems has more to do with experience and outlook than with age.

The subject matter of Hughes's blues poems is, as Jemie points out, less varied than in the blues tradition:

> No topical or occasional blues, no prison or chain gang blues, no gambling blues, no blues about someone running his mouth . . . elaborate gun bores and weaponry of popular blues are absent . . . the popular letter motif is rare . . . there are no talking blues . . . social protest is rare in Hughes as in popular blues.[44]

In general these comments are true, though it should be pointed out that Hughes wrote an impromptu "Goodbye Newport Blues" for Muddy Waters and Otis Spann, commemorating the closing down of the Newport Jazz Festival due to rioting.[45] There are also brief, peripheral references to gambling in "Ballad of the Fortune-Teller" and "Midnight Raffle." The question of social protest is somewhat more difficult. The most pertinent question is whether the fact of a black man complaining of social status, situation, lifestyle, or complaining against social institutions, constitutes social protest. The powers that be certainly seem to perceive complaints—both direct and indirect—as threats, and therefore a form of protest. In this respect, the negative description of black social conditions in blues lyrics constitutes a complaint, albeit covert. Richard Wright has suggested that protest is encoded, and that unsuccessful love relationships described in blues lyrics are sublimated racial hostilities,[46] and indeed this is a possibility. Therefore the question of protest in blues lyrics is a complicated matter arguable from both sides.

Even under Jemie's definition, though, a poem like "Southern Mammy Sings" could be considered social protest. After stanza one puts everyone in his "proper place" and expresses a world-weariness, the southern mammy leaves her "place" by overtly criticizing the white man for wars, lynching, and slavery. In the last stanza she makes an ironic apology as precursor to her most telling comment, that white folks "just ain't got no heart." Clearly the last three stanzas express what was repressed or merely hinted at in the first stanza: a movement from covert to overt protest. This type of overt protest is, however, rare both in Hughes's poetry and in traditional blues.

Both these limitations in theme and imagery may be due in part to the influence of the urban vaudeville blues singers and their lyrics on Hughes. While both traditional and vaudeville blues took relations between lovers as primary subject matter, audiences—particularly white audiences—were much more likely to run across vaudeville blues on stage. Acknowledged attempts to "touch" up the rough, earthy, overtly sexual blues for the stage could help explain vaudeville blues' contribution to these limitations in Hughes's vaudeville-blues influenced poems. The lack of this sexual perspective in Hughes's traditional blues poems also helps explain part of the problem with the authenticity of those poems. Admittedly, sexual imagery was present in vaudeville blues, as evident from the text by Margaret Carter cited earlier, and by the recorded output of "Ma" Rainey and Bessie Smith—two of Hughes's favorites, which were often close to the direct, honest, and earthy expression of the folk roots. We need, then, to look elsewhere for further explanation of the causes of these restrictions on Hughes's work.

Hughes's vantage point seems to have caused him to aim for a quaint, clever humor with sometimes overly romantic lyrics, as in "Miss Blues'es Child," as opposed to, for example, the powerful and/or double entendre lyrics of Peetie Wheatstraw's "Ice and Snow Blues," cited previously, or Robert Johnson's "Hellhound on My Trail,"

> I can tell the wind is risin'
> The leaves tremblin' on the trees
> Tremblin' on the trees.

and "Terraplane Blues,"

> I'm gonna hoist your hood, mama,
> I'm bound to check your oil.[47]

Bluesmen like Wheatstraw and Johnson were able to create stronger pure blues lyrics than Hughes because their blues were personal expressions of their own lives and experiences within the tradition; not something, as in Hughes's poems, often written about or for other people, symbolic of the souls' desires of a nation of "low down folks." In Hughes, though, those wants eliminate the sexual desires so often expressed in blues lyrics. That he was aware of the sexuality in blues lyrics is evident: in *The Big Sea* he quotes a blues from the rue Pigalle:

> Lawd, I looked and saw a spider
> Goin' up de wall.
> I say, I looked and saw a spider
> Goin' up de wall.
> I say where you goin', Mister Spider?
> I'm goin' to get my ashes hauled![48]

It is likely also that Hughes was not bawdy, violent, or extreme in much of his published work because publishers were not interested in so-called "objectionable" material like that published posthumously in *Good Morn-*

ing Revolution. Indeed Hughes himself developed a natural reticence to discuss such material. Hughes seems to have struck a compromise: a deep pride in, a deep commitment to, the blues tradition in America, tempered by a desire to present a less extreme or offensive face to the public for acceptance, and by the imposed limitations of the publishing establishment. The acceptance that Hughes sought was not only for himself, but for the black oral tradition, and it was an acceptance that provided a beat to which his poetic successors would sing more bawdy, violent, or extreme verses.

If the startling impact and poetic devices of top-drawer bluesmen like Wheatstraw and Johnson are not matched by Hughes's blues poems, Hughes's impact as a popularizer and "legitimizer" of blues and as a professional artist imposing some external intellectual constraints of the genre—in variety and violation of structure and manipulation of the benefits of a writer as opposed to oral work—more than make up for his limitations. Poems like "The Weary Blues," "Southern Mammy Sings," and "Same in Blues" are most successful, transcending the absence of an actual musical and vocal performance by capturing the spirit in the cadence of the lines, and extending the limits of the oral tradition by altering or breaking the existing structures or themes of the blues.

The range of Langston Hughes's interest in and knowledge of the blues tradition and his attempts to employ aspects of the oral blues tradition in his work reveal his genius in recognizing the blues as a truly great folk art in itself, and a worthy resource for writers of the Harlem Renaissance and beyond. While there are some obvious limitations to Hughes's work in presenting a totally forthright picture of the blues tradition, the poems he has left, in their skillful use of a tradition whose beauty and creativity is still often only suspected, deserve to be read and remembered.

A Selection of Hughes's Poems Categorized by the Blues Stanza Form
Utilized, With Identification of the Sex of the Speaker

12 Bar Blues

Morning After	Male
Widow Woman	Female
Young Gal's Blues	Female
Hard Daddy	Female
Midwinter Blues	Female
Lament Over Love	Female
Bound No'th Blues	Undetermined
Stony Lonesome	Undetermined

8 Bar Blues

Sylvester's Dyin' Bed	Male
Could Be	Undetermined
Bad Luck Card	Undetermined
As Befits A Man	Male
Midnight Raffle	Undetermined
Life is Fine	Undetermined
Southern Mammy Sings	Female
Same in Blues	Male and Female

Vaudeville Type Blues

The Weary Blues	Undetermined
Blue Monday	Undetermined
Misery	Female
Cora	Female
Blues at Dawn	Undetermined
Miss Blues'es Child	Undetermined
Down and Out	Female

Stanzaic Mixtures

Early Evening Quarrel	Male and Female
Lover's Return	Female

Notes

1. Samuel Charters, *The Bluesmen* (New York: Oak Publications, 1967), p. 166.
2. Langston Hughes, *The Big Sea* (New York: Hill and Wang, 1963), p. 215. The following lines from "The Weary Blues" are quoted from the same page.
3. Henry Thomas, "Texas Worried Blues," *Ragtime Texas*, Herwin LP 209. Throughout this work references to blues recordings will be listed not by the original 78 RPM issues, but by available 33 RPM reissues. This practice will enable the reader to procure copies of the recordings for illumination.
4. Henry Thomas, "Railroading Some," Herwin LP 209.
5. Liner notes to *Have No Fear, Big Joe Turner Is Here*, Savoy LP 2223. The following quote also occurs in these notes.
6. Charles Keil, *Urban Blues* (Chicago: University of Chicago Press, 1966), p. 61.
7. Nat Pierce, Liner Notes to *Kansas City Piano*, Decca LP 79226.
8. ARC, Columbia, Brunswick, Library of Congress, Vocalion, and Okeh, among others.
9. Ramblin' Willard Thomas, "Poor Boy Blues," *Blind Lemon Jefferson/Ramblin' Willard Thomas*, Collector's Classics LP CC5.
10. Horace Butterworth, Liner Notes to *Tex-Arkana-Louisiana Country*, Yazoo, LP 1004.
11. Jeff Titon, *Early Downhome Blues* (Urbana, Ill.: Univ. of Chicago Press, 1979), p. 104. See also Samuel Charters, *The Country Blues* (New York: Holt, Rinehart, and Winston, 1959) and Leroi Jones, *Blues People* (New York: Wiliam Morrow, 1959).
12. Langston Hughes, "Songs Called the Blues," *The Langston Hughes Reader*, ed. George Braziller (New York: George Braziller, Inc. 1958), pp. 159–61.
13. Hughes, *The Big Sea*, p. 161.
14. Langston Hughes, "Music at Year's End," *Chicago Defender*, 9 January 1943.
15. Langston Hughes, Cliff Roberts, and David Martin, *The First Book of Jazz* (New York: Franklin Watts, Inc. 1955).
16. Langston Hughes, "The Negro Artist and the Racial Mountain," The *Nation*, 23 June 1925, pp. 692–714.
17. Onwuchekwa Jemie, *Langston Hughes* (New York: Columbia University Press, 1976), pp. 77.
18. R. M. W. Dixon and John Godrich, *Recording the Blues* (New York: Stein and Day, 1970), pp. 104–5.
19. *The Langston Hughes Reader*, p. 161. The next two quotations also occur on p. 161.
20. *The Negro Renaissance*, ed. Arthur P. Davis and Michael W. Peplow (New York: Holt, Rinehart and Winston, 1975), p. 280.
21. *The Langston Hughes Reader*, p. 159.
22. Hughes, *The Big Sea*, p. 299.
23. *The Langston Hughes Reader*, p. 159.
24. Titon, p. 203.
25. Hughes, Roberts and Martin, p. 19.
26. *Arna Bontemps-Langston Hughes Letters 1925–67*. Selected and ed. by Chas. H. Nichols (New York: Dodd & Mead, 1980), p. 524.
27. Jemie, p. 77.
28. Titon, p. 179.
29. Langston Hughes, "Sylvester's Dyin' Bed," *Selected Poems of Langston*

Hughes, ed. Langston Hughes (New York: Vintage Books, 1974), p. 38. Hereafter all quotations of Hughes's poems will be from this edition, and will be documented by poem titles and page numbers in parentheses within the text.

30. Furry Lewis, "Creeper's Blues," *Frank Stokes' Dream*, Yazoo LP 1008.

31. Peg Leg Howell, "Rock and Gravel Blues," *Blues From Georgia*, Roots LP RL 309.

32. Peg Leg Howell, "Turtle Dove Blues," *Blues from Georgia*, Roots LP RL 309.

33. Mississippi John Hurt, "Got the Blues, Can't Be Satisfied," *Mississippi John Hurt 1928*. Biograph LP BLP-C4.

34. Blind Willie McTell, "Searching the Desert for the Blues," *Bluebird Blues*, RCA Victor LP V-518.

35. Peetie Wheatstraw, "Ice and Snow Blues," *Kokoma Arnold/Peetie Wheatstraw*, Blues Classics, LP PC4.

36. Tampa Red, "It Hurts Me Too," *The Guitar Wizard*, Blues Classics LP BC25.

37. George Kent, "Langston Hughes and Afro American Folk and Cultural Tradition," *Langston Hughes: Black Genius*, ed. Therman B. O'Daniel (New York: William Morrow and Co., Inc., 1971), p. 202.

38. King Solomon Hill, "That Gone Dead Train," *Tex-Arkana-Louisiana Country*. Yazoo LP 1004.

39. Tommy Johnson, "Canned Heat Blues," *The Famous 1928 Tommy Johnson Ishman Bracey Session*, Roots LP RL330; Furry Lewis, "Big Chief Blues," in *The Blues Line*, ed. Eric Sackheim, (New York: Schirmer Books, 1975), p. 253; and Sunny Boy and his Pals, "France Blues," *Really! The Country Blues*, Origin LP OJL-2.

40. Titon, p. xvi (preface), referring to Handy's published blues efforts that helped to standardize structure, much as the employment of the printing press had helped to standardize language.

41. Margaret Carter, "I Want Plenty Grease In My Frying Pan," *Pot Hound Blues*, Historical LP HLP15.

42. Edward Waldron, "The Blues Poetry of Langston Hughes," *Negro American Literature Forum* 5 (1971), 144.

43. Davis, p. 282.

44. Jemie, p. 45.

45. Muddy Waters, "Goodbye Newport Blues," *Muddy Waters at Newport*, Chess LP 1449.

46. Richard Wright, Forward to Paul Oliver's *Meaning of the Blues* (New York: Collier Books, 1972), pp. 7–12. See also Paul Oliver, *The Blues Tradition* (New York: Oak Publications, 1970), pp. 258–9.

47. Robert Johnson, "Hellhound on My Trail," and "Terraplane Blues," *King of the Delta Blues Singers*, Columbia LP CL1654.

48. Hughes, *The Big Sea*, p. 162.

◆◆◆◆◆◆◆◆◆◆◆◆◆

Hughes: His Times and His Humanistic Techniques

RICHARD K. BARKSDALE

In one of his critical essays, "Tradition and Individual Talent," T. S. Eliot suggested that there is a necessary creative tension between a given tradition and most writers who choose to write in that tradition. The tradition defines an approach and a set of guidelines that tend to restrict the creativity of the individual writer, and the writer in reaction seeks to assert his independence and modify the tradition.[1] So tradition speaks to writer and writer speaks to tradition. At times, a writer affects a given tradition little or not at all. For instance, a nineteenth-century romantic poet like Philip Freneau did not change the tradition of romantic poetry at all. On the other hand, Algernon Swinburne, because of his literary and physical encounter with sadism and various kinds of eroticism, revolted against the tradition of Victorian neo-romanticism, and the tradition was never quite the same after Swinburne.

The case of Langston Hughes is not exactly comparable, but there is substantial evidence that by 1926, with the publication of his *Weary Blues*, he had broken with one or two rather well-established traditions in Afro-American literature. By no means was he alone in this act of literary insurrection; Claude McKay, Jean Toomer, and other poets of the 1920s stood with him. First, Hughes chose to modify the poetic tradition that decreed that whatever literature the Black man produced must not only protest racial conditions but promote racial integration. There was little or no place in such a literary tradition for the celebration of the Black lifestyle for its own sake. With obviously innocuous intent, Dunbar had attempted some celebration of the Black lifestyle in the post-Reconstruction rural South, but his pictures of happy pickaninnies and banjo-plucking, well-fed cabin Blacks did not square with the poverty and racial violence that seared that period. In any event, by 1920 a poetry of strong social protest which attempted to plead cultural equality with White America had become a fixed tradition in Afro-American literature. It was thought that Black America's writers could knock on the door of racial segregation and successfully plead for admission into a presumably racially integrated society. Of course, admission would not be gained unless these writers, painters, and sculptors had all been properly

94

schooled in Western techniques and practices and thus fully qualified for acceptance. It might be pointed out in this context that to effect this end, even the so-called spirituals or sorrow-songs of the slaves were Europeanized—songs whose weird and sadly provocative melodies had had such a marked effect on northern Whites when first heard on the Carolina Sea Islands in 1862. In 1916, Harry T. Burleigh, the Black organist at New York's ultra-fashionable St. George's Episcopal Church, published his *Jubilee Songs of the United States* with every spiritual arranged so that a concert singer could sing it, "in the manner of an art song." Thus, the Black man's art in song and story was to be used primarily to promote racial acceptance and ultimately achieve racial integration. And it was clear that it had to be a Europeanized art.

Necessarily excluded from consideration in any such arrangement was the vast amount of secular folk material which had been created throughout the years of the Black man's persecution and enslavement in America. For during slavery Black people had used song and story to achieve many social and political goals. They had covertly ridiculed "massa" and "missus" in song and story and had overtly expressed their disdain and hatred for the "niggah driber." And since slavery, they had sung the blues on waterfront levees and in juke joints; they had built railroads and sung about John Henry and other laboring giants; they had been on chain gangs and as prisoners had been leased out to cruel masters to cut the tall cane on the Brazos to the tune of the slashing whip and under a blazing sun which they called "Ole Hannah." They had sung as they chopped cotton on tenant farms and scrubbed and ironed clothes in the White folks' kitchens. All of this orature, as some critics have called it, was, in the opinion of certain twentieth-century monitors of Afro-American culture, to be totally excluded from common view. Innocuous tidbits might be acceptable, like James Weldon Johnson's "Since You Went Away," which was one of the "croon songs" published in his 1916 volume *Fifty Years and Other Poems*. But generally, the richly complex burden of secular folk material—the songs and stories that came out of the sweat, sorrow, and occasional joy of Black people of the lower classes—might impede integration and hence was to be expunged from the racial literary record.

The crystallization of a tradition which outlawed Black folk literature and song inevitably fostered some attitudes which adversely affected the jazz and blues which were just beginning to be established in the early 1920s when Hughes first settled in New York City. For the indictment of folk material resulted in the cultural censure of the blues singing of Bessie and Clara Smith; the jazz playing of Duke Ellington, Louis Armstrong, and Fletcher Henderson; and the song-and-dance and vaudeville showmanship of Bill Robinson, Bert Williams, Eubie Blake, and Noble Sissell. Ironically, one of the cultural monitors of the period, James

Weldon Johnson, had written that the cakewalk and ragtime were two of Black America's principal contributions to American culture. Johnson had been a music man himself at one time in his career. But other strong-minded monitors of Black culture ignored Johnson and deemed that the dancing, singing, laughing, blues-singing, jazz-playing Black was too uncomfortably close to a despised folk tradition to project a proper integrationist image. In retrospect, one is forced to observe that in view of how deeply Black jazz and music have influenced both twentieth-century American and European lifestyles, this attempt to demean the image of the Black entertainer and music man of the early 1920s is indeed one of the great ironies in Afro-American cultural history.

So Langston Hughes and other young poets of the early years of the Harlem Renaissance had to confront a point of view which had quickly crystallized into a binding and restricting tradition. Hughes also developed a dislike for the tradition of racial exoticism which, largely promoted by White patrons, began to be an absorbing concern of Black writers by the mid-1920s. Although his resistance to racial exoticism eventually ruptured his relationship with his patron, Mrs. R. Osgood Mason, his fight against a tradition barring orature and the rich folk material of the lower classes of Blacks became his major struggle. The discussion to follow focuses not on how he waged a successful fight to change that tradition, but on the humanistic techniques which he used in his poetry to reflect and communicate the rich folk culture of Black people.

Before making any specific attempt to describe Hughes's use of humanistic techniques in his folk poetry, one may make at least three generalizations about his folk poetry. First, most of his folk poems have the distinctive marks of orature. They contain many instances of naming and enumerating, considerable hyperbole and understatement, and a strong infusion of street talk rhyming. Also, there is a deceptive veil of artlessness in most of the poems. Actually, there is much more art and deliberate design than one immediately perceives. I should point out in this context that Hughes prided himself on being an impromptu and impressionistic writer of poetry. His, he insisted, was not an artfully constructed poetry. But an analysis of some of his better monologues and his poems on economic and social class issues will reveal that much of his poetry was carefully and artfully crafted. The third generalization is that Hughes's folk poetry shares certain features found in other types of folk literature. There are many instances of dramatic ellipsis and narrative compression. Also, we find considerable rhythmic repetition and monosyllabic emphasis. And, of course, flooding all of his poetry is that peculiar mixture of Hughesian irony and humor—a very distinctive mark of his folk poetry.

The foregoing generalizations have a particular relevancy when one studies some of Hughes's dramatic monologues. In most instances, these are artfully done; the idioms of Black folk speech and street talk abound; and very often the final lines drip with irony and calculated understatement. An example is "Lover's Return":

> My old time daddy
> Came back home last night.
> His face was pale and
> His eyes didn't look just right.
>
> . . . .
>
> He says to me, "Mary, I'm
> Comin' home to you—
> So sick and lonesome
> I don't know what to do."²

First, there are two levels of monologue in this poem; the persona describes to the reader her elderly lover's return, and then, in lines which the poet italicizes, there is an interior monologue in which the persona talks to herself. These italicized lines clearly reveal the heightened anxiety and emotional tensions that haunt her:

> *Oh, men treats women*
> *Just like a pair o' shoes.*
> *You men treats women*
> *Like a pair o' shoes—*
> *You kicks 'em round and*
> *Does 'em like you choose.*

This interior monologue contains a repressed truth, and one can imagine the tremendous psychological pressure such a repressed truth has on the psyche of the persona. Moreover, these words in the interior monologue have a double-edged relevancy; they define the persona's particular dilemma and they also effectively generalize about a larger and more universal dilemma in the arena of sexual conflict. The full psychological impact of this monologue, however, is felt in the last stanza of the poem, where the conflict between outward compassion and inner condemnation is clearly delineated:

> I looked at my daddy—
> Lawd! and I wanted to cry.
> He looked so thin—
> Lawd! that I wanted to cry.
> But de devil told me:
>   Damn a lover
>   Come home to die!

Inevitably, as the result of the carefully controlled narrative compression commonly found in the well-crafted dramatic monologue, many facts remain explicitly unstated. But Hughes calls upon the perceptive and imaginative reader to fill out the details of this miniature but poignant drama. The persona, deserted by her lover many years ago, is now forced by an obviously unfair kind of social obligation to receive him once again. Her code of faithfulness and her sense of social propriety pull her in one direction. Her sense of fair play and justice pulls her in another direction. In the end, the harassed woman is torn between a deeply instinctual desire to avoid pain and distress and a strong sense of obligation to honor an elderly lover "come home to die." Characteristically, Hughes defines the dilemma and then leaves the resolution carefully unstated. By so doing, he suggests that the vulnerable, dilemma-ridden, anti-heroic persona truly counts in the larger human equation.

Further examples of Hughes's humanistic techniques can be found in certain of his blues poems and his dialogue and debate poems. In his gutsy reaction against the tradition which censured the blues as offensive and devoid of cultural import, Hughes wrote a lot of blues poems. In fact, *Fine Clothes to the Jew* (1927), *Shakespeare in Harlem* (1942), and *One-Way Ticket* (1949) have more than their fair share of such poems. Many are uncomplicated blues statements like:

> When hard luck overtakes you
> Nothin' for you to do.
> When hard luck overtakes you
> Nothin' for you to do.
> Gather up your fine clothes
> An' sell 'em to de Jew.[3]

or:

> I beats me wife an'
> I beats ma side gal too.
> Beats me wife an'
> Beats ma side gal too.
> Don't know why I do it but
> It keeps me from feelin' blue.[4]

In these poems there is a Hughesian blend of irony and humor but no psychological complexity. One contains some advice about how to handle hard luck with minimum psychological damage; the second poem describes the casual self-acceptance of a chronic woman-beater who apparently is unaware of the extent of his problem. But in "In a Troubled Key" there is a difference. The blues form is here, but the persona is emotionally insecure:

Still I can't help lovin' you,
Even though you do me wrong.
Says I can't help lovin' you
Though you do me wrong—
But my love might turn into a knife
Instead of to a song.[5]

The harassed persona is helplessly entwined in love, but there is the possibility that instead of a song of love, there will be knife-work in the night. Similarly, the blues poem "Widow Woman" has an unexpectedly ironic ending. After promising to be ever-faithful to a recently deceased "mighty lover" who had "ruled" her for "many years," in the last two lines the persona suddenly becomes aware of the full import of the freedom that is about to become hers. So the poem ends with the kind of ironic juxtaposition Hughes loved. The outwardly distraught widow stands sobbing by the open grave as she watches the drave-diggers throw dirt in her husband's face. But, inwardly, her heart soars joyfully at the prospect of freedom: ". . . you never can tell when a / Woman like me is free!"[6]

In addition to the humanizing techniques used by Hughes in some of his dramatic monologues, the poet also sometimes presented two personae in a dramatic dialogue form of poetry. In one or two instances, the dialogue broadens into a debate which the poet humanizes by carefully illuminating the two opposing points of view. For instance, in "Sister," one of the poems in *Montage of a Dream Deferred*, a dialogue occurs between a mother and her son about his sister's involvement with a married man. The brother is embarrassed by his sister's behavior and asks: "Why don't she get a boy-friend / I can understand—some decent man?"[7] The mother somewhat surprisingly defends her daughter; actually her Marie is the victim of the grim economic lot of the ghetto dweller. She "runs around with trash" in order to get "some cash." Thus a grim and dehumanizing economic determinism is in control of the lives of all three—the mother, the son, and the daughter. The son, however, still does not understand; he asks, "Don't decent folks have dough?" The mother, out of the wisdom of a bitter cynicism, immediately replies, "Unfortunately usually no!" And she continues: "Did it ever occur to you, boy, / that a woman does the best she can?" To this the son makes no reply, but a voice, probably the poet's, adds: "So does a man." Hughes is saying that, like the distressed, fragmented, and fallible personae of most folk poetry, human beings do the best that they can, and their failures and defeats are actually the mark of their humanity.

Another poetic dialogue, entitled "Mama and Daughter," has a slightly different thrust and meaning. There is no polarizing conflict between the two personae, but obviously each reacts quite differently to the same situation. The mother helps her daughter prepare to go "down the street" to see her "sugar sweet." As they talk, the mother becomes increasingly agitated because she remembers when she, too, went "down the street" to see her "sugar sweet." But now the romantic tinsel is gone forever from her life; her "sugar sweet" married her, got her with child, and then, like so many ghetto fathers, abandoned her to a life of unprotected loneliness. So a dramatic contrast develops between the naively hopeful daughter who is eager to join the young man she can't get off her mind, and the disillusioned mother who for different reasons can't get her errant husband off her mind. When the mother expresses the hope that her husband—"that wild young son-of-a-gun rots in hell today," her daughter replies: *Mama, Dad couldn't be still young.* The anger of the mother's final comment is the anger of all the abandoned women of all of America's urban ghettos. And what she leaves unsaid is more important than what she actually says:

> He *was* young yesterday,
> He *was* young when he—
> Turn around!
> So I can brush your back, I say![8]

Love and sex have tricked the mother and left her lonely and full of bitter memories, but the "down-the-street" ritual must be repeated for the daughter. Disappointment and disillusionment very probably await her later; but to Hughes disappointment and disillusionment await all lovers because these are, once again, the necessary and essential marks of the human condition.

There are three other poems by Hughes which provide interesting examples of his use of humanistic techniques. The first, "Blue Bayou," is a tersely wrought dramatic monologue in which the persona describes the circumstances leading to his death by lynching. In essence, it is an age-old southern tale of an inter-racial love triangle that inevitably turns out badly for the Black man. What is striking about the monologue is the poet's use of the folk symbol of the "setting sun." In some of the old blues standards, this image is a recurring motif with various overtones of meaning:

> In the evenin', in the evenin'
> When the settin' sun go down
> Ain't it lonesome, ain't it lonesome
> When your baby done left town.

or:

> Hurry sundown, hurry sundown
> See what tomorrow bring
> May bring rain
> May bring any old thing.

And at the beginning of "Blue Bayou," the "setting sun" could be a symbol of "any old thing." The persona says: "I went walkin' / By de Blue Bayou / And I saw de sun go down."⁹ Using the narrative compression and dramatic ellipsis usually found in the folk ballad, the persona then tells his story:

> I thought about old Greeley
> And I thought about Lou
> And I saw de sun go down.
> > White man
> > Makes me work all day
> > And I works too hard
> > For too little pay—
> > Then a White man
> > Takes my woman away.
> I'll kill old Greeley.

At this point, the persona's straight narration ends. In the next stanza, sundown as a reddening symbol of violent death is introduced, and the italicized choral chant of the lynchers is heard:

> De Blue Bayou
> Turns red as fire.
> *Put the Black man*
> *On a rope*
> *And pull him higher!*

Then the persona returns to state with a rising crescendo of emotional stress: "I saw de sun go down."

By the time the final stanza begins, "De Blue Bayou's / A pool of fire" and the persona utters his last words:

> And I saw de sun go down,
> > Down,
> > > Down!
> Lawd, I saw de sun go down.

The emphasis in this last stanza is on the word "down," used four times in the four lines, and in lines two and three "down, down!" are the only words used. And Hughes arranges the monosyllabic words so that the second literally is placed "down" from the first. Thus concludes this grim little tragedy of a triangular love affair that ended in a murder and a lynching.

Several additional critical observations may be made about this poem. First, it is interesting to note how Hughes manipulates the meaning of the setting sun. It is done with great verbal economy and tremendous dramatic finesse. At the beginning, when the persona views the setting

sun, it is part of a beautiful Blue Bayou setting. But the persona's mood
is blue just like the anonymous blues singer who shouts:

> In the evenin', in the evenin'
> When the settin' sun go down
> Ain't it lonesome, ain't it lonesome
> When your baby done left town.

Hughes's persona quickly and succinctly relates what has happened to
his baby, Lou. We do not know whether she left voluntarily with old
Greeley or had no choice. In any event, as the sun is setting, the persona
decides to assert his manhood and kill old Greeley. A short time after
the deed is done, the lynchers catch him by the Blue Bayou. Again the
sun is setting, but now all nature begins to reflect and mirror the victim's
agony. The bayou turns red with his blood; and then it becomes a pool
of fire mirroring the flames that begin to burn his hanging, twisting
body. Finally, the victim symbolically sees his own death as he repeats,
"Lawd, I saw de sun go down." It is through his poetic technique that
Hughes, the "artless" poet, conveys to the reader the brutal and agoniz-
ing slowness of the persona's death. Just as the setting sun in the American southland provides a scene of slow and lingering beauty as it sinks
down, down, down over the rim of the earth, so the death of the victim
is a slow and lingering agony as he sinks down, down, down into the pit
of death.

It should also be stressed that, although this poem has a recurring
blues motif in its use of the setting-sun image, it has a finality hardly
ever found in the standard blues. In fact, all good blues reflect survival
and recovery. In "Stormy Monday Blues," for instance, it takes Lou
Rawls six days to get rid of his blues; then, after the "ghost walks on
Friday," on Saturday he "goes out to play" and on Sunday he goes "to
church to pray." In the real blues the persona is always waiting hopefully
to see "what tomorrow brings." But in Hughes's "The Blue Bayou," the
persona has no tomorrow. Had the poem described a tomorrow, the
reader would have seen a bayou flooded with the bright colors of a beautiful sunrise; and, mirrored in the bayou's sun-flecked waters, one would
see the persona's body slowly twisting in the early morning breeze. The
stench of burning flesh would be everywhere and no birds would sing to
greet the multi-colored dawn.

A discussion of Hughes's humanistic techniques in poetry should include two additional poems: "Jitney," an experimental poem celebrating
a highly particularized mode of the Black lifestyle, and "Trumpet Player:
52nd Street," which reflects the poet's consummate artistry in one mode
of genre description. Essentially, both are folk poems. "Jitney" is an
exuberant salute to the jitney cabs that used to wind up and down South
Parkway in Chicago and Jefferson Street in Nashville, Tennessee. They

have long been supplanted by better modes of transportation, but in the 1930s and 1940s the jitneys were very much part of Black Chicago and Black Nashville.

In his poem, Hughes attempts to capture the uniqueness of the experience of riding a jitney cab on two round trips between Chicago's 31st and 63rd street. Like the cab, the poem snakes along; each stop—31st, 35th, 47th—is a single line, thus providing the reader with the sense of movement in space. Not only does the form reflect the content in this poem; the form is the content.

The great merit of the poem is not its experimental form, however. "Jitney" is a microcosm of a moving, surging, dynamic Black Chicago. Thus the poem celebrates not so much a mode of transportation unique to Chicago's Black Southside; rather it celebrates the Southside folk who ride jitneys and hustle up and down South Parkway to go to church, to go to the market, to go to night school, to go to nightclubs and stage shows and movies. Or sometimes the time spent riding in a jitney becomes a peaceful interlude in the hectic struggle to survive in a swiftly paced urban society—an interlude to gossip or signify:

> Girl, ain't you heard?
> *No, Martha, I ain't heard.*
> I got a Chinese boy-friend
> Down on 43rd.
> 47th,
> 51st,
> 55th,
> 63rd,
> Martha's got a Japanese!
> Child, ain't you heard?[10]

As people come and go, facts and circumstances obviously change; but apparently the mood in a jitney cab is one of warm, folksy friendliness—the kind Chicago's Black residents remembered from their "down-home" days. Indeed, the poem suggests that in a large metropolis like Black Chicago, one refuge from the cold anonymity of urban life is the jitney cab:

> 43rd,
> I quit Alexander!
> Honey, ain't you heard?
> 47th,
> 50th Place,
> 63rd,
> Alexander's quit Lucy!
> Baby, ain't you heard?

. . . .
If you want a good chicken
You have to get there early
And push and shove and grab!
I'm going shopping now, child.

The pervasive mood of "Jitney," then, is one of racial exuberance and vitality. As the cab moves up and down South Parkway, the Southside folks who jump in and out and are busy about their business have no time to talk about deferred dreams. Obviously, Chicago's Black citizens had as many as Harlem's Black citizens; but the jitney provided neither the time nor the place for in-depth discussions of racial dilemmas. It is significant that by the time Black urban American exploded into riot and racial confrontation, the jitneys of Chicago's South Parkway and Nashville's Jefferson Street had long since disappeared from the urban scene.

Finally, "Trumpet Player: 52nd Street" reveals a fine blending of the best of Hughes's humanistic techniques. In the portrait of the musician we see both a particular person and a folk symbol. For Hughes, who had started writing about "long-headed jazzers" and weary blues-playing pianists back in the 1920s, regarded the Black musician as a folk symbol with deep roots in the racial past. Thus in the poem's first stanza we greet the symbol, not the man. What the persona remembers, all Black musicians have remembered throughout all of slavery's troubled centuries:

The Negro
With the trumpet at his lips
Has dark moons of wariness
Beneath his eyes
Where the smoldering memory
Of slave ships
Blazed to the crack of whips
About his thighs.[11]

The instrument he is playing has no significance; it could be a banjo, a drum, or just some bones manipulated by agile Black fingers; the memory is the same. And the memory makes the music different. Etched in pain, the sound is better, the beat more impassioned, the melody more evocative. And the music flows forth with greater ease, as Dunbar's Malindy proved in "When Malindy Sings." Actually these musicians have found the "spontaneous overflow of powerful emotions" that the youthful Wordsworth was in search of and actually never found, for too often in Western artistic expression, traditional structures intervene and negate spontaneous creativity.

The poem also has its fair share of Hughesian irony. Where in ancient times man through his music sought the moon and the beautiful, ever-surging sea, now matters have changed:

> Desire
> That is longing for the moon
> Where the moonlight's but a spotlight
> In his eyes,
> Desire
> That is longing for the sea
> Where the sea's a bar-glass
> Sucker size.

So no fanciful escape from the hard facts of nightclub life is permitted. We can and must remember the past but we cannot escape the present, and through Hughes's gentle reminder one stumbles on one of history's great and o'erweening truths. If art does provide an escape from the present, it is but a temporary escape. But the memory of past pain and the awareness of the present's difficulties and deferred dreams are themes that make the *comédie humain* so truly comic.

Finally, as the poem draws to a close, the poet presents the trumpeter himself:

> The Negro
> With the trumpet at his lips
> Whose jacket
> Has a *fine* one-button roll,
> Does not know
> Upon what riff the music slips
> Its hypodermic needle
> To his soul.

The figure of the hypodermic needle penetrating the soul of the music man suggests that the music provides only temporary relief from the difficulties of the present: jazz is a useful narcotic to allay the world's woes. But the poetic image of the hypodermic needle also suggests that jazz lovers can develop addictive personalities and become dependent on a little music that excludes the terror and woe of human existence. It is not only good for the soul but absolutely necessary for the psyche.

The final stanza of this extraordinarily well-made poem repeats what was said at the beginning of the poem about the historical role of the Black maker of music.

> But softly
> As the tunes come from his throat
> Trouble
> Mellows to a golden note.

The music anesthetizes both performer and listener against remembered pain. In fact, the 52nd Street trumpeter with his "patent-leathered" hair and his jacket with "a *fine* one-button roll" disappears from view and a folk music man of ancient origin reappears. His role has long been to convert "trouble" into beautiful music. But Hughes humanizes the function of art and music. In "Trumpet Player: 52nd Street" the poet suggests that the Black man's music nullifies the pain of the past and seals off the woe of the present. Admittedly, the poem, with its sophisticated imagery, is probably not orature of the kind found in other poems discussed above, but the Black music man described herein has long been a focal figure in producing the songs and stories that Black people have orated and sung down through the centuries.

There are many more instances of Hughes' use of humanistic techniques throughout the full range of his poetry. But this discussion has been limited to his folk poetry—to his orature. It is now clear that Hughes's devotion to this kind of poetry had two major consequences: he broke the back of a tradition which sought to exclude secular folk material from the canon of Black literature. And, in his use of the language of the Black lower classes, Hughes prepared the way for the use and acceptance of the revolutionary Black street poetry of the late 1960s.

Notes

1. T. S. Eliot, "Tradition and Individual Talent," in *Modern Criticism* (New York: Sutton and Foster, 1963), p. 142.
2. *Selected Poems* (New York: Knopf, 1959), p. 112.
3. *Fine Clothes to the Jew* (New York: Knopf, 1927), p. 4.
4. "Bad Man," in *Fine Clothes to the Jew*, p. 21.
5. *Shakespeare in Harlem* (New York: Knopf, 1942), p. 49.
6. *Selected Poems*, p. 139.
7. *Montage of a Dream Deferred* (New York: Holt, 1951), p. 7.
8. *One-Way Ticket* (New York: Knopf, 1949), pp. 31–32.
9. Ibid., pp. 53–54.
10. Ibid., pp. 131–33.
11. *Selected Poems*, pp. 114–15.

♦♦♦♦♦♦♦♦♦♦♦♦♦

"Some Mark to Make": The Lyrical Imagination of Langston Hughes

R. BAXTER MILLER

W. R. Johnson, a superior theorist, illuminates the lyric well:

> We want the pictures, yes, but we also want the hates and loves, the blame
> and the praise, the sense of a living voice, of a mind and heart that are
> profoundly engaged by a life they live richly, eagerly. Art, then, any art, is
> not a reproduction of what is seen: it is a highly complex action (action both
> by artist and audience) in which what is outer and what is inner—things,
> perceptions, conceptions, actualities, emotions, and ideas—are gathered into
> and made manifest by emotional and intelligible forms. The artist cannot be
> undisciplined in searching for such forms; . . . he can no more be slovenly in
> his habits of feeling and thinking than he can be slovenly in his habits of
> looking and listening or of using the implements of his craft; but neither can
> he be dispassionate, emotionless, unconcerned. The lie in modern imagism is
> that no one snaps the picture. But the difference between a bad or mediocre
> photo and a good or great one is precisely who takes the photo—and the
> photographer, like any other artist, is defined not merely by his technique or
> his mastery of his instrument but also by the quality of his feeling, by the
> precision and vitality . . . which his composition captures and reveals . . . the
> thing that called his mind and heart into action. . . .[1]

The words describe well many poems by Langston Hughes, one of Black
America's greatest lyricists. Over nearly sixty years one has hardly
dared think so. While the Greeks believed the lyric to be a communal
performance in song, the shared epiphany between the singer and the
audience, the form implied the aristocratic elitism at court during the
Middle Ages and the Elizabethan period. In the romantic and Victorian
eras, the genre suggested privacy and isolation from the masses. Today,
somewhat diminished in favor of the dramatic monologue, as poetry has
possibly ebbed into esoterism, those who prefer personal lyric often dis-
claim the social rhetoric of direct address. Indeed, one might almost take
Langston Hughes at his word and accept the distinction between the
forms. But while the margins between genres are convenient, they are
yet flexible and partly illusory. Literary forms really mean only variations in degree. "The Negro Speaks of Rivers" (*Crisis*, June 1921),
Hughes's first published poem, displaces the personal reflection, or the
narrative, through a sequence of shifts from ancient Egypt in 3,000 B.C.
to the United States in the nineteenth century. Through the speaker's
placement in history, it leads back to the present. Drawing upon the

narrative and the dramatic elements, the poem celebrates Black America and humankind.

But, ironically, Black American history complicates the appreciation of Hughes as a lyricist. In a personal voice the poet revises the tradition he inherited. Where Phillis Wheatley praised George Washington, he honors the Black Everyman and, indeed, Everyperson. Though his contemporary, Countee Cullen, depended on sources in the poetry of John Keats, Hughes relied on allusions to the folk ballads of 1830–50 and on the nature and prophetic poems of Walt Whitman. Hughes drew upon the more contemplative verse of Vachel Lindsay. Where Paul Laurence Dunbar had earlier accommodated himself to the Old South, Hughes revised the pastoral for the times. But, as regards the folk integrity, Hughes was less native.

From *Weary Blues* in 1926, to "Daybreak in Alabama" at the end of *Panther and the Lash* in 1967, the lyric serves to open and close Hughes's literary life and work.[2] When other genres attract his attention, this one retains particular resilence. But the impulse wanes in the fifties and sixties. For Langston Hughes the lyric illuminates the graphic and timeless. Against the backdrop of time, he invokes dynamic feeling in order to subordinate and control personal loneliness, but he never excludes the communal response. In retrospection, he downplays the narrative of miscegenation ("Cross") and the allegorical tragedy ("Pierrot") into precise understatement. Or he sometimes disguises the lyrics themselves as dramatic performances through the blues song and the jazz instrument. What one finds ultimately in the lyricist concerns the sensitive self who speaks to Nature and the masses. In an epiphany the solo and the chorus face each other, at the height of the performance, itself timeless through intensity and will, but the personae live within three deades (1920–40), no matter how universal the writer dreams them to be. Whether in the twenties or the forties, one ultimately redescends from "The Negro Speaks of Rivers" or from "Oppression" to the fallen world.[3] From the poetic re-creation of Black American history in particular and the American South in general, the narrator inevitably returns to a certain death in Harlem. Sequential history is fact.

For Langston Hughes the lyric highlights the human and social dream. Incarnated in the blues singer and player, it signifies the artistic performance in general. It suggests the oral teller and the cultural priest, who recount the sacred story about experience and the past. From the history of 1855–65, the lyric records the poetic remembrance of the Civil War and the presence of one poet, Walt Whitman, who wrote it down.[4] Almost indifferent to the historical context, the speaker never mentions whom Whitman met, or when, or says why so. Including the death of Abraham Lincoln, the narrator overlooks the troubled circumstances. But what he manages yet involves a frozen moment in human and self-communion. Sometimes disguised as the blues performance, Hughes's lyric first subsumes social rhetoric into epiphany (*The Weary Blues*, 1926). Then it encourages inquiry into the technical means for the evocation of awe and wonder, for astonishment, and for the sublime.[5] Finally, the lyric demonstrates the compression and acrostic power in *Fields of Wonder* (1947). Over the years Langston Hughes abandons much lyricism to the use of dramatic monologue.

Largely to assess the significance of the change, it profits one to define the purpose and function of lyric.[6] The genre involves poetic emotion which, expressed in time, insists that time itself or, sequential thought, is illusion. Just as the lyric quality displaces the narrative poem on the grand scale, so it often represses from itself much analytic idea and dramatic action. Yet lyric situates itself in the dramatic context from which emotion emerges. Though drama takes place in history and time, the lyric distances itself from them. While the drama tends to move, the lyric remains still. The drama reveals the development of plot and character, but the lyric illuminates the progression of emotion. While the drama signifies the narrative and historical action, the lyric signifies the story of the self. At times Langston Hughes succeeds through the projection of the lyric personality into the narrator who speaks and feels truly. While the implicit dramatic action depends upon time and space, the particular situation, the lyric quality suspends them. And though a play such as *Mulatto* benefits from a precise setting, "The Negro Speaks of Rivers" reveals the permanency of memory and human existence.

However academic the overtones, any elitist assessment of Langston Hughes's lyrics must fail. Open to the range of human emotion, they express misanthropy, egoism, or cynicism.[7] In the display of the solo self, they reveal a concern for the choral one as well.[8] Here the individual talent speaks within cultural and racial tradition. So even Hughes's lyrics are covertly rhetorical. Where poetic images exist, as part of human language, they necessarily contribute to emotive and moral discourse. For the Black American and social poet, they intensely reconfirm the tension between the pictured world (American Dream) and the real one (racial lynching): "A totally unrhetorical poetry will be, as we have come to know all too well, a poetry void of passion, void of choosing, void of rational freedom—it will be in Paul Valery's metaphor, the rind of the orange without the pulp and the juice."[9] Even lyric distills the sublime, the humane and social spirit that informs figurative language: "In our technological societies, when the individual human began more and more to feel cut off from his fellows and from the world, when inwardness became less matter of anger and terror, the modern chorists, in their different ways, attempted to countervail this process of alienation by reaffirming our kinship with each other and with the world that begets us and nourishes us, by denying that the exploitations of empire and the degradations worked by the machine had or would or could succeed. . . ."[10]

To recognize the covert rhetoric in lyric means to appreciate the overlap between emotive and discursive poetry,[11] Rooted in song, the lyric reestabishes the ritual of human communion. From the ancients who sang out the odyssey, to Woody Guthrie and Bob Dylan, to Roberta Flack and Lionel Richie, the flow contains an inspirational power nearly akin to religion. What one remembers, finally, concerns the double presence that allows Langston Hughes to speak at once within and without history, to participate in the dynamic story, yet inertly reflect upon it, to read as well as feel the meaning.

For Langston Hughes the lyric imagination bridges the prelapsarian and lapsarian worlds. Aware of the discrepancy between the American word and deed, he hardly mistakes the country itself for the ideal. The imagination and social mind separate only in the failure to impose the coherent vision upon the entire range of human experience. While the tragic *Mulatto*, or the comic *Semple* [sic] *Takes a Wife* represents the diverse sides present, the lyrics express the duality of the whole imagination. The poems convert fact into value, power into thought, and the "dualism of word and deed into an orphic unity."[12] While Hughes's speakers perform the historical rites from the Harlem Renaissance (1920–28), from the Great Depression (1930s), from World War II (1940s), and from the Civil Rights Movement (1954–68), they supersede historical sequence. They contain ideals that transcend time or, indeed, Time (human pattern): "'words' and 'silence' denote two different states of feeling, the second higher and purer than the first. Words issue from time *(tempus)* and are vitiated by the penury of our daily concerns. However, they know enough to aspire to a higher and purer state, given in Eliot's lines as 'form' and 'pattern' in which the mere contents of form are not transcended but enhanced, fulfilled, redeemed. Silence is therefore a scruple which attends upon the local satisfaction of words, the voice which says that words are often self-delusions, trivial gratifications. Silence speaks against time to redeem time. Silence therefore corresponds to the fine excess of the imagination."[13] Hughes's lyric voice clarifies his own signature to Black American history. Shaped through words themselves become symbols,[14] it mediates between antonyms which are untranslatable, at least completely, into each other, including Black and White, Harlem and Africa, war and peace. However apparently private, the lyrics ultimately implode back into the folk center implied. Where the images suggest cutural beliefs and myths, the values are Black American: "Expressions cannot save us from temporality, but thanks to symbols, we can ascend to the realm of eternity."[15] While Hughes's lyricism displaces the drama and narrative of Black American history, it nevertheless signifies the passage from the Harlem Renaissance to the Civil Rights Movement. The lyrics imply the very drama which they displace, the advance from tragedy to peace.[16] While Hughes confines racial suffering and conflict to the half-light, he clarifies the need for reconciliation. Langston Hughes reclaims from American history the right to reimagine Black humanity and, indeed, humankind.[17]

A broad overview of *The Weary Blues* clarifies the thematic unity and diverse technique. Grouped according to seven romantic ideas, sixty-eight poems appear under seven headings. While the emphasis goes to the collective consciousness derived from African ancestry in particular and human history in general, other concerns are personal loneliness, isolation, and loss. Still signifying the Harlem Renaissance and the jazz age, a third set presents the cabarets, infusing interracial sex within overtones of the exotic. In a deftness often overlooked, Hughes uses anaphora to narrate an imperial self so as to sustain the blues stanza as countermelody and ironic understatement. What most complements the lyric skill concerns the dramatic movement of feeling. Through the impulse, he portrays the child's maturation into the state of the lost imagination and the transmutation of suffering into art. In narrative distancing his speakers achieve a double identification. While they situate themselves in the dramatic situation implied, they share the reader's historical consciousness. The lyric hardly represents all of the range, but the formal movement does counterplay to the dramatic tragedy suggested.

Indeed, the performance in the title poem completes the ritualistic conversion from Black American suffering into epic communion. On 1 May 1925, during a banquet at an "elegant" Fifth Avenue restaurant in New York City, the poem won a prize from *Opportunity* magazine, where it subsequently appeared. The thirty-five-line lyric presents a singer who plays one night on Harlem's Lenox Avenue. Having performed well in the club, the pianist goes to bed, as the song still sounds in the mind. In the dull pallor, and beneath the old gas light, he has played his ebony hands on the ivory keys. During the "lazy sway" from the bar stool, he has patted the floor with his feet, done a few chords, and then sung some more. Finally, he sleeps "like a rock that's dead," the artistic spirit exhausted.[18]

His performance clearly implies several dramatic actions. While one sets the dynamic playing, the Black self-affirmation against what fades, a second concerns a vital remaking of the Black self-image. A third shows the transcendence through racial stereotype into lyrical style. From the dramatic situation of the player, both musical as well as performed, the poem imposes the isolation and loneliness, yet the refusal to accept them. The song marks a metonym for the human imagination.

When Hughes's speakers step back from the dramatic performance into the lyric perception, they delimit the space of dream, sometimes in covertly sexual metaphor. At the detached distance from any dramatic situation, they even remake the iconography of Black and White, often revising and neutralizing the traditional code of culture, race, and value. Written in two stanzas, "Dream Variations" has nine lines in the first part and eight in the second one. While the persona longs for his dream, he sees the externalization in Nature, the place and the sun. What confronts him concerns the very duality of dream, which exists only in the lyric moment of timelessness. For the player within the concealed story, on the night in 1924, the performance must be completed in time to assure the customary paycheck.

While the lyric dream may therefore seem static, it finally has a meaning in the dynamic world of social change, where it would decay. In "Dream Variations" the Black self impregnates the lighted world and even Time itself. While the phallic drive into the Harlem Renaissance, the advance in chronological time, is finite, the vaginal response to sentiment, as the imaginative reassertion, remains infinite. Insofar as the Western world asserts the priority of linear time over the natural frontier, the view ultimately vanishes into darkness. Survival depends upon universal harmony with the world.

> whirl
> Till the white day is done
> Then rest at cool evening
> Beneath a tall tree
>
> . . . . . .
>
> A tall, slim tree
> Night coming tenderly
> Black like me

Here the speaker balances the double compulsion toward reason and light (white day) with the mythic sentiment which justifies life.

While the double identification with phallic time and vaginal timelessness appears perhaps most notably in "The Negro Speaks of Rivers" (*Crisis*, June 1921), a poem dedicated to the late W. E. B. Du Bois, it is more essential to the well-crafted and allegorical "Jester." "Rivers" presents the narrator's skill in retracting known civilization back to the source in East Africa. Within thirteen lines and five stanzas, through the evocation of wisdom and anagoge, one marks human consciousness. Then the speaker affirms the spirit distilled from human history, ranging from 3,000 B.C., through the mid-nineteenth century to the author himself at the brink of the Harlem Renaissance.[19] The powerful repetend, "I've known rivers. / Ancient, dusky rivers," closes the human narrative in nearly a circle, for the verse has subtly turned itself from an external focus to a now unified and internal one: "My soul has grown deep like the rivers." Except for the physical and spiritual dimensions, the subjective "I" and the "river" read the same.

So East Africa marks the source for both physical and spiritual humanity. When the Euphrates flows from East Turkey southeast and southwest into the Tigris, it recalls the rise as well as the fall of the Roman Empire. For over two thousand years, the water helped delimit the domain. Less so did the Congo which south of the Sahara demarcates the natural boundaries between White and Black Africa. The latter empties into the Atlantic Ocean, just as the Nile flows northward from Uganda into the Mediterranean. In the United States, the Mississippi River flows in the southeast from North Central Minnesota to the Gulf of Mexico. Whether north or south, east or west, the rivers signify in concentric half-circles the fertility as well as the dissemination of life. For the imaginative mind, the liquid externalizes the flow and depth. In suggesting the challenge to explore brave new worlds, Europe and the Americas, "The Negro Speaks of Rivers" reclaims the origins in Africa.

Just as the speaker in "The Negro Speaks of Rivers" stands outside of historical time, so the narrator in "Jester" distances himself from literary forms as well:

> In one hand
> I hold tragedy
> And in the other
> Comedy—
> Masks for the Soul

Detached from the dramatic situation, the narrator makes a choral appeal without didacticism, not excuding the epigrammatic twist, abruptly closing the lyric in understatement and rhetorical question. Here appears the invocation to chorus through recovery of the solo:

> Laugh at my sorrow's reign.
> I *am* the Black jester
> The dumb clown of the world,
>
> . . . .
> Once I was wise
> Shall I be wise again?

What some would mistake for simplistic discourse is thoughtful reflection.

While the lyric dream in Langston Hughes suggests the personal solo, the sea implies the choral response in Nature. Sometimes the parts coalesce in an epiphany. "As I Grew Older" tells about the persona's loss of a dream and the subsequent disillusion. The poem opens with a memory of the ideal, but the rising wall eclipses it. In color the "dark hands" resemble the shadow. What challenges the speaker concerns the need to deconstruct the negative associations and to reimage himself as positive Black light.

While the social restrictions (the wall) exist during the 1920s, they ironically imply the dream that transcends Time. In the rise, the wall demonstrates the dynamic recurrence. The social eclipse appears as "dimming" and "hiding." When dynamism leads finally to stasis, the solo self invokes Nature:

> Find my dream!
> Help me to shatter this darkness,
> To smash this night;
> To break this shadow
> Into a thousand lights of sun,
> Into a thousand whirling dreams
> Of sun!

Where color was descriptive ("my dark hands"), it becomes metaphorical, for any real "darkness" exists within.

Whatever the imminent dangers, the sea provides a means for lyric escape. Written in two stanzas, "Water-Front Streets" is simply a romantic ballad that shows a movement from external nature to the poetic mind. Hughes achieves the personal revision of the pastoral tradition in English. Evolved from Edmund Spenser, the genre was already decadent by the time of Alfred Lord Tennyson, but it subsisted in the lyrics of the Georgians near the turn of the century, just as it does today in confessional and neo-romantic poetry. While biographical and autobiographical sources generally note Lindsay and Lowell as the major influences on Hughes's verse, the diction and tone suggest Tennyson's "Crossing the Bar" (1889). The placement of life and death reverses itself, "But lads put out to sea / Who carry their beauties in their hearts / And dreams, like me." From Milton's "Il Penseroso" to Gray's "Elegy Written In A Country Churchyard," Gothic ascent and romantic isolation suggest the evolution of English lyricism. When the sailor (the poet) lifts anchor in "A Farewell," those on shore hardly miss him. Realists lack patience with dreamers. The gypsies and the sailors are metonyms, or the "wanderers of the hills and seas." Seeking the fortune, they leave "folk and fair." For Hughes's speakers, the invoked chorus provides only silence, for the "you" who live between the hills / And have never seen the seas." And they counterplay to the poet, the Black Odysseus. In "Seascape" Hughes's narrator redescends from lyric heights to sequential history. When a ship passes off the coast of Ireland, the seamen view a line of fishing ships etched against sky. Later, off the coast of England, the seamen ride ("rode") the foam where they observe an Indian merchant "coming home." Still, realism infringes upon the dreamworld. While the seascape is a revelation, the speaker rides in time as well, not merely toward his literal "home" but toward death.[20]

For Langston Hughes the lyric arrests the movement of the personal narrative toward extinction. "Death of an Old Seaman" portrays a persona who has returned home. Through alliteration and assonance, he appears against the background of the hill and sea. In facing the winds, he sets into relief all of the natural elements except fire, possibly because his life now ends. The musical recovery may exist as much within the narrative content as in the sentimental rhythm. Clearly a ballad more than a lyric, "Beggar Boy" dramatizes the mysterious performance of a black flute player. Despite the poverty, he incarnates the creativity that eludes all imagery. Distilled from Black American deprivation, the introspection tells: "And yet he plays . . . / As if Fate had not bled him. . . ." However much the final line bumps, the beggar boy remains a "shadow," but the narrator truly reads the "Fate." The story resembles the boy's "flute," the "sun." What the child feels but cannot articulate, the speaker understands well. As the signs for self-determination, the story and song oppose dark fate.

In *Fields of Wonder* (1947) Hughes disproves the critic's arbitrary and condescending claim: "His lyric poetry is no doubt of secondary importance in his work; yet, as usually happens with the minor work of great artists, his minor (lyric) poetry is high enough in quality and great enough in quantity to have sustained the reputation of a lesser poet."[21] Where the prescriptive critic favors the "social" verse he accepts too readily the distinction between lyric and rhetoric.[22] But what generates the lyrical power in *Fields* conceals the real concern with community. While the persona feigns privacy, he addresses the men and women who would hear him, for the lyric, like the dramatic monologue, implies the respondent. Sometimes the hearer is anthromorphic Nature, almost elegaic in the counterplay and impervious to Time.

In *Fields* Hughes makes the external world (fields) parallel the personal sentiment (desire and tears). The language shows greater compression. Derived from the acrostic design, it displays alliteration as well as assonance. What sometimes begins as a skillful apostrophe ends in rhetorical and cryptic counterpoint.[23] Published originally in the *Christian Register* (May 1947), a twelve-line lyric, "Birth," signifies the artistic credo. Without direct address to the social mission, as does the "cool poet" in "Motto,"[24] it images the creative calling into the metonyms of stars, moon, and sun. Just as the lyric emotion subsides into the lyric process, so the pictorial frieze fades into the surge of dramatic action. Private feeling has become public deed. Where the social revolutionary seems displaced, he still speaks in undertone. Indeed, he imposes the signature and voice upon human history: "stroke / Of lightening / In the night / Some mark to Make / Some Word / to Tell." Indirectly, the persona partially confirms: "The imagination deals with feelings preferably wayward, congenitally wild, and it wants to move them not into formulae but toward the state of value and purity for which Eliot's 'form' and 'pattern' at once moving and still. . . . The imagination makes nothing happen, but it lets things happen by removing obstacles of routine and providing a context of feeling from which they appear naturally to emerge."[25] But for Langston Hughes the lyrical imagination is dynamic and fertile.

"Carolina Cabin," a neglected poem, displaces lyricism into the dramatic situation. In twenty-two lines and four stanzas, two lovers take warm refuge near a fireplace. Viewed first as an imaginative landscape, the setting has hanging moss, holly, and "tall straight pine." The unfolding drama parallels the narrator's silent movement inward. Near the cracking fire and rare red wine, the narrator hears good laughter. When he looks then outward, the gloomy world has

> The winds of winter cold
> As down the road
> A wandering poet
> Must roam.

Still, the plot peacefully evolves itself in reinforced laughter. Where love's old story recurs, people make a home. The poem reveals the angle on post-World War II alienation in the United States. While the aesthetic world lures the narrator, he must eventually return to realistic commitment. The diction has both secular and religious connotations. As a participant in the racial narrative implied, the speaker achieves the mythic dimensions of the Wandering Jew. In the way, he perceives the limits of literary myth and historical reality.

"Old Sailor," far less dramatic and well-structured, subordinates the lyric quality to greater narrative. For twenty lines, a paralyzed mariner fancies women all over the world lament his absence. Indebted to Hughes's own days as a sailor (1923–24), the tragicomic poem completes the career vicariously. The literary work closes the frame on the historical life. In the first twelve lines, the narrator has "tasted" mysteries in Oriental cities. With Bohemian joy and international sorrow, he pursues the Dionysian urge. Then, in the last eight lines, he deteriorates into a poor dreamer. Unable to perform "heroic" deeds, he remembers from youth the sexual prowess and laughter. Yet while the mind itself faces decay, it "re-minds" itself of the spiritual recovery that resists physical death. Embodied in Time, the poetic urge remains timeless.

In twenty-four lines and four stanzas, "Sailing Date" tells the story of old mariners who face the fading years. Here are the twist, strangeness, and "bitter rage" of the lives. The sailors have deteriorated from youthful adventure ("salt sea water") to lushness ("whiskey shore"). While the decline marks the broken dreams and the imminent aging, the men narrate the past. Experienced in a thousand storms, they have survived world wars. Since the days when submarines once threatened them, they have mastered an ironic indifference.

For the tone Hughes draws heavily upon the poetry of England and the United States, especially from the nineteenth century, though the sources still merit original consideration.[26] In "O Captain! My Captain!" Whitman alludes to Abraham Lincoln (history) and to God (eternity). For "Crossing the Bar," on the contrary, Tennyson allegorizes God (the Pilot) alone. And Hughes himself celebrates Whitman in "Old Walt,"[27] a poem which appropriately reappeared in a chapbook called *The Pilot* (26 December 1954). Whether about the president during the Civil War or the God beyond, the narrator portrays events within historical time, but imaginatively projects himself beyond them. The implicit drama of history underscores Lincoln's death and Tennyson's life, but the lyric highlights the symbolic actions of mourning and faith. Thus in the repressed rhetoric Hughes's lyrics bridge the disparate worlds of fact and value.

In "Trumpet Player: 52nd Street," as in "The Weary Blues," the dramatic performance completes the lyrical impulse.[28] The quality implodes in the instrumental metaphor rather than in the choral rhetoric. During the forty-four lines, the player distills jazz from old desire and hardship. Then, with the trumpet at his lips, he blows against and through the ambivalence for acculturation, the paradox of racial identity. In the "tamed down hair," the straightened "process" he demonstrates more than style, for he would resemble Whites whose hair is naturally so. But what the player has accepted socially, he rejects artistically. The inner Black light, the implicit metaphor, "glows" brilliantly through the "process" and "gleams" as "jet [Black] were yet a crown."

What gives the image dramatic power concerns the lighted frieze in the counterplay to the persona's inner light and, indeed, to the musical time in the played song as well as to Time. The light on the player moves so fast as to feign no movement. But the music, the movement of which is clearly heard, sounds rhythmically. And the music reminds the reader that the temporal lapse between 1947 and 1985, indeed the future, is hardly the static illusion by which speeding light tricks the eye. Immediate in the challenge to lyrical experience, history and time are real. Distanced from them, the narrator focuses on different angles for the trumpeter and for the performance. Partly identifying with the sound and light, he narrates the communion of the dramatic performance. In the arrestment of time, both auditory (sound) and visible (light), the player mixes "honey" with "liquid fire," an oxymoron in flowing and "burning" sweetness. The dynamic performance merely plays out the inert desire. Though the scene gives the illusion of permanence, he expresses "longing for the moon" and "longing for the sea." In the reflection of the moonlight, from earth at night, he has resolved a paradox, for if fire can flow yet appropriate to itself the quality of the contrasting element, water, so the imagination might reverse the very racial terms through which poets image human experience. Literary light, like the trumpeted song, may well be Black. And the Black light exorcises the previous self-disillusion. When the repetend reinforces the dramatic performance, including the frieze, the player sports his "one-button roll" or jacket. In the convenient shift from the dramatic mode to the lyric one, the narrator wonders about the trumpeter's motivation.

While the performance obscures the lyric form itself, the latter subsides in the instrumental music. Herein modernity only appears to have displaced the pastoral world. Through rhetorical convention, the soloist delivers the song to the chorus but expects no answer. While any reaffirmations are silent from the poem, they are yet implied. Thus Langston Hughes, like Ezra Pound, "found that he loved and praised only what Pindar and Horace and Johnson and Whitman had loved and praised: perfection of good order, the kinship of earth, the earth herself in her epiphanies of fertility, Nature, and culture, the paradises of earth and the unearthly paradises that engender them, the dignity of humankind and of the universe. Like his predecessors in choral, he had also blamed what offered to harm or destroy what he loved and praised, but he had spent too much time in blaming. And the joy and celebration survived even that."[29]

Even the sensitive insight implies the illusions that Western critics impose upon human history. At least three thousand years before Pindar, the lyric in Africa must have made for the communal recitation during which the original humans listened to history from the oral teller. Today the lyric still marks the ritual through which the self and society collectively reaffirm community. Whether the song is vocal or instrumental, the writer's narrators merely displace the racial history that the speakers inevitably signify. The lyric implies both the social narrative and the dramatic event. Never completely detoured into aristocratic and private poetry, Langston Hughes helps restore the ancient form to rhetorical timelessness.

Notes

1. W. R. Johnson, *The Idea of Lyric* (Berkeley: University of California Press, 1982), 23.
2. See R. Baxter Miller, "'A Mere Poem': 'Daybreak in Alabama,' Resolution to Langston Hughes's Commentary on Music and Art," *Obsidian* 2 (1976): 30–37.
3. I am mainly concerned here with *The Weary Blues* (1926; reprint, New York: Alfred A. Knopf, 1945) and *Fields of Wonder* (New York: Alfred A. Knopf, 1947).
4. See Donald B. Gibson, "The Good Black Poet and the Good Gray Poet: The Poetry of Hughes and Whitman," in *Modern Black Poets*, ed. Donald B. Gibson (Englewood Cliffs, N.J.: Prentice-Hall, 1973), 43–56; reprinted from *Langston Hughes: Black Genius*, ed. Therman B. O'Daniel (New York: William Morrow, 1971).
5. Edmund Burke, *The Philosophy of Edmund Burke*, ed. Louis I. Bredvold and Ralph G. Ross (Ann Arbor: University of Michigan, 1967), 256–67.

6. See Felix E. Schelling, *The English Lyric* (Boston: Houghton Mifflin, 1913), 1–2; Barbara Hardy, *The Advantage of Lyric* (Bloomington: Indiana University Press, 1977), 1–3.
7. The position disagrees with Schelling's (*The English Lyric*, 5–12).
8. The distinction is Johnson's (*The Idea of Lyric*).
9. Ibid., 23.
10. Ibid.
11. Ruth Finnegan, *Oral Poetry* (London: Cambridge University Press, 1977), 25–29; Thomas R. Edwards, *Imagination and Power: A Study of Poetry on Public Themes* (New York: Oxford University Press, 1971), 6.
12. Denis Donoghue, *The Sovereign Ghost* (Berkeley: University of California Press, 1976), 221–22.
13. Ibid., 228.
14. Seiichi Hatano, *Time and Eternity*, trans. Ichiro Suzuki (Tokyo: Ministry of Education, 1963), 20.
15. Ibid., 20, 148.
16. See Albert William Levi, *Literature, Philosophy, and the Imagination* (Bloomington: Indiana University Press, 1962), 274.
17. See Peter Conrad, *Imagining America* (New York: Oxford University Press, 1980), 5.
18. See Faith Berry, *Langston Hughes: Before and Beyond Harlem* (Westport: Lawrence Hill, 1983), 61.
19. See Chancellor Williams, *The Destruction of Black Civilization* (Chicago: Third World Press, 1976), 139.
20. "Home," the metaphor of death, occurs in "Soul Gone Home," in *Five Plays by Langston Hughes*, ed. Webster Smalley (Bloomington: Indiana University Press, 1963).
21. Onwuchekwa Jemie, *Langston Hughes* (New York: Columbia University Press, 1976), 139.
22. See Johnson, *The Idea of Lyric*, 1–23.
23. The groupings are Fields of Wonder, Border Line, Heart of the World, Silver Rain, Desire, and Tearless.
24. Arthur P. Davis, "Langston Hughes: Cool Poet," *CLA Journal* 11 (June 1968): 276–83.
25. Donoghue, *The Sovereign Ghost*, 226–27.
26. Though Gibson ("The Good Black Poet") deals satisfactorily with the sources in Whitman, nearly everyone overlooks the Victorians.
27. "Old Walt," *Beloit Poetry Journal*, no. 5 (1954): 10.
28. For a folk reading, see Richard K. Barksdale, "Langston Hughes: His Times and Humanistic Techniques," in *Black American Literature and Humanism*, ed. R. Baxter Miller (Lexington: University Press of Kentucky, 1981), 23–25.
29. See Johnson, *The Idea of Lyric*, 195.

◆◆◆◆◆◆◆◆◆◆◆◆◆◆

Langston Hughes: Evolution of the Poetic Persona

RAYMOND SMITH

Langston Hughes's career as a poet began with the publication of "The Negro Speaks of Rivers" in the June, 1921 issue of *The Crisis*. By 1926, before the poet had reached the age of twenty-five, he had published his first volume of poems, *The Weary Blues*. Of this volume Alain Locke, the leading exponent of "The New Negro," announced that the black masses had found their voice: "A true people's poet has their balladry in his veins; and to me many of these poems seem based on rhythms as seasoned as folksongs and on moods as deep-seated as folk-ballads. Dunbar is supposed to have expressed the peasant heart of the people. But Dunbar was the showman of the Negro masses; here is their spokesman."[1] With the publication of his second volume of poems, *Fine Clothes to the Jew* (1927), Hughes was being referred to as the "Poet Laureate of the American Negro." During a visit to Haiti in 1932, he was introduced to the noted Haitian poet Jacques Roumain, who referred to Hughes as "the greatest Negro poet who had ever come to honor Haitian soil."[2] When the noted Senegalese poet and exponent of African negritude, Léopold Senghor, was asked in a 1967 interview "In which poems of our, American, literature [do] you find evidence of Negritude?" his reply was "Ah, in Langston Hughes; Langston Hughes is the most spontaneous as a poet and the blackest in expression!"[3] Before his death in 1967, Hughes had published more than a dozen volumes of poetry, in addition to a great number of anthologies, translations, short stories, essays, novels, plays, and histories dealing with the spectrum of Afro-American life.

Of the major black writers who first made their appearance during the exciting period of the 1920s commonly referred to as "the Harlem Renaissance," Langston Hughes was the most prolific and the most successful. As the Harlem Renaissance gave way to the Depression, Hughes determined to sustain his career as a poet by bringing his poetry to the people. At the suggestion of Mary McLeod Bethune, he launched his career as a public speaker by embarking on an extensive lecture tour of the South. As he wrote in his autobiography: "Propelled by the backwash of the 'Harlem Renaissance' of the early 'twenties, I had been drifting along pleasantly on the delightful rewards of my poems which seemed to please the fancy of kindhearted New York ladies with money to help young writers. . . . There was one other dilemma—how to make a living from *the kind of writing I wanted to do*. . . . I wanted to write seriously and as well as I knew how about the Negro people, and make *that* kind of writing earn me a *living*."[4] The Depression forced Hughes to reconsider the relation between his poetry and his people: "I wanted to continue to be a poet. Yet sometimes I wondered if I was barking up the wrong tree. I determined to find out by taking poetry, *my* poetry, to *my* people. After all, I wrote about Negroes, and primarily *for* Negroes. Would they have me? Did they want me?"[5]

Though much of the poetry Hughes was to write in the thirties and afterward was to differ markedly in terms of social content from the poetry he was producing in the twenties, a careful examination of his early work will reveal, in germinal form, the basic themes which were to preoccupy him throughout his career. These themes, pertaining to certain attitudes towards American and vis-à-vis his own blackness, had in fact been in the process of formulation since childhood. Hughes's evolution as a poet cannot be seen apart from the circumstances of his life which thrust him into the role of poet. Indeed, it was Hughes's awareness of what he personally regarded as a rather unique childhood which determined him in his drive to express, through poetry, the feelings of the black masses. Hughes's decision to embark on the lecture tour of Southern colleges in the 1930s is not to be taken as a rejection of his earlier work; it was merely a redirection of energies towards the purpose of reaching his audience. Hughes regarded his poetry written during the height of the Harlem Renaissance as a valid statement on Negro life in America. The heavily marked volumes of *The Weary Blues, Fine Clothes to the Jew*, and *The Dream Keeper* (published in 1932 but consisting largely of selections from the two earlier volumes) used by Hughes for poetry readings during the thirties and forties and now in the James Weldon Johnson Collection at Yale University, indicate that Hughes relied heavily on this early work and in no way rejected it as socially irrelevant.

Hughes's efforts to create a poetry that truly evoked the spirit of Black America involved a resolution of conflicts centering around the problem of identity. For Hughes, like W. E. B. Du Bois, saw the black man's situation in America as a question of dual consciousness. As Du Bois wrote in his *Souls of Black Folk* (1903): "It is a peculiar sensation, this double-consciousness, this sense of always looking at oneself through the eyes of others, of measuring one's soul by the tape of a world that looks on in amused contempt and pity. One ever feels his twoness,—an American, a Negro; two souls, two thoughts, two unreconciled strivings; two warring ideals in one body, whose dogged strength alone keeps it from being torn asunder."[6] Hughes was to speak of this same dilemma in his famous essay, published in 1927, concerning the problems of the black writer in America, "The Negro Artist and the Racial Mountain": "But this is the mountain standing in the way of any true Negro art in America—this urge within the race toward whiteness, the desire to pour racial individuality into the mold of American standardization, and to be as little Negro and as much American as possible."[7] In *The Weary Blues* (New York: Alfred Knopf, 1926), Hughes presented the problem of dual consciousness quite cleverly by placing two parenthetical statements of identity as the opening and closing poems, and titling them "Proem" and "Epilogue." Their opening lines suggest the polarities of consciousness between which the poet located his own persona: "I Am a Negro" and "I, Too, Sing America." Within each of these poems, Hughes suggests the interrelatedness of the two identities: the line "I am a Negro" is echoed as "I am the darker brother" in the closing poem. Between the American and the Negro, a third identity is suggested: that of the poet or "singer." It is this latter persona which Hughes had assumed for himself in his attempt to resolve the dilemma of divided consciousness. Thus, within the confines of these two poems revolving around identity, Hughes is presenting his poetry as a kind of salvation. If one looks more closely at Hughes's organization of poems in the book, one finds that his true opening and closing poems are concerned not with identity but with patterns of cyclical time. "The Weary Blues" (the first poem) is about a black piano man who plays deep into the night until at last he falls into sleep "like a rock or a man that's dead." The last poem, on the other hand, suggests a rebirth, an awakening, after the long night of weary blues: "We have tomorrow/Bright before us/Like a flame."[8] This pattern of cyclical time was adopted in the opening and closing poems of *Fine Clothes to the Jew*, which begins in sunset and ends in sunrise. Again, it is the blues singer (or poet) who recites the song: "Sun's a risin',/This is gonna be ma song."[9] The poet's song, then, is Hughes's resolution to the problem of double consciousness, of being an American and being black.

Hughes viewed the poet's role as one of responsibility: the poet must strive to maintain his objectivity and artistic distance, while at the same time speaking with passion through the medium he has selected for himself. In a speech given before the American society of African Culture in 1960, Hughes urged his fellow black writers to cultivate objectivity in dealing with blackness: "Advice to Negro writers: Step *outside yourself*, then look back—and you will see how human, yet how beautiful and black you are. How very black—even when you're integrated."[10] In another part of the speech, Hughes stressed art over race: "In the great sense of the word, anytime, any place, good art transcends land, race, or nationality, and color drops away. If you are a good writer, in the end neither blackness nor whiteness makes a difference to readers." This philosophy of artistic distance was integral to Hughes's argument in the much earlier essay "The Negro Artist and the Racial Mountain," which became a rallying call to young black writers of the twenties concerned with reconciling artistic freedom with racial expression: "It is the duty of the younger Negro artist if he accepts any duties at all from outsiders, to change through the force of his art that old whispering 'I want to be white' hidden in the aspirations of his people, to 'Why should I want to be white? I am a Negro—and beautiful!'"[11] Hughes urged other black writers to express freely, without regard to the displeasure of whites *or* blacks, their "individual dark-skinned selves." "If white people are glad, we are glad. If they are not, it doesn't matter. We know we are beautiful. And ugly too. If colored people are pleased we are glad. If they are not, their displeasure doesn't matter either. We build temples for tomorrow, strong as we know how, and we stand on top of the mountain, free within ourselves." In this carefully thought-out manifesto, Hughes attempted to integrate the two facets of double consciousness (the American and the Negro) into a single vision—that of the poet. His poetry had reflected this idea from the beginning, when he published "The Negro Speaks of Rivers" at the age of nineteen. Arna Bontemps, in a retrospective glance at the Harlem Renaissance from the distance of almost fifty years, was referring to "The Negro Speaks of Rivers" when he commented: "And almost the first utterance of the revival struck a note that *disturbed* poetic tradition."[12] (Italics mine)

In Hughes's poetry, the central element of importance is the affirmation of blackness. Everything that distinguished Hughes's poetry from the white avant-garde poets of the twenties revolved around this important affirmation. Musical idioms, jazz rhythms, Hughes's special brand of "black-white" irony, and dialect were all dependent on the priority of black selfhood:

> I am a Negro
> Black as the night is black
> Black like the depths of my Africa.[13]

Like Walt Whitman, Hughes began his career as a poet confident of his power. Unlike Whitman, however, who celebrated particular self ("Walt Whitman, the Cosmos"), Hughes celebrated racial, rather than individual, self. Hughes tended to suppress the personal element in his poetry, appropriating the first person singular as the fitting epitome of universal human tendencies embodied in race. "The Negro Speaks of Rivers" seems almost mystical in comparison to Whitman's physicality:

> I've known rivers:
> Ancient, dusky rivers.
> My soul has grown deep like the rivers.[14]

One could venture too far in this comparison; of course, Whitman declared himself the poet of the soul as well as the body. Few would deny he had mystical tendencies.

In Hughes, however, there is little hint of the egotism in which Whitman so frequently indulged. Indeed, Hughes was hesitant to introduce the element of the personal into his poetry. In an essay published in the journal *Phylon* in 1947 on his "adventures" as a social poet, Hughes remarked that his "earliest poems were social poems in that they were about people's problems—whole groups of people's problems—rather than my own personal difficulties."[15] Hughes's autobiographical account of the writing of "The Negro Speaks of Rivers" confirms this point, and sheds light on the process by which Hughes transformed personal experiences into archetypal racial memories. The poem had evolved out of personal difficulties with his father, who had emigrated to Mexico when Langston was a child, and had not seen his son in over a decade. Hughes had been summoned unexpectedly by his father to join him in the summer of 1919, hoping to persuade the son to enter into the business world. The elder Hughes felt nothing but contempt for the country and the race he had left behind. The following conversation, recorded in Hughes's autobiography *The Big Sea*, suggests the irreconcilable differences between the two:

> "What do you want to be?"
> "I don't know. But I think a writer."
> "A writer?" my father said. "A writer?
> Do you think they make money? . . . Learn something you can make a living from anywhere in the world, in Europe or South America, and don't stay in the States, where you have to live like a nigger with niggers."
> "But I like Negroes," I said.[16]

The following summer, on a train trip to Mexico, Hughes's dread of the eventual confrontation with his father over his future vocation led to the writing of the poem: "All day on the train I had been thinking about my father, and his strange dislike of his own people. I didn't understand it, because I was Negro, and I liked Negroes very much."[17] Despite Hughes's severe emotional state, the poem itself displays little hint of the personal anxiety that led to its creation.

Perhaps the closest Hughes ever came to incorporating his personal anxiety into a poem was his "As I Grew Older," published initially in 1925, and later included in *The Weary Blues*. The poem is almost reduced to abstractions; it is a landscape of nightmare, a bleak and existential examination of blackness. The poet begins by recalling his "dream," once "bright like a sun," but now only a memory. A wall which separates the poet from his dream suddenly appears, causing him severe anxiety. It is at this point that the poet is thrust back upon himself and forced to seek an explanation for his dilemma:

> Shadow.
> I am black.

These two lines appearing at the center of the poem provide the key to his despair and to his salvation. As he begins to realize that his blackness is the cause of his being separated from his dream, he simultaneously realizes that blackness is central to his ontology. It is as much a physical reality as it is a metaphysical state of mind. In order for the dream to be restored, the spiritual and the physical blackness must be reintegrated. As the poet examines his hands, which are black, he discovers the source of his regeneration as a full person:

> My hands!
> My dark hands!
> Break through the wall!
> Find my dream!
> Help me to shatter this darkness,
> To smash this night,
> To break this shadow
> Into a thousand lights of sun,
> Into a thousand whirling dreams
> Of sun![18]

In order for the poet to transcend his temporal despair, he must accept the condition of his blackness completely and unequivocally. The poem thus ends, not in despair, but rather in a quest for self-liberation, dependent on the affirmation "I am black!"

The words had been used much earlier by another poet, W. E. B. Du Bois, far better known as the founder of the NAACP, editor of *The Crisis*, and lifelong champion of black pride. His poem "The Song of the Smoke," published in the magazine *Horizon* in 1899, opened with the words:

> I am the smoke king,
> I am black.

Later in the poem, Du Bois wrote these ringing lines:

> I will be black as blackness can,
> The blacker the mantle the mightier the man,
> My purpl'ing midnights no day may ban.
>
> I am carving God in night,
> I am painting hell in white.
> I am the smoke king.
> I am black. [19]

The poem, published when Hughes was five years old, prefigures the point in time, fifteen years later, when the careers of the two—Du Bois and Hughes—would converge, with the publication of Hughes's poem "The Negro Speaks of Rivers," in Du Bois's journal *The Crisis*, with the poem's dedication also going to Du Bois.

This early connection between Hughes and Du Bois is important, for it was Du Bois who was calling for a renaissance of black culture as early as 1913, in an essay on "The Negro in Literature and Art": "Never in the world has a richer mass of material been accumulated by a people than that which the Negroes possess today and are becoming conscious of. Slowly but surely they are developing artists of technic who will be able to use this material."[20] By 1920, Du Bois was actually using the word "renaissance" in referring to the new awakening of black creativity in the arts: "A renaissance of Negro literature is due; the material about us in the strange, heartrending race tangle is rich beyond dream and only we can tell the tale and sing the song from the heart."[21] This editorial in *The Crisis*, almost certainly read by Hughes, must have encouraged him to submit the poem for publication. In his autobiography, Hughes credited Du Bois and *The Crisis* for publishing his first poems and thus giving his literary career its first official boost: "For the next few years my poems appeared often (and solely) in *The Crisis*. And to that magazine, certainly, I owe my literary beginnings, insofar as publication is concerned."[22]

While Hughes certainly owed Du Bois a debt of gratitude for his official entrance upon the literary scene, it seems that Hughes's very special sensitivity as a budding young poet developed organically from his experiences as child. Though he did credit Dunbar and Sandburg among his influences, these literary mentors pale in light of what Hughes had to say about his method of poemwriting: "Generally, the first two or three lines come to me from something I'm thinking about, or looking at, or doing, and the rest of the poem (if there is to be a poem) flows from those first few lines, usually right away". This spontaneity of approach worked both for and against Hughes. Many of his poems, written in hasty response to some event reported in yesterday's newspaper, for example, have badly dated. The spontaneity that resulted in his best poetry came from the depths of his own experiences as a black man in America, though these personal experiences often were disguised as archetypal ones.

The tension between his awareness of growing up black and his acceptance of the "dream" of America, however tenuously defined, provided the dynamic for his poetry. From an early age, Hughes developed the distinction between the social versus the physical implications of black identity in America: "You see, unfortunately, I am not black. There are lots of different kinds of blood in our family. But here in the United States, the word 'Negro' is used to mean anyone who has *any* Negro blood at all in his veins. In Africa, the word is more pure. It means *all* Negro, therefore *black*". During a trip to Africa as a merchant seaman in 1922, he discovered that the Africans who "looked at me . . . would not believe I was a Negro". The semantic confusion was of American origin. Whatever the semantic distinctions, Hughes desired to be accepted as Negro by the Africans, and was disappointed with their reaction to him.

Hughes's middle-American background (he grew up in Lawrence, Kansas) sheltered him from some of the more blatant forms of racial prejudice toward Negroes in other regions of the country. When he lived in Topeka, he attended a white school, his mother having successfully challenged the school board to have him admitted. Most of his teachers were pleasant, but there was one "who sometimes used to make remarks about my being colored. And after such remarks, occasionally the kids would grab stones and tin cans out of the alley and chase me home". For a while he lived with his maternal grandmother, from whom he heard "beautiful stories about people who wanted to make the Negroes free, and how her father had had apprenticed to him many slaves . . . so that they could work out their freedom. . . . Through my grandmother's stories always life moved, moved heroically toward an end. . . . Something about my grandmother's stories . . . taught me the uselessness of crying about anything". Hughes's poem "Aunt Sue's Stories," published in *The Crisis* in July of 1921, furnishes an example of how Hughes transformed such memories into poetry. His childhood was not a happy one in Lawrence, as he related in his autobiography, and he turned to books for solace. Parallels between his childhood experiences and later poems abound. Many of his poems focused on unhappy or wrongly treated children, for whom the American dream had no relevance. This empathy with wronged children had its origins in Hughes's own unhappiness as a child.

Many of his poems about black laborers originated out of his difficulties in finding work while in school. A job he had in a hotel, cleaning toilets and spitoons, while only in the seventh grade, was to result in one of his more well-known poems, "Brass Spitoons," included in his second volume of poetry *Fine Clothes to the Jew* (1927). Four decades after a local theatre owner put up a sign "NO COLORED ADMITTED" in Lawrence, Kansas, Hughes would recall the event in *ASK YOUR MAMA:*

> IN THE QUARTER OF THE NEGROES
> WHERE THE RAILROAD AND THE RIVER
> HAVE DOORS THAT FACE EACH WAY
> AND THE ENTRANCE TO THE MOVIE'S
> UP AN ALLEY UP THE SIDE[23]

A beating administered by a group of white toughs in Chicago the summer before the Chicago riots would be transformed into "The White Ones" seven years later:

I do not hate you,
For your faces are beautiful, too.
I do not have you,
Your faces are whirling lights of loveliness
and splendor, too.
Yet why do you torture me,
O, white strong ones,
Why do you torture me?[24]

These parallels between Hughes's early life and his later poetry indicate that he had formulated certain attitudes towards his race and towards white America before he had ever considered the idea of becoming
a poet.

It was only by accident that he became a poet. He was elected to
the position of class poet at Cleveland's Central High because, as he
humorously recalled, he was a Negro, and Negroes were supposed to
have "rhythm." "In America most white people think, of course, that *all*
Negroes can sing and dance, and have a sense of rhythm. So my classmates, knowing that a poem had to have rhythm, elected me unani-
mously—thinking, no doubt, that I had some, being a Negro. . . . It had
never occurred to me to be a poet before, or indeed a writer of any
kind."[25] Thus the role of poet was thrust upon Hughes by accident, or
perhaps, by design, because he was Negro in a white society. It was the
social implications of his blackness, however, that fitted him for the role.
The incidents of his childhood and youth had marked Langston Hughes
as a black man, and his poetry would affirm his acceptance of the mission,
to be a spokesman for the black masses.

At the same time, Hughes could not deny the double nature, the dual-
consciousness of being an American as well as a black. The very fact that
he had been chosen by his classmates as class poet *because* he was Negro
only accentuated his separateness from them. By the same token, he had
never been completely exposed to the full brunt of prejudice, American-
style, during his youth. Up until the time of his Southern lecture tour of
1931, his acquaintance with Southern mores had been merely peripheral.
Indeed, he often began these programs by explaining how truly "American" his upbringing had been: "I began my programs by telling where I
was born in Missouri, that I grew up in Kansas in the geographical heart
of the country, and was, therefore very American."[26] His audiences,
which consisted largely of Southern Negroes, must have found his initial
declaration of Americanism rather disorienting. As Hughes himself explained in his autobiography, this first-hand encounter with racial prejudice in the South provided an introduction to an important aspect of
racial heritage to which he had never been fully exposed: "I found a great
social and cultural gulf between the races in the South, astonishing to

one who, like myself, from the North, had never known such uncompromising prejudices."[27]

In a poem published in *The Crisis* in 1922, Hughes outlined his ambivalence towards the region in rather chilling imagery:

> The child-minded South
> Scratching in the dead fire's ashes
> For a Negro's bones.

He indicated in the poem's conclusion that the South had a strong attraction, but that he was more comfortable in resisting its allure:

> And I, who am black, would love her
> But she spits in my face
> And I, who am black,
> Would give her many rare gifts
> But she turns her back upon me.[28]

In the same year that Hughes published "The South," Jean Toomer published *Cane*. One of the poems in *Cane*, "Georgia Dusk," evoked similar imagery:

> A feast of moon and men and barking hounds,
> An orgy for some genius of the South
> With blood-hot eyes and cane-lipped scented mouth,
> Surprised in making folk-songs from soul sounds.[29]

Where Toomer's *Cane* was the product of direct experience (a six-month sojourn in Georgia as a rural schoolteacher), Hughes's South was an imaginatively evoked nightmare. The last lines of Hughes's poem suggest that he was not yet ready to embrace the Southern experience as Toomer had done. Hughes's Gothic South was a far cry from Toomer's seductive lines in "Carma":

> Wind is in the cane. Come along.
> Cane leaves swaying, rusty with talk,
> Scratching choruses above the guinea's squawk,
> Wind is in the cane, Come along.[30]

If Hughes feared the direct Southern confrontation during the twenties, he found much to admire in those Southern blacks who came to settle in the teeming cities of the North, and from them he derived material for his poetry. In seeking communal identity through them, Hughes overemphasized the exotic, as this passage from *The Big Sea* indicates: "I never tired of hearing them talk, listening to the thunderclaps of their laughter, to their troubles, to their discussions of the war and the men who had gone to Europe from the Jim Crow South. . . . They seemed to me like the gayest and the bravest people possible—

these Negroes from the Southern ghettoes—facing tremendous odds, working and laughing and trying to get somewhere in the world". The passage suggests the attitude of a sympathetic observer rather than that of an engaged participant. In some ways, Hughes's attitude towards Southern Negroes was directly counter to that of his father's. According to Langston, the elder Hughes "hated Negroes. I think he hated himself, too, for being a Negro. He disliked all of his family because they were Negroes and remained in the United States". Hughes, on the other hand, proudly affirmed his racial heritage. Where his father rejected both race and country, Hughes could reject neither.

At the end of his lecture programs in the South, Hughes would recite his poem "I, Too, Sing America." As often as he invoked this poem, he would be reaffirming his faith in the American dream. Some of Hughes's earliest poems reveal an almost childlike faith in the American ideal, as in the opening lines of the following first published in 1925:

> American is seeking the starts,
> America is seeking tomorrow,
> You are America,
> I am America
> America—the dream,
> America—the vision.
> America—the star-seeking I.

The same poem affirmed the unity of black and white America:

> You of the blue eyes
> And the blond hair,
> I of the dark eyes
> And the crinkly hair,
> You and I
> Offering hands . . .[31]

This affirmation of racial unity had a direct relation to Hughes's experience with racial integration at Cleveland's Central high, where he was often elected to important class positions because of his acceptability to various white ethnic factions: "Since it was during the war, and Americanism was being stressed, many of our students, including myself, were then called down to the principal's office and questioned about our belief in Americanism. . . . After that, the principal organized an Americanism Club in our school, and . . . I was elected President" (*The Big Sea*). While this experience might serve to strengthen his faith in an ideal America, it also, paradoxically, reinforced his sense of separateness as a Negro. His race was clearly an advantage in terms of popularity among his peers; still, it was his color which marked him as different.

At the same time, Hughes's experience in racial integration set him apart from the experience of those Negroes from the South whose lifestyle he so admired. Hughes must have realized that his experience vis-à-vis that of most black Americans was rather unique. Though he claimed at times to have had a typical Negro upbringing, it was nevertheless different, as he pointed out in this passage from *The Big Sea:* "Mine was not a typical Negro family. My grandmother never took in washing or worked in service or went to church. She had lived in Oberlin and spoke perfect English, without a trace of dialect. She looked like an Indian. My mother was a newspaper woman and a stenographer then. My father lived in Mexico City. My grandfather had been a congressman". In addition, Hughes harbored no grudges against white society: "I learned early in life not to hate *all* white people. And ever since, it has seemed to me that *most* people are generally good, in every race and in every country where I have been".

Hughes often sought to dispel the distinction between American and Negro by affirming his nationality in no uncertain terms. The following incident from his autobiography illustrates this point. He had been teaching English to Mexicans during his final summer in Mexico with his father. The teacher who was to replace him was a white American woman who found it incredible that a Negro could be capable of teaching anything:

> When she was introduced to me, her mouth fell open, and she said: "Why, Ah-Ah thought you was an American."
> I said,: "I am American!"
> She said: "Oh, Ah mean a white American."
> Her voice had a Southern drawl.
> I grinned.

Another incident from his autobiography concerns his refusal to deny his race. On the return trip to the United States from Mexico after his first summer there, Hughes attempted to purchase an ice cream soda in St. Louis. The following exchange took place:

> The clerk said: "Are you a Mexican or a Negro?"
> I said: "Why?"
> "Because if you're a Mexican, I'll serve you," he said. "If you're colored, I won't."
> "I'm colored," I replied. The clerk turned to wait on someone else. I knew I was home in the U.S.A.

These incidents were to have their counterparts in his poetry, where he could affirm with equal assurance his two credos of identity: "I am a Negro" and "I, Too, Sing America." But while affirming these polar commitments, Hughes was alienated from both of them. As a black man, he was aware that his race had never been granted full participation in the American dream. His exposure to the possibilities of that dream, however, through his experience with racial integration, and his relative innocence (this was to disappear, of course) in matters of Southern mores, would distinguish his circumstances from the lot of the black masses, with whom he sought to identify to the extent of becoming their spokesman. This peculiar set of conditions allowed Hughes to assume a degree of sophistication in racial matters quite unusual among his contemporaries, white or black. This sophistication, coupled with his insistence on maintaining the necessary aesthetic distance of the artist, provided the stimulus for his poetry and endowed the poet with a sense of mission. He was absolutely confident of his self-imposed mission as a poet of the black masses. His familiarity with white Bohemian intellectual circles in New York during the twenties provided him with the additional stimulus of communicating his message across racial lines. Thus two kinds of poetry emerged in the twenties: the black vernacular poetry, utilizing dialect, jazz talk, and everyday subject matter; and "message" poetry, which concentrated on the position of the black man in white America. *The Weary Blues*, Hughes's first book, contained much of this message poetry, besides some experiments in jazz poetry ("The Cat and The Saxophone," "Blues Fantasy," "Negro Dancers"), and additional non-racial lyrics. The second book, *Fine Clothes to the Jew*, concentrated almost entirely on the vernacular subject matter, and contained many poems written in blues dialect. These two tendencies in Hughes's early work were to predominate throughout his career.

Shakespeare in Harlem (1942), for example, may be considered a sequel to *Fine Clothes*, while *Montage of a Dream Deferred* (1951) integrated the vernacular subject matter with the thematic concerns introduced in *The Weary Blues*. *Montage*, along with *ASK YOUR MAMA* (1961), will probably remain Hughes's most important achievements in poetry since his work of the twenties. *ASK YOUR MAMA*, permeated with humor, irony, and exciting imagery, contains echoes of "The Negro Speaks of Rivers," "As I Grew Older," and "The Cat and the Saxophone." As in these earlier poems, Hughes transforms personal experiences and observations into distillations of the Black American condition.

Hughes wrote in his autobiography: "My best poems were all written when I felt the worst. When I was happy, I didn't write anything". When he first began writing poetry, he felt his lyrics were too personal to reveal to others: "Poems came to me now spontaneously, from somewhere inside. . . . I put the poems down quickly on anything I had a [at] hand when they came into my head, and later I copied them into a notebook. But I began to be afraid to show my poems to anybody, because they had become very serious and very much a part of me. And I was afraid other people might not like them or understand them". These two statements regarding his poetry suggest deep underlying emotional tensions as being the source of his creativity. And yet the personal element in Hughes's poetry is almost entirely submerged beneath the persona of the "Negro Poet Laureate." If, as Hughes suggested, personal unhappiness was the cornerstone of his best work, it then follows that, in order to maintain the singleness of purpose and devotion to his art, he would be required to sacrifice some degree of emotional stability. Thus poetry became a kind of therapy, masking deeper emotional tensions. We know from his autobiography that Hughes experienced two severe emotional breakdowns. The first one had to do with a break with his father over the course of his vocation: the second followed upon a break with his wealthy white patroness in the late twenties over the kind of poetry he was writing. Both of these emotional traumas were directly related to his decision to become a poet of his people.

The persona of the poet was the role Hughes adopted in his very first published poem, as *the Negro* in "The Negro Speaks of Rivers." It was a persona to which he would remain faithful throughout his lengthy career. The link between his personal experiences and his poetry has been suggested in this paper. It cannot be defined because it seems clear that Hughes suppressed the more frightening excursions into his own personal void. Poetry was an outlet as well as a salvation. Only occasionally, as in the poem "As I Grow Older," does Hughes provide a window upon his inner anxieties, and even in this poem the real root of these anxieties is hidden, and the poem becomes an allegory of the black man's alienation in white America.

Hughes's early attempts in the twenties to fill the role of Poet Laureate of the Negro led him to create a body of work that was organic in nature. The traditional literary sources of inspiration were for the most part bypassed. The source of his poetry was to be found in the anonymous, unheard black masses: their rhythms, their dialect, their life styles. Hughes sought to incorporate this untapped resource of black folk language into a new kind of poetry. His personal experiences, as related in his autobiography, combined with this folk material to provide thematic dimension to his work. The basic themes regarding the American dream and its possibilities for the black man were always present in his poetry. The tension between the unrealized dream and the realities of the black experience in America provided the dynamic. This tension between material and theme laid the groundwork for the irony which characterized Hughes's work at its best.

Notes

1. "The Weary Blues" (Review), *Palms*, 4, No. 1 (October 1926), 25.
2. Langston Hughes, *I Wonder As I Wander* (1956; rpt. New York: Hill and Want, 1964), p. 31.
3. Quoted in Arthur P. Davis, "Langston Hughes: Cool Poet," in *Langston Hughes: Black Genius: A Critical Evaluation*, ed. Therman B. O'Daniel (New York: William & Morrow & Company, 1971), p. 25.

4. *I Wonder As I Wander*, pp. 4–5.
5. *I Wonder As I Wander*, pp. 41–42.
6. *The Souls of Black Folk*, rpt. Greenwich, Conn.: Fawcett Publications, 1961), pp. 16–17.
7. *Nation*, 122 (June 23, 1926), 692.
8. *The Weary Blues*, p. 109.
9. Langston Hughes, *Fine Clothes to the Jew* (New York: Alfred A. Knopf, 1927), pp. 17–89.
10. "Writers: Black and White," in *The American Negro Writer and his Roots* (New York: American Society of African Culture, 1960), p. 44.
11. "Negro Artist and Racial Mountain," *p. 694.*
12. "Negro Poets, Then and Now," in *Black Expression: Essays by and about Black Americans in the Creative Arts*, ed. Addison Gayle, Jr. (New York: Weybright and Talley, 1969), p. 83.
13. Hughes, *The Weary Blues*, p. 108.
14. *The Weary Blues*, p. 22.
15. "My Adventures as a Social Poet," *Phylon*, 8 (Fall 1947), 205.
16. *The Big Sea* (1940); rpt. New York: Hill and Wang, 1963), pp. 61–62.
17. *The Big Sea*, p. 54.
18. *Weary Blues*, pp. 55-56.
19. W. E. B. Du Bois, "The Song of the Smoke," (1899) rpt. in *Dark Symphony: Negro Literature in America*, ed. James A. Emmanuel and Theodore L. Gross (New York: Free Press, 1968), p. 44.
20. *The Seventh Son: The Thought and Writings of W.E.B. Du Bois*, ed. Julius Lester (New York: Random House, 1971), I, 451.
21. *The Emerging Thought of W. E. B. Du Bois: Essays and Editorials from The Crisis*, ed. Henry Lee Moon (New York: Simon and Schuster, 1972), p. 354.
22. *The Big Sea*, p. 72. Subsequent references to *The Big Sea* will appear parenthetically in the text.
23. Langston Hughes, *ASK YOUR MAMA: 12 MOODS FOR JAZZ* (New York: Alfred Knopf, 1961), p. 5.
24. *Weary Blues*, p. 106.
25. *The Big Sea*, p. 24.
26. *I Wonder As I Wander*, p. 57.
27. *I Wonder As I Wander*, p. 52.
28. *Weary Blues*, p. 54.
29. *Cane* (1923); rpt. (New York: University Place Press, 1967), p. 22.
30. *Cane*, p. 16.
31. "America," *Opportunity*, 3 (June 1925), 175.

◆◆◆◆◆◆◆◆◆◆◆◆◆

Or Does It Explode?

ONWUCHEKWA JEMIE

I

Amiri Baraka (LeRoi Jones) once defined the black writer's function as follows:

> The Black Artist's role in America is to aid in the destruction of America as he knows it. His role is to report and reflect so precisely the nature of the society, and of himself in that society, that other men will be moved by the exactness of his rendering and, if they are black men, grow strong through this moving, having seen their own strength and weakness; and if they are white men, tremble, curse, and go mad, because they will be drenched with the filth of their evil.[1]

The statement is at once descriptive and prescriptive, not unlike Aristotle's *Poetics* which is both a description of the practice of leading Greek playwrights of his day and a recommendation or prescription to future playwrights. Except for the anticipated effect of the work of art on the audience (and such effect is always a theoretical ideal and difficult to measure), Baraka's statement accurately describes the main tradition of Afro-American writing from the slave narratives and abolitionist fiction to the novels of Wright, Himes, and Ellison, the essays of DuBois, Baldwin, and Cleaver, and the poetry and drama of the Black Consciousness era of the 1960s and 70s. Certainly, it describes Hughes's lifelong artistic theory and practice. We have already seen, in the blues and jazz poems, how precisely Hughes reports and reflects the nature of American society and the black man's life in it. His other poems, those not modeled on black musical forms, are informed by the same vision.

Hughes's "report" includes a picture of America as a cage, a zoo, a circus, a gory monster cannibal and a syphilitic whore, and the black man as deracinated, alienated, exiled, groping for reconnection with his African past. Africa is "time lost," surviving only in fragments and in dim racial memories felt, like the music that is its chief surrogate, in the blood and bones, in received culture not fully understood.[2] Hughes was more fortunate than most of his contemporaries in that he had actually visited the coastal areas of West Africa, a region rich in history for Afro-Americans. But the contact was brief—too brief to save his early evocations of Africa wholly from the romanticism which characterized, for instance, Countee Cullen's "Heritage" or Claude McKay's "In Bond-age," "Outcast," and "Africa."

In any case, what is crucial is not so much Hughes's image of Africa as his image of America. In his early poems, Africa is for him a distant ideal, foil and backdrop for his portrait of the present reality that is America. America to him is a cold, joyless wilderness, Africa a carefree tropical paradise,[3] a land where it would be customary, for instance, to "work maybe a little today, rest a little tomorrow. Play awhile. Sing awhile. O, let's dance."[4] Uprooted from a natural environment of palms and forests and silver moons, blacks in America suffocate in a prison of skyscrapers and industrial smog.[5] And as lions, tigers, and elephants, nature's majestic creatures created to live free, are trapped and harnessed for entertainment and profit, so have the non-white peoples of the world been converted from human beings into natural resources in the Western "circus of civilization."[6]

Forced to play "the dumb clown of the world," the black man finds a limited victory in laughter,[7] hiding his "tears and sighs" (to use Dunbar's phrase) behind a mask that "grins and lies."[8] The comic exterior is the black entertainer's particular stereotype. Hughes himself muffles a blazing rage behind his genial mask. But in "Summer Night" and "Disillusion" in the solitude of privacy, the public mask is momentarily lifted, and we feel in full the anguish of the poet or his persona. Like the rest of his brethren trapped in this circus, he tosses weary and sleepless, his soul "empty as the silence."[9] The mask, the music, the wild laughter of Harlem's nights are but temporary escapes. And he longs for a return to the wholeness both of childhood and of the African past:

> I would be simple again,
> Simple and clean
> Like the earth,
> Like the rain. . . .[10]

In "Danse Africaine" we glimpse a possible ritual of at-one-ment, with the priestess, "night-veiled girl," whirling softly to the low beating of tom-toms, drawing her audience into the unifying circle of light.[11] In the overwhelming compulsion toward spiritual reunion with the fatherland, first expressed in *The Weary Blues* in "Dream Variation" and "Our Land," the two halves of Hughes's dream theme—the dream deferred and the dream as romantic fantasy—merge.

The "Proem," later titled "Negro," which introduces *The Weary Blues*, is both a catalogue of wrongs against the black man over the centuries and a celebration of the strength by which he has survived those wrongs. That strength, a strength rooted in hope where there is no visible basis for hope, is, as we have seen, the essence of the blues. Outside of the blues, its most profound expressions in Hughes's poetry are in "Mother to Son," "The Negro Mother," "I, Too," and "The Negro Speaks of Rivers."

MOTHER TO SON

Well, son, I'll tell you:
Life for me ain't been no crystal stair.
It's had tacks in it,
And splinters,
And boards torn up,
And places with no carpet on the floor—
Bare.
But all the time
I'se been a-climbin' on,
And reachin' landin's,
And turnin' corners,
And sometimes goin' in the dark
Where there ain't been no light.
So boy, don't you turn back.
Don't you set down on the steps
'Cause you finds it's kinder hard.
Don't you fall now—
For I'se still goin', honey,
I'se still climbin',
And life for me ain't been no crystal stair.[12]

"The Negro Mother"[13] is a narrative version (dramatic monologue) of the more compact and earlier "Mother to Son." Both poems share the metaphor of life as a journey, in particular a climbing up the ladder of success, or "up the great stairs" to heaven's golden gate. For the rich the stairs are crystal and smooth and the climb easy; for the poor the stairs are splintered and torn up and dark, not unlike the ghetto stairway of "Ballad of the Landlord," and the climb is slow and arduous. (Or: the rich ride up in elevators, but tenement dwellers must walk up.) To get to the top, one must keep moving, cannot stop and sit. "I *had* to keep on! No stopping for me." To stop is to become a sitter on stoops and stander on street corners (the ghetto versions of the beach bum), or to become a prostitute, pimp, hustler, or thief. To despair is, in short, to wither and die. And as one conscious of her destiny as bearer of "the seed of the Free," one therefore on whom the future depended the Black Mother chose to keep climbing. This is her achievement, that she survived to bear and nourish new generations, a staggering achievement under the circumstances. It is from this perspective that we must view Hughes's later summoning of "Uncle Tom on his mighty knees,"[14] or the mild mannered grandfather in Ellison's *Invisible Man* describing himself as a sophisticated saboteur and guerrilla. These men and women acquiesced in their own humiliation and kept climbing on in order to prepare the way for "the coming Free." Their reward is in their vision of the possibility of freedom for their children. They are conservers and transmitters of the national soul, an example of love, wisdom, perseverance, and triumph for the younger generations to emulate.

Both poems reflect the form of a church testimony, with the lesson: "It's a sin to give up. I'm pressing toward the mark." This along with the traditional religious image of the stairs, and the stark endurance, fuelled by the "dream like steel in my soul" and expressed in "A song and a prayer," show both poems as emerging from the same big sea as the traditional spirituals and blues.

I, TOO

I, too, sing America.

I am the darker brother.
They send me to eat in the kitchen
When company comes,
But I laugh,
And eat well,
And grow strong.

Tomorrow,
I'll sit at the table
When company comes.
Nobody'll dare
Say to me
"Eat in the kitchen,"
Then.
Besides,
They'll see how beautiful I am
And be ashamed,—

I, too, am America.[15]

"I, Too" is as stoical as it is affirmative. Hughes accepts the brotherhood of black and white as beyond question. In addition, white and mulatto are brothers by immediate blood. The "darker brother" is America's secret shame, the kitchen his secret kingdom. Banished from polite company, he laughs, transforming his "yeah" into a "nay," as the grandfather in *Invisible Man* advised. He bides his time, eats well and grows strong, confident in his own beauty, and confident that "tomorrow" he will share the table (of communion) with the others. The domestic context lends mythic depth to the poem; for what we are witnessing is the career of the young prince dispossessed and suppressed by his wicked relatives. The certainty of his return and reinstatement is foretold in the archetypes.

The poem seems in particular response to Walt Whitman's insistent singing of his American soil and genealogy:

> My tongue, every atom of my blood, form'd from this
> soil, this air,
> Born here of parents born here from parents the same,
> and their parents the same. . . .[16]

The black man's roots in American soil are as deep, indeed deeper than the roots of most whites. Therefore Hughes, too, celebrates America, but unlike Whitman, not the America that is but the American that is to come. The demoratic vistas which Whitman saw all about him are, to Hughes, still distant on the horizon, yet to be.

THE NEGRO SPEAKS OF RIVERS

I've known rivers:
I've known rivers ancient as the world and older than the
    flow of human blood in human veins.
My soul has grown deep like the rivers.

I bathed in the Euphrates when dawns were young.
I built my hut near the Congo and it lulled me to sleep.
I looked upon the Nile and raised the pyramids above it.
I heard the singing of the Mississippi when Abe Lincoln
    went down to New Orleans, and I've seen its muddy
    bosom turn all golden in the sunset.

I've known rivers:
Ancient dusky rivers.

My soul has grown deep like the rivers.[17]

"The Negro Speaks of Rivers" is perhaps the most profound of these poems of heritage and strength. Composed when Hughes was a mere 17 years old, and dedicated to W. E. B. DuBois, it is a sonorous evocation of transcendent essences so ancient as to appear timeless, predating human existence, longer than human memory. The rivers are part of God's body, and participate in his immortality. They are the earthly analogues of eternity: deep, continuous, mysterious. They are named in the order of their association with black history. The black man has drunk of their life-giving essences, and thereby borrowed their immortality. He and the rivers have become one. The magical transformation of the Mississippi from mud to gold by the sun's radiance is mirrored in the transformation of slaves into free men by Lincoln's Proclamation (and, in Hughes's poems, the transformation of shabby cabarets into gorgeous palaces, dancing girls into queens and priestesses by the spell of black music). As the rivers deepen with time, so does the black man's soul; as their waters ceaselessly flow, so will the black soul endure. The black man has seen the rise and fall of civilizations from the earliest times, seen the beauty and death-changes of the world over the thousands of years, and will survive even this America. The poem's meaning is related to Zora Neale Hurston's judgment of the mythic High John de Conquer, whom she held as a symbol of the triumphant spirit of black America: that John was of the "Be" class. *"Be* here when the ruthless man comes, and *be* here when he is gone."[18] In a time and place where black life is held cheap and the days of black men appear to be numbered, the poem is a majestic reminder of the strength and fullness of history, of the source of that life which transcends even ceaseless labor and burning crosses.

One of Hughes's fullest representations of this black strength is in his twelve-poem sequence on the life and times of Alberta K. Johnson, "Madam to You."[19] Madam Alberta Johnson is hewed out of solid rock, yet soft flesh and rollicking soul. She is a contemporary of Jesse B. Semple, and her life and times, like Simple's, are the stuff of the blues. She once owned a beauty parlor, then a barbecue stand, but the depression and a no-good man took care of those. Now she works as a domestic. She bears her losses bravely. Her spirit is resilient; she is strong, outspoken, determined not to be taken advantage of, determined to survive. The people she comes in contact with, each with his hustle, each aiming to exploit her, feel the lash of her tongue and recoil from the sharp edge of her resistance: the employer with her twelve-room house and spine-breaking cooking, ironing, scrubbing, baby-nursing, and dog-walking, who nevertheless professes concern ("You know, Alberta, / I love you so! / I said, Madam, / That may be true— / But I'll be dogged / If I love you!"); the rent man who wants his money but wouldn't make repairs; the telephone operator who wants payment for a collect call she says she didn't authorize; the social worker who knows very well you can't raise a foster child on four dollars a week, yet keeps coming around asking for a report ("Last time I told her, / Report, my eye! / Things is bad— / *You* figure out why"); the fortune teller, pretending a mystery, who wants another dollar and a half to read the other palm; Mr. Death himself who has come before his time (". . . Alberta / Ain't goin' with you today!"); and the census man who wants to change her name to suit his bureaucratic convenience ("I said, I don't / Give a damn! / Leave me and my name / Just like I am!"). Everyone of them is quickly put in his place. Hers is the same spirit which, years later, in response to similar pressures, issued in the sassy "Ask your Mama" retorts. Nothing and no one will dominate her. With the printer she insists on her American identity, wants her business cards in American letters, not in Old English or

Roman letters: "There's nothing foreign / To my pedigree: / Alberta K. Johnson— / American that's me." The minister by preaching sin strives in vain for hegemony over her mind: "He said, Sister / Have you backslid? / I said, it felt good— / If I did." Not even love can rule or ruin her. She grew up the hard way, has had two husbands, and when she met a man who was "always giving / And never taking," who swore "All I want is you"—

> Right then and there
> I knowed we was through. . . .

> Nobody loves nobody
> For yourself alone.

The world is too harsh, her emotional equilibrium too hard-earned to permit the turbulence of love to disrupt it.

> I said, I don't want
> My heart to bust.

"Madam's Past History" offers us a glimpse of the total destitution blacks are required to suffer before they are considered in need. Just as in "Out of Work" the WPA turned down a man who had not lived in the city a year and a day, they turn down Alberta because she has insurance. Her reaction is much like his—not anger or bitterness or self-pity, but the sassy humor of the blues:

> I said,
> DON'T WORRY 'BOUT ME!
> Just like the song,
> Take care of yourself—
> And I'll get along

—as though the WPA and other social welfare agencies ever took care of anyone but themselves, which is part of the intended irony. Now she may be a domestic—but she is still "Madam." Her dignity will hold up, for it is not the position that makes the person.

"Madam and Her Madam" tears down the myth that the black woman ever had it easy because she could easily get a job (as a domestic) because of white folks' love for her. The employer is not mean, she just happens to have too much work for one domestic. Still she lives in the illusion that she is doing Alberta a favor, and is shocked to discover otherwise. Not only does Alberta speak up for herself, showing none of the false humility of the black servant stereotype which the employer no doubt expected, but she boldly rips off the employer's own sentimental-master mask.

The employer's false concern is echoed in the rent collector's polite

"Howdy-do?" in "Madam and the Rent Man." Alberta is sharp, matches him word for word. She is polite ("What / Can I do for you?") when he is, but when he sheds his mask and talks tough, she does too, producing a rapid inventory of needed repairs comparable to that in "Ballad of the Landlord." But the rent man claims he is only an agent, not responsible; the owner is absent, distant, never there to accept responsibility.

The impersonal owner reappears in "Madam and the Phone Bill." To Alberta, the telephone operator is simply "Central," a disembodied voice representing an invisible empire. But she is not intimidated: she is concerned about what is central to her, not what is central to the phone company. In "Madam's Past History" the words important to her—the name plates over her business establishments—were capitalized; here it is the words important to the phone company that are capitalized. What is central to her is not to them, and vice versa. They don't care to hear about her private affairs, and she doesn't care to hear about their phone bill. As with the rent man, her wit matches her spunk. Her long monologue on Roscoe and his girl friends in Kansas City is a deliberate ploy, the traditional nigger jive used to confuse white folks, wear out their patience and force them to give up. And Alberta is a mean player.

Alberta's frivolous, gentle side is seen in "Madam's Calling Cards," "Madam and the Number Writer," and "Madam and the Fortune Teller." There is a comic incongruity in her desire for calling cards, but it is an understandable bit of compensation and wish-fulfillment which is common with poor folks. The scene with the fortune teller is a farce. This is a jive fortune teller, saying and doing all the wrong things. Alberta sees through her, offers to pay her "some mind," not some money. That contest is a draw; but when it comes to the number writer she loses out. This is the only time someone out-raps her. But with the number man she is light-hearted and relaxed; she knows he is not out to swindle her out of a lot of money. He is even willing to risk a dime himself. He is playful and she is game—and lets herself be taken. And in the end they find themselves in the same fix (they lost), and there is no hostility. Her irreverence (heaven as a place in which not only to gamble but to win continuously) is echoed in her flippant replies to Rev. Butler in "Madam and the Minister," an irreverence common enough in a culture in which the line between the religious and the secular is often quite thin.

Alberta K. Johnson is the kind of black woman so frequently portrayed as a simple-minded nonentity. What Hughes has done, in effect, is to turn the stereotype inside out. Alberta is bright, strong, knows who she is, and insists on her identity. Her middle initial, which stands for nothing but itself, is a symbol of her unique person. Her battle with the census-taker is a battle that black people, individually and collectively, have fought over and over: the battle over *names*, the battle for *self-definition*. The man came to take the census, but turns around and attempts to *censor*, define, and confer identities. He came to count her, ends up attempting to *discount* her. But neither her name nor her life will be subsumed under anyone else's control. She stands on her dignity, demands respect: she is "Madam" to him.

We would have to go to Hughes's prose to find (in Simple) a comparably complete and arresting portrait of a black man. In Hughes's poetry no man, and for that matter no other woman, is presented so memorably.

In describing America Hughes pays particular attention to the South, for the obvious reason that the black man's unfreedom is most starkly evident there. The South with its lynchings is, in his view, the measure of America. In "Magnolia Flowers"[20] the poet goes South looking for the region's storied beauty, but finds instead "a corner full of ugliness." That ugliness is delivered with devastating finality in his early poem "The South":

> The lazy, laughing South
> With blood on its mouth.
> The sunny-faced South,
>   Beast-strong,
>   Idiot-brained.
> The child-minded South
> Scratching in the dead fire's ashes
> For a Negro's bones.
>   Cotton and the moon,
>   Warmth, earth, warmth,
>   The sky, the sun, the stars,
>   The magnolia-scented South,
> Beautiful, like a woman,
> Seductive as a dark-eyed whore,
>   Passionate, cruel,
>   Honey-lipped, syphilitic—
>   That is the South.
> And I, who am black, would love her
> But she spits in my face.
> And I, who am black,
> Would give her many rare gifts
> But she turns her back upon me.
>   So now I seek the North—
>   The cold-faced North,
>   For she, they say,
>   Is a kinder mistress,
> And in her house my children
> May escape the spell of the South.[21]

The poem is a fierce portrait etched with fire. In its masculine aspect the South is bestial, sub-human, a predator and scavenger, and in its feminine aspect a degenerate *femme fatale*, a syphilitic whore. These are not Hughes's sad, gentle black prostitutes and pathetic black clowns but their malicious and deadly white counterparts. The masculine image elicits total repulsion, the feminine mixed attraction and repulsion. It is the seductive female principle that entangles the unwary black man, delivering him up finally to be hanged, maimed, and burned by the male of the species, as the community watches and cheers. The landscape too is innocently seductive, but those who yield to its sunshine and magnolia fragrance (which becomes the sickly-sweet smell of flowers on a coffin) will have to live under constant threat of destruction by the human predators who roam the region as their preserve and hunting ground. The "rotten meat" of the lynched body defaces the landscape. Nature's beauty is desecrated by the brutal acts committed within it.[22]

The poem's metaphors conform to history and experience. For the usual excuse for lynching a black man is that he raped a white woman.

> "No I didn't touch her
> White flesh ain't for me."[23]

Protestations of innocence are useless. A black man accused of molesting a white woman is as good as dead. The rope around his neck, the knife at his genitals, and the fire all over him is all the due process he could ever hope for. When the lynch fever seizes the mob, any excuse will do. They will lynch a black man for threatening a white man who not only works him too hard for too little pay, but in addition has raped his wife.[24] They will lynch a black man for speaking of freedom:

> Last week they lynched a colored boy.
> They hung him to a tree.
> That colored boy ain't said a thing
> But we all should be free.[25]

And they will lynch a black man for resisting their claims of racial superiority:

> They hit me in the head
> And knocked me down. . . .
>
> A cracker said, "Nigger,
> Look me in the face—
> And tell me you believe in
> The great white race."[26]

Whatever the excuse, ultimately blacks are lynched because they are powerless, because they have none but God to protect them:

> Way Down South in Dixie
> (Bruised body high in air)
> I asked the white Lord Jesus
> What was the use of prayer.[27]

And while this grisly ritual is taking place, the men, women, and children, "little lads, lynchers that were to be," as Claude McKay called them,[28] dance and cheer "in fiendish glee":

> Pull at the rope! Oh!
> Pull it high!
> Let the white folks live
> And the black boy die.
>
> Pull it, boys,
> With a bloody cry
> As the black boy spins
> And the white folks die. . . .[29]

Most lynchings are for rape. But it is common knowledge that in the South it is extremely rare that a black man has actually raped or attempted to rape a white woman. In the South, sexual contact between black men and white women, from slavery times to the present, has almost always been initiated by the white woman. And every black man in the South knows that if he is unlucky enough to become the object of a white woman's affections, he must leave town or die. When a white woman invites you to love, you are doomed. If you accept and it is found out, as it will sooner or later, she will cry rape, and you will be lynched. If you refuse, she will in humiliation and revenge cry rape, and you will be lynched.

The rape-and-lynch psychosis must be viewed in the context of the perverted sexual mythology whereby white Americans first reduced black people to subhumans, then invested them with a hypersexuality, forced access of white males to black females, blocked access of black males to white females, and proceeded to project white lust and puritan guilt onto black males and victimize them for the sins of white males. For Southern white men to publicly admit that in liaisons with black men, Southern white women are usually willing accomplices, most often the provocateurs, is for them to lose control of reality as they wish to know it. Instead, that secret knowledge drives them even more rabidly violent. It is this psychological cat and mouse game that gives a poem like "Silhouette" its ironic power:

> Southern gentle lady,
> Do not swoon.
> They've just hung a black man. . . .

> For the world to see
> How Dixie protects
> Its white womanhood.
> Southern gentle lady,
>   Be good!
>   Be good![30]

The most prolonged and deeply moving of Hughes's lynch poems is "The Bitter River,"[31] a dirge for two black youths lynched in Mississippi in 1942. Hughes conceives of the lynch terror as a bitter, poisonous river flowing through the South, a river at which black people have been forced to drink too long. Its water galls the taste, poisons the blood, and drowns black hopes. The "snake-like hiss of its stream" strangles black dreams. The bitter river reflects no stars, only the steel bars behind which are confined numberless innocents—the Scottsboro Boys, share-croppers, and labor leaders. The bitter river makes nonsense of liberal rhetoric:

> "Work, education, patience
> Will bring a better day."
> The swirl of the bitter river
> Carries your "patience" away.

Patience is useless, the hope in work and education a slim and distant one. The poem ends in bitter complaint, weariness and gloom:

> I'm tired of the bitter river!
> Tired of the bars!

Hughes's most brilliant lynch poem is "Christ in Alabama," one of the four poems accompanying the title play in *Scottsboro Limited* (1932). The Scottsboro Boys, eight black youths falsely accused of rape on the forced testimony of a group of disreputable white women, were in jail awaiting a legal lynching. This was the occasion of Hughes's epigrammatic "Justice":

> That Justice is a blind goddess
> Is a thing to which we black are wise:
> Her bandage hides two festering sores
> That once perhaps were eyes.[32]

In the poem "Scottsboro" the youths are identified with Jesus Christ, John Brown, Nat Turner, Gandhi, and other martyrs. These men are not dead, Hughes declares, they are immortal; and "Is it much to die when immortal feet / March with you down Time's street . . .?"[33] In "Christ in Alabama" Jesus is pictured as a lynched black man:

> Christ is a nigger,
> Beaten and black:

Oh, bare your back!

Mary is His mother;
Mammy of the South,
Silence your mouth.

God is His father:
White Master above
Grant Him your love.

Most holy bastard
Of the bleeding mouth,
   Nigger Christ
   On the cross
   Of the South.[34]

"Christ is a nigger" in two senses: in the historical sense as a brown-skinned Jew like other Jews of his day, with a brown-skinned mother—both later adopted into the white West and given a lily-white heavenly father; and in the symbolic sense of Jesus as an alien presence, preaching an exacting spirituality, a foreign religion as it were, much as the black man, with his different color and culture, is an alien presence in the South. Each is a scapegoat sacrificed for the society's sins. In particular, the white sin of lust has created a mongrel mulatto race ("most holy bastard") with black slave mothers ("Mammy of the South") and white slavemaster fathers ("White Master above"). And, once created, this race is cast out, disinherited, crucified.

A later poem, "Bible Belt," amplifies and illuminates "Christ in Alabama":

It would be too bad if Jesus
Were to come back black.
There are so many churches
Where he could not pray
In the U.S.A.,
Where entrance to Negroes,
No matter how sanctified,
Is denied,
Where race, not religion,
Is glorified.
But say it—
You may be
Crucified.[35]

If they remembered Jesus in his historical identity ("nigger"), the white people of the United States would not so readily call themselves Christians. Hughes recalls an occasion when students at the University of

North Carolina at Chapel Hill printed "Christ in Alabama" on the front page of their newspaper on the day he was scheduled to speak at the university. Some of the townspeople, including the sheriff, suggested that the poet be run out of town: "It's bad enough to call Christ a *bastard*. But when he calls him a *nigger*, he's gone too far!"[36]

The cryptic simplicity of "Christ in Alabama" exhibits Hughes at his best. Profound insight is carelessly draped in the most facile diction and form, the most commonplace images. There is no decoration or pedantry. The poem is so stark it could almost have been written by a child. It reminds one of classic African sculpture, with its bold lines and geometric precision. The poem evokes the feeling that great art so often evokes: that it could not have been done any other way. It commands both accessibility and depth. Hughes is a master at clothing the complex and profound in simple garb; and perhaps it is this more than any other quality that marks him as a great poet.

Lynching is the ultimate weapon of the Southern terror; but other bitter tributaries feed its bitter stream. What Hughes said of the people and town of Scottsboro may be said of many small towns of the South:

> Scottsboro's just a little place:
> No shame is writ across its face—
> Its court, too weak to stand against a mob,
> Its people's heart, too small to hold a sob.[37]

Sharecroppers, cotton pickers and other rural laborers, regardless of how hard they work, will remain in drastic poverty:

> The cotton's picked
> And the work is done
> Boss man takes the money
> And we get none,
>
> Leaves us hungry, ragged
> As we were before.[38]

And sooner or later many come to the conclusion that there is no reason to stay. Life anywhere else could hardly be worse:

> Cause it's hard for a jigaboo
> With a wife and children, too,
> To make a livin'
> Anywhere
> Today.
>
> But in West Texas where de sun
> Shines like de evil one,
> There ain't no reason

> For a man
> To stay!³⁹

And therefore many buy a ticket and head north, not intending to return:

> I pick up my life
> And take it with me
> And I put it down in
> Chicago, Detroit,
> Buffalo, Scranton,
> Any place that is
> North and East—
> And not Dixie. . . .
>
> I am fed up
> With Jim Crow laws,
> People who are cruel
> And afraid,
> Who lynch and run,
> Who are scared of me
> And me of them.⁴⁰

This is the Great Migration, and they come sometimes in a trickle, sometimes in an avalanche. And what do they find up north? As Hughes was to show in *Montage of a Dream Deferred*, the migrant discovers that he still can't own anything up north, but at least he is thankful that "there ain't no Ku Klux / on a 133rd." However, his gratitude will diminish considerably when he discovers police brutality.

Hughes equates the Northern police violence of "Third Degree" and "Who But the Lord?" with the Southern violence of "Ku Klux." The police have the same "faces like jack-o-lanterns" as the members of the KKK in *Ask Your Mama*.

KU KLUX

> They took me out
> To some lonesome place.
> They said, "Do you believe
> In the great white race?"
>
> I said, "Mister,
> To tell you the truth,
> I'd believe in anything
> If you'd just turn me loose."
>
> The white man said, "Boy,
> Can it be

You're a-standin' there
A-sassin' me?"

They hit me in the head
And knocked me down.
And then they kicked me
On the ground.

A cracker said, "Nigger,
Look me in the face—
And tell me you believe in
The great white race."[41]

Like Madam Alberta Johnson in "Madam and the Phone Bill," the narrator of "Ku Klux" is signifying and clowning around, sassing the white
folks. He knows that anything he says will be used against him, and his
knowledge gives him a certain freedom. He mocks his attackers' beliefs
by saying he would believe in anything if they would just turn him loose;
that is, he would accept their reading of reality only under duress. They
are desperate to persuade him, but they also know it's useless. And the
fact that he knows and says as much makes them even more frantic. The
poem holds five hundred years of history in capsule, spotlighting the
physical violence by which the West established and enforced the myth
of its superiority over the rest of the world.

"Third Degree," a later poem, repeats the structure and drama of
"Ku Klux."

THIRD DEGREE

Hit me! Jab me!
Make me say I did it.
Blood on my sport shirt
And my tan suede shoes.

Faces like jack-o-lanterns
In gray slouch hats.

Slug me! Beat me!
Scream jumps out
Like blow-torch.
Three kicks between the legs
That kill the kids
I'd make tomorrow.

Bars and floor skyrocket
And burst like Roman candles.

When you throw

> Cold water on me,
> I'll sign the
> Paper. . . .[42]

"Ku Klux" is a leisurely account after the event; the victim has lived to tell his story, and can afford to mellow its memory with humor and sass. But in "Third Degree" the drama is more immediate, taking place in the present, and there is no room for humor. We are inside the victim looking out, feeling the blows and watching physical objects blurr [sic] and merge. The intensity of pain is suggested in the fire images: blow-torch, skyrocket, candles. As in "Ku Klux" the victim is defiant and his confession is forced.

It is perhaps no accident that organized white violence, actuated by the myths breeding sexual paranoia, so frequently focusses on black male genitals: lynch mobs shear them off; Southern sheriffs attacked them with electric cattle prods during the civil rights movement of the 1960s; and in "Third Degree," Northern white police attempt to crush them ("Three kicks between the legs / That kill the kids / I'd make tomorrow").

WHO BUT THE LORD?

> I looked and I saw
> That man they call the law.
> He was coming
> Down the street at me!
> I had visions in my head
> Of being laid out cold and dead,
> Or else murdered
> By the third degree.
>
> I said, *O Lord, if you can,*
> *Save me from that man!*
> *Don't let him make a pulp out of me!*
> But the Lord he was not quick.
> The law raised up his stick
> And beat the living hell
> Out of me!
>
> Now I do not understand
> Why God don't protect a man
> From police brutality.
> Being poor and black,
> I've no weapon to strike back
> So who but the Lord
> Can protect me?[43]

"Who But the Lord?" is the most humorous of the trio. Like "Ku Klux,"
a leisurely after-the-fact account, the poem establishes a comic equation
between the Lord and the law. Both presume to protect, but in the course
of the poem we learn that the law destroys and the Lord fails to protect.
The victim had been taught to live in fear of God, but as it turns out, in
the real world the law carries greater weight, is the one to be feared.
The Lord may be Savior, but the law moves so much faster that one has
to have something else for protection. The narrator's "I do not understand" is ironic, for he does; and his wisdom is in the knowledge that at
least in dealing with police brutality God is but a weak wish, that black
folks need some other real power to protect them.

The poem ends in one of those tense moments where Hughes leaves
a question hanging fire. That his intention is not only to censure God and
criticize black religiosity, but also to make a radical political statement,
is confirmed in the ominous closer which he added to the version of the
poem that appeared years later in *The Panther and the Lash*. To the
question: who but the Lord can protect me? the rejoinder is a subterra-
nean "We'll see."[44]

Taken together, these three key poems on white physical brutality
reveal Hughes as sharing the sentiment, quite common among blacks,
that as long as you're south of the Canadian border, you're south; that
Mississippi is in New York.

Through the four decades of his career Hughes's poetry reflected
public concerns, borrowing insights from the spirit of each era. The 1930s
and 60s were the particular decades of radicals and extremists, and for
Hughes each was an ideological and rhetorical decade, the 30s perhaps
more so than the 60s: the difference was between the fire and enthusiasm
of a young man in his thirties and the weariness and disappointment of
an old man in his sixties who finds his dreams still deferred.

Some of Hughes's political poetry of the 30s was collected in two
pamphlets: *Scottsboro Limited* (1932) and *A New Song* (1938). Both are
party-line statements calling for revolution, calling on black and white
workers to sink their racial antagonisms and band together to overthrow
their common enemy, the capitalist ruling class and its agents.

> Let us forget what Booker T. said,
> "Separate as the fingers."
>
> Let us become instead, you and I,
> One single hand
> That can united rise
> To smash the old dead dogmas of the past—
> To kill the lies of color
> That keep the rich enthroned

> And drive us to the time-clock and the plow
> Helpless, stupid, scattered, and alone—as now—
> Race against race,
> Because one is black,
> Another white of face.[45]

The union is to be forged under the communist banner. In the verse play "Scottsboro Limited" the Communist Party offers aid, and the eight youths accept: "Who else is there to help us out o' this?" The Communist Party made a *cause célèbre* of the Scottsboro case. In the strength of this new alliance, the youths declare:

> Now out of the darkness
> The new Red Negro will come:
> That's me!
> No death in the chair![46]

The "New Negro" of the 20s has become the "Red Negro" of the 30s. The onset of the depression, which brought early death to all the high optimism of the Harlem Renaissance, made the alliance of the black struggle with the communist labor movement, in history as well as in Hughes's poetry, almost inevitable. *A New Song* was published by the International Workers Order, with an introduction by Michael Gold, editor of *New Masses* magazine. In it Hughes champions the cause of the oppressed of all races—blacks, Indians, poor whites, and new immigrants—against "the same old stupid plan / Of dog eat dog, of mighty crush the weak."[47] In "Justice", reprinted from *Scottsboro*, it is no longer "we black" but "we poor" who know that American justice is not merely blindfolded but horribly eyeless. The derelict in "Park Bench" who threatens to invade wealthy Park Avenue is not necessarily black, nor is the militant of "Pride". The people—and their enemies—come from all races; the division is class, not race. The "Kids Who Die" are murdered with the aid of the pseudoscience of "the gentlemen with Dr. in front of their names, / White and black, / Who make surveys and write books". The powerful proletarian chants and ballads ("Chant for May Day," "Chant for Tom Mooney," "Ballad of Ozie Powell," "Ballads of Lenin," "Song of Spain") are rendered in the multinational voices of workers the world over. The workers are of one mind, their voices are strident, and they are determined to push the world forward into a future better than the past.

> The past has been
> A mint of blood and sorrow—
> That must not be
> True of tomorrow. ("History")

The "New Song" of the title is a song of unity and revolt:

> Revolt! Arise!
>
> The Black
> And White World
> Shall be one!
> The Worker's World!

Hughes's ideological interest in communism may indeed have commenced with the Scottsboro case in 1931; however, his sympathies were radical and his voice defiant years before that, as exemplified in "God to Hungry Child" (1925):

> Hungry child,
> I didn't make this world for you.
> You didn't buy any stock in my railroad,
> You didn't invest in my corporation.
> Where are your shares in standard oil?
> I made the world for the rich
> And the will-be-rich
> And the have-always-been-rich.
> Not for you,
> Hungry child.[48]

Or in "Johannesburg Mines" (1928):

> In the Johannesburg mines
> There are 240,000 natives working.
>
> What kind of poem
> Would you make out of that?
>
> 240,000 natives working
> In the Johannesburg mines.[49]

Nor did his Marxist vision subside with the Nazi-Soviet Pact of 1939 and the onset of World War II. The exposure of poverty and oppression and the call for world-wide revolution in *Scottsboro Limited* and *A New Song* are duplicated and reinforced not only in his uncollected poetry of the same period, e.g., "Advertisement for the Waldorf-Astoria,"[50] "Goodbye, Christ," "Good Morning, Revolution," "The Same," "Air Raid Over Harlem," and "White Man," but also in such later works as the series of laudatory essays on the Soviet Union in his weekly column in the *Chicago Defender* of June, July, and August of 1946, and on China in "The Revolutionary Armies of China—1949." However, by 1943, when his next two pamphlets of political poetry, *Jim Crow's Last Stand* and *Freedom's Plow*, were published, Hughes had indeed beat a tactical retreat—*but only in his collected works*—from the broad-based multiracial Marxist workers' platform, to concentrate once more on black people's particular American dream, without specifying an ideology or method for fulfilling that dream. In these two later pamphlets he focusses most closely on America's avowed principles and the contradiction between those principles and the oppression of blacks. The dominant mood is bewilderment, the tone is hurt. The black man who speaks in "The Black Man Speaks" just "can't see / Why Democracy means / Everybody but me." The question is all the more urgent in a time of war (1943):

> If we're fighting to create
> A free world tomorrow,
> Why not end *right now*
> Old Jim Crow's sorrow?[51]

Roosevelt's "Four Freedoms" should be made a reality here at home:

> Freedom's not just
> To be won Over There.
> It means Freedom at home, too—
> Now—*right here!*[52]

And Freedom is immortal, will not be destroyed by burning books, imprisoning Nehru, or lynching black men.[53]

In *Jim Crow* and *Freedom's Plow* Hughes takes America's democratic rhetoric seriously. Nowhere is he more patently patriotic. These poems pick up where "I, too, sing America" left off. They are protest poems in the classic sense, addressed to white America, and not so much to their hearts as to their heads. The poet attempts to *reason* with white folks. He urges them to return America to first principles. There might even be no need to go hunting for foreign ideologies. The blueprint is right here at home, it's just a matter of building upon it:

> The plan and the pattern is here,
> Woven from the beginning
> Into the warp and Woof of America.[54]

But until this is done, he urges black folks to hold on to the plow and never let go. This, he says, is the song the slaves sang long ago: "Keep Your Hand on the Plow! Hold On!" This is the invariable message of the spirituals and blues, the meaning of black history thus far: no solution at hand, only endurance, a continuing struggle.

But the dream may not be deferred indefinitely without repercussions. In "Roland Hayes Beaten" (1949) Hughes warned that black people will not always be patient and nonviolent, that the dream will explode. *The Panther and the Lash* (1967) is a poetic record of the beginning of that explosion. When such a dream is deferred overlong, paramilitary groups such as the Black Panthers are liable to appear, followed by the usual white backlash—and the scene is set for violent clashes. This is the meaning of the book's title.

The Panther and the Lash is subtitled "Poems of Our Times"; and it is a testimony to Hughes's deep insight and enduring quality that of the 70 poems in the collection, 28 (or over a third) are reprints from earlier works, are poems of other times which speak just as directly to the high-strung 60s. "Christ in Alabama" reflects America as accurately in 1967 as in 1932. Not much has changed in the black situation, nor in Hughes's perception of it. His vision was from the beginning pan-African in scope, with the black man in America closest to home and squarely in the center. Africa at first inhabited the vague, outer reaches of that vision-scope, until the proletarian 30s; then, starting in the late 50s and 60s, modern communications and international politics dramatically transformed time, distance, and visibility, bringing Africa so much closer and providing the details and drama which make Africa so much more real in *Ask Your Mama* and *The Panther and the Lash*, than, for instance, in *The Weary Blues* or *One-Way Ticket*. The transformation of time, distance, and visibility had a great deal to do with the black consciousness revolution of the 1960s, which in turn set the stage for the reemergence in his collected poems of Hughes's own Third World consciousness and his vision of the possibility of world-wide revolution—although this possibility is rendered in more deliberately circumspect terms than in his radical poetry of the 30s.

In *The Panther and the Lash*, as elsewhere, Hughes is a poet of his age, up to date, viewing the same black life through the lenses of the particular day. Whatever the era, his lenses are usually well fitted and focussed. He knows what he is looking for, and he captures it with astonishing clarity, in all its beauty, sordidness, or violence.

The Panther and the Lash is a book of the tense and violent 60s—in its title, in the occasional topicality of its verse, and in its Third World awareness. It is dominated by public issues. In it Hughes brings together some of his best political poems, with the result that the book is more consistently, directly, and bitingly political than any of his earlier poetry volumes, not counting the pamphlet of the 30s. There is no sweetness here. The energetic proletarian optimism of *Scottsboro Limited* and *A New Song*, which by 1943 had given way to the bewilderment and disappointment of *Jim Crow's Last Stand* and *Freedom's Plow*, has by the mid-60s soured into a full-bodied disillusionment and bitterness. And yet Hughes has not repudiated the dream. For although he says in "Oppression" that dreams are now no longer available to the dreamers, "Nor songs / To the singers," he hastens to add that "the dream / Will come back, / And the song break its jail."[55] And in "Dream Dust" he urges his readers to gather out of the broken pieces of their dreams "One handful of dreamdust / Not for sale." "Hold Fast To Dreams," he titled a speech around the same period.[56]

No, he has not given up the dream, but he is beginning to look elsewhere (away from white America, whether workers or liberal Northerners) for sources for fulfilling it. And while the means is not specified, the complex out of which that means is likely to develop is broadly hinted at. The hope (distant, but nevertheless a hope) is in the emerging modern powers of the African homeland, and in China; in other words, in a gathering of Third World forces, all of whom have suffered oppression from the white man. There is a threat in Hughes's voice, a threat which disappeared from his collected poetry after the 1930s, and the frequency and strength of that threat in *The Panther and the Lash* is supported by that Third World hope.

"The Backlash Blues", the one clearly political blues in his collected poems, warns that nonwhites are the majority of the world's peoples; and when they join together, as they are about to, then, Mister Backlash,

> You're the one,
> Yes, you're the one
> Will have the blues.

The youngster of "Junior Addict", suffering from poverty and ignorance, and rapidly destroying himself with drugs, has no way of knowing that there is about to emerge a saving "sunrise out of Africa." And the poet calls out to the African nations to do their "emerging quickly and get to the job at hand:

> Quick, sunrise, come!
> Sunrise out of Africa,
> Quick, come!
> Sunrise, please come!
> Come! Come!

Hughes envisages revenge and redress, this time from a powerful China, for the four little girls killed in Birmingham, Alabama, in September 1963 when their church was bombed by white terroists. For centuries China made explosives, but used them for entertainment (fireworks). Europeans borrowed China's explosives, harnessed them to weapons of death and conquered the world with them. Now history has run full circle. China, borrowing modern technology from the West, has now harnessed those same explosives for death, although China's power is as yet unfelt, least of all in Dixie. But not for long. China too is building a nuclear arsenal; and on the Day of Judgment (the day of the nuclear destruction of the world) these four little girls will have their revenge ("Birmingham Sunday").

The threats in "Who But the Lord" ("We'll see") and in "Office Building: Evening" ("But just wait, chile. . ."), are less pointed and therefore perhaps even more ominous. China and Africa are distant threats, but these others may prove to be something more immediate, something on a local or even a personal scale but equally devastating and final. "Who But the Lord" is in its original 1949 version—except for the added threat, "We'll see." God has not protected black folks from police brutality. Somebody surely will: but who? If we wait long enough, it will be the avenging forces of the Third World. But before that, right now, on a local scale, it might be the Panthers, or their successors. Right now, the Panthers are all brashness and youth. Their "fist is clenched / Today— / To strike your face" ("Militant"). Desperate in their boldness, they hide nothing, wear "no disguise" ("Black Panther"). But their successors are likely to be more sophisticated—and deadly. The threat renews itself daily.

Finally, the greatest threat is simply in the people themselves, the black masses, in their continued existence, their refusal to disappear. The Pilgrims of Jamestown made the fatal error, and black people are here, a hard-rock reality. The sons of former slave owners may wish them away all they want, but these "Ghosts of 1619" will continue to haunt them, to "rape, rob, steal, / Sit-in, stand-in, stall-in, vote-in," until it's either liberation or genocide, freedom or death. Hughes sums it all up in "Final Call". To pipe the rats away, he suggests sending for the Pied Piper and other men of power; and he proceeds with a fantastic roll call of persons and shades, of all those who might, however vaguely, be connected with the case: the dead as well as the living, here and abroad; figures of history and figures of myth; black people and white people; miracle workers and makers of laws, declarations, and decrees, preachers and politicians; monarchs and rebels and revolutionaries; artists and freedom fighters; "old John Brown who knew slavery couldn't last," and "Uncle Tom on his mighty knees" (for even the Uncle cried "Freedom Now!" as best he knew how—*that* was his way of crying "Freedom Now!"—and as though his archetypal greatness does not loom large enough, he is described as having "mighty knees"). The one obvious omission is Booker T. Washington, and it is not clear why. Even Adam Clayton Powell, a Congressman-fugitive from New York State law, might come in "on a non-subpoena day" (a line weighted with all the ambiguity, all the sorrow and jest of the blues; a line as bitterly ironic as the man's career). The rats are the real rats infesting the ghetto, therefore poverty; but they are also the black masses, those same ghosts of 1619 whom the children of former slaveholders so desperately wish some pied piper would pipe away. The rats symbolize America's problems in general, and the poet is engaged in malicious fun (although this is humor that, as in the blues, cuts both ways): white America will try everything, however far-fetched or fantastic, except the one and only remedy that would work. The poem is, among other things, a poem about national bad faith and lack of commitment, about "experts" and their cartoon theories and programs. It is a majestic and stately poem, anticipating those militant poems of the late 60s and 70s which will find their strengths in forceful repetition, their shrillness a mark of the stresses and dynamic energies of their times. It is a dangerous poem.

First comes the prolonged crash and roar:

SEND FOR THE PIED PIPER AND LET HIM PIPE THE RATS
    AWAY.
SEND FOR ROBIN HOOD TO CLINCH THE ANTI-POVERTY
    CAMPAIGN.
SEND FOR THE FAIRY QUEEN. . . .
SEND FOR. . . .
SEND FOR. . . .
SEND FOR. . . .

Then, silence. And then, the quiet last line, its triumphant humility accentuated by the parenthesis: "(And if nobody comes, send for me.)"

For all its calm, that closing line is in the sassy tradition of the dozens: If nobody comes, send for your mother. She's the pied piper. Your mama will pipe the rats away. It is also a boast: If no one else can, I can. Me, I'll take care of business. If I can't do it, it can't be done. The line also carries the ironic humor and ambiguity of the blues: Well, I can't do it either, and then too I can. If you'd listen to me (Langston Hughes, *vox populi*) you'd know how it could be done.

As a public poet, Hughes normally uses the personal pronoun to weld himself tightly to his people, making his voice their voice, their joys and sorrows his joys and sorrows: "I am a Negro: / Black as the night is black / . . . . I brushed the boots of Washington"; "I, too, sing America. / . . . They send me to eat in the kitchen / When company comes"; "O white strong ones, / Why do you torture me?" But in the closing line of "Final Call," and in a number of other places, Hughes uses the personal pronoun not to merge but rather to disengage himself from the generality. We find this "movement away," usually with "me" as its pronoun-signature, in the title "Stokely Malcolm Me", or in the line "The land that's mine—the poor man's, Indian's Negro's, ME—" ("Let America Be America Again"). In *Ask Your Mama* it appears in a half-comic, half-defiant phrase:

LOVELY LENA MARIAN LOUIS PEARLIE MAE
GEORGE S. SCHUYLER MONTO BENE
COME WHAT MAY LANGSTON HUGHES. . . .[57]

(He will not let a false modesty write him out of the rolls of the celebrities). In each of these examples the poet's reference to himself is tossed in carelessly like an afterthought, not unlike a painter's signature tucked away in a corner of his canvas. "Me" is Hughes's way of establishing, publicly, a private, personal relationship to the emotion or action at hand. It is his way of being a public voice without ceasing to be a flesh-and-blood member of the community; his way of being a spokesman without becoming an oracle. This occasional effort to disengage himself from the crowd and to momentarily relish his individuality ("our individual dark-skinned selves") is a salutary one. It is not egotism—on the contrary: I may be all black men, but not all the time, even in verse. Sometimes I just got to be me, just *me*, Langston Hughes!

II

The deferred dream was overwhelming, yet not even its great weight could crush the purely lyric impulse totally. The world of beauty and lyricism may have been distant from Hughes's daily life and the concerns of his art, as he claims in "My Adventures as a Social Poet," but, all the same, he made frequent and pleasurable excursions into that world. Especially in his early years he maintains a respectable balance between social and lyric poems. Of his first five books, only *Fine Clothes to the Jew* and *The Negro Mother* are entirely social and/or modeled on black folk forms.[1] Lyric poetry with no immediate social or political content occupies most of *Dear Lovely Death* (1931) and roughly a half of *The Weary Blues* (1926) and of *The Dream Keeper* (1932) (although two-thirds of the latter were reprints). But after that it was three or four lyric poems per volume, except for *Fields of Wonder* (1947), which was almost entirely lyric.

The most prominent feature of Hughes's lyric verse is its brilliance of imagery. Hughes makes frequent use of poetic conceits as we find them in Shakespeare, the Metaphysical Poets, and Emily Dickinson, and of the brief and bright flashes that characterize Japanese haiku and the early 20th century Imagists. The lyric poem is the particular vehicle of the dream as romantic fantasy and wish fulfillment ("love, roses, and moonlight"). And in *The Weary Blues* the dreamers include the lovers of the "Black Pierrot" section, seeking relatedness; the sailors of "Water Front Streets" who seek adventure in farway lands; and the wretched bits of humanity in "Shadows in the Sun" who endure as best they can life's heavy foot that crushes all of their dreams.[2] "Pierrot" is a ballad of desertion and elopement. "A Black Pierrot" and "Songs to the Dark Virgin" are in the surrealistic, imagistic mode in the one, the rejected lover weeps "until the red dawn / Dipped blood over the eastern hills," his "once gay-colored soul / Shrunken like a balloon without air"; and in the other, the lover conceives of himself in three stages—as a shattered jewel falling humbly at his loved one's feet, as a silken garment wrapping her body close, and as a leaping flame enveloping and annihilating her. "Ardella," "Poem: To the Black Beloved," and "When Sue Wears Red" are lyrical celebrations of female beauty.

> I would liken you
> To a night without stars
> Were it not for your eyes.
> I would liken you
> To a sleep without dreams
> Were it not for your songs.
>
> ("Ardella")

"When Sue Wears Red" is perhaps the most powerful of Hughes's love poems:

> When Susanna Jones wears red
> Her face is like an ancient cameo
> Turned brown by the ages.
> Come with a blast of trumpets,
> Jesus!
>
> When Susanna Jones wears red
> A queen from some time-dead Egyptian night
> Walks once again.
> Blow trumpets, Jesus!
>
> And the beauty of Susanna Jones in red
> Burns in my heart a love-fire sharp like pain.
>
> Sweet silver trumpets,
> Jesus!

Like "The Negro Speaks of Rivers," which it rivals in brilliance, this too is an early poem, written while Hughes was in high school, a poetically mature 17. And just as that poem fuses into one timeless flow the soul-deep rivers of the black experience through the ages, so does this reincarnate in one woman the feminine beauty and majesty of the ages. The poem derives its power from its vision of eternity and from the holler and shout of religious enthusiasm ("Come with a blast of trumpets, Jesus!"). In addition, it has its literary antecedents in Dunbar's "The Colored Band" and "When Malindy Sings":[3] Malindy, whose voice in "Come to Jesus" sets sinners' hearts atremble and compels their feet Christ-ward; Malindy, whose "Swing Low, Sweet Chariot" echoes "from de valley to de hill / . . . Th'oo de bresh of angels' wings, / Sof' an' sweet."

In both poets the vision is of transfiguration through art/magic: through
Sue's red dress, a type of magic mantle, which resurrects in her the
queens of other ages; through the Colored Band's syncopated rhythms
in response to which "de hea't goes into bus'ness fu' to he'p erlong de
eah"; and through the mesmeric power of Malindy's down-home voice.

The sailors and cabin boys of "Water Front Streets" pursue their
dreams of romance on the waters and faraway lands. Abandoning the
constricted life "between the hills," they haul off to sea carrying "beauties in their hearts." The waterfront streets themselves are unbeautiful,
but their denizens are in touch with the sea, which is a vehicle of the
dream, the sea on which "dream ships sail away / To where the spring
is wondrous rare / And life is gay," to where the sunset is like God's
hemorrhage "coughed across the sky." And in that land of romance the
young sailor, like the long-headed jazzers and other habitués of Harlem
nights, lives for the moment, bearing "his own strength / And his own
laughter, / His own today / And his own hereafter." His sojourn on land
is a circus of wine, women, and laughter, "and nothing hereafter." It is
at sea that his soul flowers and is fulfilled.

The sea itself is acutely characterized: it is "a wilderness of waves, /
A desert of water" endlessly dipping and diving, rising and rolling, all
day and all night. It will not stand still; tranquility is not in its nature.
And when it is calm, it is ominously calm—"It is not good / For water /
To be so still that way"—reminding us of its double nature as a gateway
to dreams fulfilled and a destroyer. The sea is "strong / Like God's hand"
and holds "a wide, deep death." Not even the sea's own children understand its fascination, they only feel in their marrows that they belong to
it. So that when the old seaman dies and is buried "high on a windy hill,"
his "sea-soul" refuses the weight and confinement of earth and reverts
to the freedom of the sea:

> Put no tombstone at my head,
> For here I do not make my bed.
> Strew no flowers on my grave,
> I've gone back to the wind and wave.
> Do not, do not weep for me.
> For I am happy with my sea.
>
> ("Death of an Old Seaman")

From the gypsies and seafarers it is only a half-step to "Shadows in
the Sun," a series of vignettes of broken and forgotten humanity, bits of
human clay hardly more than shadows. Through each the poet discovers
and exposes the cord that binds him and the reader to all mankind.
Something in each which he can "neither hear nor feel nor see . . . nor
understand" reaches for him like a magnet, compelling sympathy and
identification, bringing communion. So that the poet—and the reader—

becomes in turn the beggar boy playing "upon his flute a wild free tune / As if Fate had not bled him with her knife"; the "troubled woman / Bowed by / Weariness and pain / Like an autumn flower / In the frozen rain"; the suicide who could not resist the call of water ("The calm, / Cool face of the river / Asked me for a kiss"); the sick woman lying under "a sheet of pain . . . between two lovers— / Life and Death"; the aged Mexican woman who sits on the ground "day in, day round . . . selling her scanty wares"; the young bride dead; and the man who loved and lost his friend ("I loved my friend. / He went away from me. / There's nothing more to say").

To the poet and the reader, and to the lovers, sailors, gypsies, and other bits of unfulfilled humanity, the vast mysterious figure of "The Dream Keeper" stretches out his arms and calls:

Bring me all of your dreams,
You dreamers.
Bring me all of your
Heart melodies
That I may wrap them
In a blue cloud-cloth
Away from the too rough fingers
Of the world.

There is consolation in the dream, for when all else is lost, the dream is the one thing that can be saved, sacred, personal, and inviolate. And the poet is an articulator, protector, and transmitter of the dream. He too is The Dream Keeper.

Hughes's nature poems share the power of imagery of his other lyric verse. In "Poème D'Automne"[4] the trees are "dressed in scarlet gold / Like young courtesans / Waiting for their lovers," and their lovers, the winter winds, first strip and then attack their bare bodies with "sharp, sleet-stung / Caresses of the cold." The "March Moon,"[5] though more distant, fares no better: the winds strip away her cloud-garments and abandon her naked and shameless.

Hughes holds a carnival to wild nature in *Fields of Wonder*. This book in unique among his works in that it is almost all sweetness, with hardly a discordant note. Even the poems on Harlem are tender and wistful. Images flame and burst like stars upon the page. The book is a literary heaven, "the place where / Happiness is / Everywhere" and animals and birds and stones sing and salute each other.[6] Here, one might say, the poet is at peace with himself and the world. He is what Jean Toomer once called himself: Earth-Being.[7] Here are earth-songs of an earth-being, celebrating nature and all living creatures, the stars, sun and moon, and the changing seasons; the spring sprouting of plants and flowers, the rain and the rainbow; bird, snake, and snail; the global dew; the cycles of birth, life, death, and rebirth, the ineffable powers of night, sleep, love, and desire.

The influence of Emily Dickinson is very strong in such poems as "Heaven," "Snail," "Border Line," "Luck," "Walls," "Personal," "Gifts" ("To some people / Love is given. / To others— / Only heaven,"); and the influence of Imagism and haiku in "One," "Montmartre," "Fragments," "Motherland," "Big Sur" ("Great lonely hills. / Great mountains. / Mighty touchstones of song"). One is reminded of Pound's "In a Station of the Metro" by Hughes's characterization of "Gypsy Melodies" as

> Songs that break
> And scatter
> Out of the moon:
> Rockets of joy
> Dimmed too soon

All the same, these poems are not mere imitations but imaginative and fresh originals.

The most intriguingly mystical poem in the collection is "A House in Taos", in which a weary trinity, "you, she, and I . . . smitten by beauty," seek the wilderness, "waiting for nothingness." And they pray to the cosmic forces to sweep Through the red, white, yellow skins / Of our bodies," watering and mellowing their barren hearts and whipping their divided racial souls into "one snarl of souls," into human unity and divine oneness.

Brilliant and unusual imagery is also what makes Hughes's poems on so common a subject as death so engaging. His habit is through the use of metaphors to draw parallels between death and human activity, objectifying and defining death into its niche in the cycle of existence. He looks on death with a cold, detached poetic eye. His basic definition is the common one of death as change:

> Dear lovely Death
> That taketh all things under wing—
> Never to kill—
> Only to change
> Into some other thing. . . .
> Dear lovely Death,
> Change is thy other name.[8]

Death is "a drum / Beating for ever / Till the last worms come / To answer its call," till atoms, stars, time, and space have come and danced themselves to exhaustion and are no more.[9] Death's call is magnetic, powerful, and inescapable as the music: when the drum beats, willy-nilly, the body responds. Death is like an absent mother for whom the child longs and waits: "I'm waiting for ma mammy,— / She is Death."[10] It is "a nothingness / From where / No soul returns."[11] It is "a tower / To which the soul ascends / To spend a meditative hour— / That never ends."[12]

For the musicians and hedonists, death is the cessation of music and fun: life for them is

> The shivering of
> A great drum
> Beaten with swift sticks
> Then at the closing hour
> The lights go out
> And there is no music at all
> And death becomes
> An empty cabaret
> And eternity an unblown saxophone
> And yesterday
> A glass of gin
> Drunk long
> Ago.[13]

As for the grave, it is the "Cheapest boarding house; / Some of these days / We'll all board there."[14] It is "that sleeping place, / Long resting place, / No stretching place, / That never-get-up-no-more / Place."[15] And beyond death is eternity, where "I, / Who am nobody, / Will become Infinity, / Even perhaps / Divinity."[16]

In the same unintimidated spirit, Hughes's people die nonchalant, doing whatever they love to do best. Some ask to be accompanied by their favorite music. One requests the "St. Louis Blues" and "St. James Infirmary": "I want some fine music / Up there in the sky."[17] Another wants "a stormy song" to drown the rattle of his dying breath:

> Beat the drums of tragedy for me,
> And let the white violins whir thin and slow,
> But blow one blaring trumpet note of sun
> To go with me
>   to the darkness
>   where I go.[18]

The cabaret girl dying quietly on Welfare Island regrets just one thing— that she did not die as she lived, "drunk and rowdy and gay . . . / where the band's a-playin' / Noisy and loud."[19] Old seamen who have "weathered / A thousand storms, / Two wars, / And submarines / From here to there," set out on yet another voyage, not knowing and not caring whether this one is "To the Nevermore— / Perhaps— / Or just another / Trip."[20] And when they die, all they want is to be buried with their sea, to be one forever with their element.[21]

Aside from "Death in Harlem," Hughes's most exuberant death poem is "Sylvester's Dying Bed."[22] Great lover that he is, Sylvester is surrounded, in his hyperbolic imagination, by "All de womens in town / . . . Sweet gals . . . a-moanin' / . . . And a hundred pretty mamas" crying and begging him not to die; "Daddy! / Honey! Baby! . . . / You can't leave us here!" So he decides to love them all one more time. "I's still Sweet Papa 'Vester, / Yes, sir! Long as life do last!" But life doesn't last much longer; and as he reaches up to hug them, "de Lawd put out de light," and all is darkness, his dying simultaneous with the symbolic moment of consummated love. Hughes's people carry their love of life into death.

Hughes's lyric poetry is no doubt of secondary importance in his work; yet, as usually happens with the minor work of great artists, this minor (lyric) poetry is high enough in quality and great enough in quantity to have sustained the reputation of a lesser poet.

A brief word about Hughes's prose works which, though perhaps not of secondary importance in his overall *opus*, are nevertheless peripheral to the present study. His prose is of a piece with his poetry. His essays and speeches over the years reiterate and reinforce the esthetic first advanced in "The Negro Artist and the Racial Mountain." His first novel, *Not Without Laughter* (1930), contrasts the blues-filled life of itinerant minstrel man Jimboy, who in his wanderings neglects his wife and son, with the upward-bound austerity of his wife's sister Tempy, both against the background of family poverty. Jimboy's son, Sandy, seems destined for one or the other of these worlds; but his aunt Harriett's success on the concert circuit as a blues queen, and her assumption of moral and financial responsibility for him, rescues him from Tempy's joyless household and ensures that he would indeed acquire education and money— but "not without laughter." In Sandy's future Hughes envisions a life in which it would not be necessary to abandon the folk culture in order to progress; a life in which one could be comfortable and middle class and still affirm the black heritage.

True to its title, Hughes's first collection of short stories, *The Ways of White Folks* (1934), focusses on what to black folks are the strange, contradictory, and absurd customs and attitudes of white folks. As one character puts it, "the ways of white folks, I mean some white folks, is too much for me. I reckon they must be a few good ones, but most of 'em ain't good—leastwise they don't treat me good. And the Lawd knows, I ain't never done nothin' to 'em, nothin' a-tall."[23] Hughes is gently vicious (his usual manner); his wit is razor-sharp, and it cuts precisely and deeply. The areas probed include the white "cult of primitivism" during the Harlem Renaissance ("Rejuvenation Through Joy"); the ironies of white patronage of blacks ("Slave on the Block," "The Blues I'm Playing," "Poor Little Black Fellow"); lynching ("Home"); and the bitter complex of interracial love, miscegenation and passing ("A Good Job Gone," "Mother and Child," "Red-Headed Baby," "Passing," "Father and Son"). "Passing," which consists of a son's letter to his mother explaining why he had to pretend not to know her when they passed each other in the street, is an almost clinical dissection of the tragedy of the mulatto. Characteristically, Hughes is sympathetic without being sentimental, ironic without being frivolous. There is a cold, brutal adherence to the facts, with a concise intimation of the complex emotions of the parties involved. Hughes dramatizes the attitudes of those who could and did pass as effectively in these five brief pages as some full-length novels on the subject.

His second and third collections of short stories, *Laughing to Keep From Crying* (1952) and *Something in Common* (1963) (the latter consisting mostly of reprints from the former), take up some of the same themes. Black folks can be just as strange in their ways as white folks. White folks and black folks do indeed have something in common, and they need not travel all the way to Hong Kong to find out, as the characters of that title story did.

Hughes's best known prose is his Tales of Simple. Originating as a regular column in the *Chicago Defender* in 1943, Jesse B. Semple's conversations with Ananias Boyd finally grew to fill four volumes: *Simple Speaks His Mind* (1950), *Simple Takes a Wife* (1953), *Simple Stakes a Claim* (1957), and *Simple's Uncle Sam* (1965), plus a volume of selections, *The Best of Simple* (1961). These conversations, reported by Boyd, are witty, rich in folkways and folk humor. The language is sometimes uneven (possibly due to the tyranny of newspaper deadlines), wavering between formal English and black urban dialect. Simple's life is the stuff of the urban blues: he grew up poor in the South, made a bad marriage, left his wife, and migrated North. Now he is a Harlemite, living in a furnished room and carrying on the usual battles with difficult landladies, trying to save money to pay for his divorce, patronizing Paddy's bar and rapping with his buddies there, including Boyd. We are exposed to Simple's life and loves in cumulative detail, and to his views on a broad range of subjects, the same subjects which preoccupied Hughes during the same period. In fact, the Tales of Simple closely parallel Hughes's poetry of the 40s, 50s and 60s.

Simple's views are those of the average Harlemite, the simple folk; to a large extent they are also Hughes's views. Simple's interlocutor, Boyd, is not so much an antagonist as a foil, a wall against which ideas are bounced, a dialectical proposition. It takes two to make conversation, and if you don't want a chorus or a dirge, you need a dissenting voice, however mild. Boyd plays devil's advocate; he is, firstly, a listener and recorder, and secondly, a stand-in for all those who insist that every truth must have two sides. He articulates the conventional, often conservative opinion on all things; but he doesn't push it. It's Simple's scene, not his. His function is to disagree just long enough to drive Simple to his swift anecdotes and witty but pithy conclusions. With Boyd, Hughes is running a game and fooling no one (intending to fool no one)—no more than Plato fools us with Socrates' respondents. In both writers the respondent is a protodramatic device to provide the main character an audience and the reader a bit of human excitement. Simple/Socrates is the preordained winner of every argument; but the argument is presented, not as a dry socio-philosophical treatise, but as a human drama.

There is no real difference of opinion between Simple and Boyd. Simple speaks for Boyd about as often as he speaks for Hughes and the black masses, which is most of the time. Those who say that Boyd is Hughes's alter ego but Simple is not, miss the picture. Boyd is Hughes's alter ego, but so is Simple; Hughes's identity embraces both. For, though college educated, Boyd is, like Hughes, not a member of the "black bourgeoisie" in the classic sense (the "black bourgeoisie" do not hang out in "low-down" Harlem bars). Like Hughes, Boyd is the writer as social enquirer, as recorder and recaller of the lives of the folk (this is the only view of Boyd we are permitted to see, a functional and deliberately incomplete view); and Simple is a representative of the folk of whom this breed of writer is a part. The writer (Boyd) and the folk (Simple) are aspects of Hughes's own identity. They belong harmoniously together. And where there is no opposition, there is no choice to be made. They are one.

In another sense, Simple is a dreamer-idealist-Quixote, Boyd his realist-Sancho Panza. This would seem the primary sense in which these dialogues were influenced by Hughes's reading of Cervantes.[24] Simple and the Don are the ones who insist that the ideal and the real can and should be done. Their dream is so powerful, its logic so implacable that it attains the status of a force of nature. They themselves are larger than life, heroic, dwarfing the Boyds and Sancho Panzas—those loyal, sane, and quite necessary reminders of our human limitations and common mortality. But still, limited as men are, they dare not lose the vision of the Simple/Quixotes, or they will perish in the narrow prison of the quotidian. In myth and story, and in real life, it is the Simples and Quixotes, the stretchers of possibility, not the Boyds and Sancho Panzas, the literalists, who command our profoundest allegiance. *Simple's Uncle Sam*, the last of the series, closes with Boyd prostrate before Simple's overwhelming dream—Hughes's deferred dream that will not die—crying a deep Amen: "Dream on, dreamer. . . . dream on."

The tales of Simple are about as difficult to classify as Jean Toomer's *Cane*. They have been variously designated as short stories, sketches, novels, humor, epic, and the like. Perhaps a term like "editorial fiction" or "documentary fiction" captures more accurately their central character, namely, a fictionalized commentary both on Afro-American life and culture and on American public affairs from a black perspective.

Hughes's drama includes nine full-length plays, two one-act plays, four gospel musicals, a Christmas cantata, four opera librettos, and one screenplay. In addition, over forty of his poems and lyrics have been set to music and performed by well-known artists. His drama is a cut of the same rich fabric as his poetry and fiction. The themes are variations of the same abiding one, presented, again, with the aid of the vast resources of Afro-American musical, religious, and comic traditions. On occasion, Hughes tells the same story in two genres, as in *Mulatto* (drama, 1931) and "Father and Son" (short story, 1934); *Tambourines to Glory* (drama, 1949; novel, 1958); *Simple Takes a Wife* (documentary fiction, 1953) and *Simply Heavenly* (drama, 1956). But even these do not give us any immediate sense of redundancy; each is freshly adapted to its genre.

Notes

I

1. LeRoi Jones (Amiri Baraka), "State/Meant," *Home Social Essays* (New York, Apollo, 1966), p. 251.
2. "Afro-American Fragment," *Dear Lovely Death*, n.p.
3. See "Dream Variation" and "Our Land," *Weary Blues*, pp. 43, 99.
4. "The Negro Artist and the Racial Mountain."
5. "Afraid," "Poem: For the Portrait of an African Boy," *Weary Blues*, pp. 101, 102.
6. "Lament for Dark Peoples," ibid., p. 100
7. "The Jester," ibid., p. 53; "The Black Clown," *The Negro Mother* (New York, Golden Stair Press, 1931), pp. 8–11.
8. Paul Laurence Dunbar, "We Wear the Mask," *Complete Poems* (New York, Dodd, Mead, 1913), p. 71.
9. "Summer Night," *Weary Blues*, p. 103.
10. "Disillusion," ibid., p. 104.
11. "Dance Africaine," ibid., p. 105.
12. "Mother to Son," ibid., p. 107.
13. "The Negro Mother," *Negro Mother*, pp. 16–18.
14. "Final Call," *Panther*, p. 21.
15. "I, Too" ("Epilogue"), *Weary Blues*, p. 109.
16. Walt Whitman, "Song of Myself" [1855], *Leaves of Grass and Selected Prose* (New York, Holt, Rinehart, 1964), p. 23.
17. "The Negro Speaks of Rivers," *Weary Blues*, p. 51.
18. Zora Neale Hurston, "High John de Conquer," *Book of Negro Folklore*, p. 95. Italics hers.
19. "Madam to You," *One-Way Ticket*, pp. 3–27.
20. "Magnolia Flowers," *Fine Clothes*, p. 70.
21. "The South," *Weary Blues*, p. 54.
22. "Mulatto," *Fine Clothes*, p. 71.
23. "Flight," *Dear Lovely Death*, n.p.
24. "Blue Bayou," *Jim Crow*, p. 10.
25. "Southern Mammy Sings," *Shakespeare*, pp. 75–76.
26. "Ku Klux," ibid., pp. 81–82.
27. "Song For a Dark Girl," *Fine Clothes*, p. 75.

28. Claude McKay, "The Lynching," *Selected Poems* (New York, Bookman Associates, 1953), p. 37.
29. "Lynching Song," *A New Song* (New York, International Workers Order, 1938), p. 30.
30. "Silhouette" *One-Way Ticket*, p. 56. For a discussion of America's sexual mythology, see Calvin C. Hernton, *Sex and Racism in America* (New York, Doubleday, 1965). LeRoi Jones, "American Sexual Reference: Black Male," *Home*, pp. 216–33. Eldridge Cleaver, *Soul on Ice* (New York, McGraw-Hill, 1968), pp. 155–210. Nathan Huggins, *Harlem Renaissance*, ch. 6.
31. "The Bitter River," *Jim Crow*, pp. 11–13.
32. "Justice," *Scottsboro Limited*, n.p.
33. "Scottsboro," ibid.
34. "Christ in Alabama," ibid.
35. "Bible Belt," *Panther*, p. 38.
36. "My Adventures as a Social Poet." Also, *I Wonder As I Wander* [1956] (New York, Hill and Wang, 1968), p. 46.
37. "The Town of Scottsboro," *Scottsboro Limited*, n.p.
38. "Sharecroppers," *Shakespeare*, p. 77.
39. "West Texas," ibid. p. 79. Cf. Malcolm X contrasting house slaves and field slaves: "If someone came to the field Negro and said, 'Let's separate, let's run,' he didn't say, 'Where we going?' He'd say, 'Any place is better than here.'" "Message to the Grassroots" [1963], *Malcolm X Speaks* (New York, Grove Press, 1966), p. 11.
40. "One-Way Ticket," *One-Way Ticket*, pp. 61–62.
41. "Ku Klux," *Shakespeare*, pp. 81–82.
42. "Third Degree," *One-Way Ticket*, p. 130.
43. "Who But the Lord?," ibid., p. 73.
44. *Panther*, p. 17.
45. "Open Letter to the South," *New Song*, p. 27.
46. "Scottsboro Limited," *Scottsboro Limited*, n.p.
47. "Let America Be America Again," *New Song*, p. 9. Subsequent references to this volume will be cited in parentheses in the text.
48. "God to Hungry Child," *The Workers Monthly*, March 1925, p. 234, reprinted in *Good Morning Revolution*, p. 36.
49. "Johannesburg Mines," *The Crisis*, February 1928, p. 52, reprinted in *Good Morning Revolution*, p. 10.
50. "Advertisement for the Waldorf-Astoria," *New Masses*. December 1931, pp. 16–17. This and the poems and essays cited below are reprinted in *Good Morning Revolution*.
51. "The Black Man Speaks," *Jim Crow*, p. 5.

II

1. See chapter 1, n. 24 for my definition of social and lyric poetry.
2. Unless otherwise indicated, the poems immediately following are cited from these three sections of *The Weary Blues*.
3. Dunbar, *Complete Poems*, pp. 82, 178.
4. "Poème D'Automne," *Weary Blues*, p. 45.
5. "March Moon," ibid., p. 47.

6. "Heaven," *Fields of Wonder*, p. 3. The poems immediately following are cited from this volume unless otherwise indicated.
7. *Earth-Being: The Autobiography of Jean Toomer* (unpublished), excerpted in *The Black Scholar* 2, January 1971, pp. 2–13.
8. "Dear Lovely Death," *Dear Lovely Death*, n.p.
9. "Drum," ibid.
10. "Mammy," *Fine Clothes*, p. 76.
11. "Exits," *Fields of Wonder*, p. 65.
12. "Tower," *Dear Lovely Death*, n.p.
13. "Sport," *Fine Clothes*, p. 40.
14. "Boarding House," *One-Way Ticket*, p. 119.
15. "Grave Yard," *Fields of Wonder*, p. 21.
16. "There," ibid., p. 88.
17. "Request for Requiems," *One-Way Ticket*, p. 115.
18. "Fantasy in Purple," *Weary Blues*, p. 46.
19. "Cabaret Girl Dies on Welfare Island," *Shakespeare*, p. 66.
20. "Sailing Date," *Fields of Wonder*, p. 86.
21. "Death of an Old Seaman," *Weary Blues*, p. 81.
22. "Sylvester's Dying Bed," *Shakespeare*, p. 67.
23. "Berry," *The Ways of White Folks* (New York, Knopf, 1934), p. 175.
24. *I Wonder as I Wander*, p. 291.

◆◆◆◆◆◆◆◆◆◆◆◆◆◆

The Christ and the Killers

JAMES A. EMANUEL

Way Down South in Dixie
(Bruised body high in air)
I asked the white Lord Jesus
What was the use of prayer.
—"Song for a Dark Girl"

The world is curious about how religious attitudes, man's most distinctively human disposition, have operated in the formation and in the productivity of its creative people. American curiosity is heightened in the case of Negro authors because religion, through its shape-shifting perseverance under the eyes of slaveholders and their legion descendants South and North, has long held the strands of Negro togetherness. Perhaps the secret of the toughness of those strands, so frequently knotted today as to portend a social revolution, lies partly in the religious affections expressed by Negro writers. For the tie between religion and violence is ancient. America "stubbed its toe," to use a phrase from a poem by Hughes, on the rock that has divided the active Christian conscience from the act of enslaving and dehumanizing the millions for whom it assumed the responsibilities that accompany total arbitrary power. A trail of racial violence and bloodshed under specious Biblical sanction criss-crosses the path of every American and grits the memory of every Negro author, regardless of occasional appearances to the contrary.

The ruts of violence in the wash of a failing Christianity harshly surface some of Hughes's poetry and fiction. His uses of Jesus need to be seen in the perspective of Negro experience and the author's purposes. Extra light gleams over Hughes's fusion of Christ and black people when one sees how his early lapses might have worked with his lifelong attraction to gospel song rituals and fellowship-with-Christ fervor to evolve his concept of an earth-oriented Jesus. In *The Big Sea*, Hughes writes of his hot night, at the age of twelve, on the mourners' bench in Lawrence, Kansas. Some time after he and another boy had been left alone to await the light of Jesus, he heard the boy whisper, "God damn! I'm tired o' sitting here," and saw him rise to be saved. Alone then in a swirl of adjuring songs and prayers, and implored by the sobs of his beloved Auntie Reed, young Hughes finally let the minister lead him to the platform.

Reading Hughes's description of his ordeal later that night, one thinks of the boy Luigi Pirandello, his tears drowned in drums and songs as he marched in the lottery processional to his rich father's house. Like Hughes, the playwright felt his boyhood spiritual integrity thwarted by a sycophantic priest who defrauded him of the good conscience due from his generous attempt to transfer his winning lottery ticket to a poor boy of the church. Hughes records the aftermath of his discovery that prolongation of his "waiting serenely for Jesus" would tilt the ritual askew: "That night, for the last time in my life but one . . . I cried. . . . [my aunt] told my uncle I was crying because . . . I had seen Jesus. But I was really crying because I couldn't bear to tell her that I . . . hadn't seen Jesus, and that now I didn't believe there was a Jesus any more. . . ."

In 1960, Hughes's answer to a question put to him on the radio and television show "Viewpoint" relegated that sad night to its proper place in his development. The question was whether "religious faith of any kind" influenced his work. The author replied: "'Yes, I would think very much so. I grew up in a not very religious family, but I had a foster aunt who saw that I went to church and Sunday school . . . and I was very much moved, always, by the, shall I say, rhythms of the Negro church, . . . of the spirituals, . . . of those wonderful old-time sermons. . . . And when I began to write poetry, that influence came through. . . .'"[1]

I *Christ on the Road*

Religion in Hughes's poetry is predictably nonsectarian. His faintly satirical cast at the mourners' bench in "Mystery" is far from dogmatic. His stand on one issue, however, could not be more resolute: his opposition to the misuse of religion. In "Sunday Morning Prophecy" (*The New Yorker*, 1942), an old Negro minister, after loudly ending a sin-ripping sermon in a vivid burst of devil's exultation and backsliders' vain cries for deliverance, tersely closes with a "give freely/In the collection basket/That I who am thy shepherd/Might live./Amen!" The poem, typical in its lively actability, is almost insensibly altered by this infusion of straight-faced humor. Incipiently a poem on the misuse of religion by its unduly mercenary agents, the lines lose their faultfinding strength in the old pastor's sudden candor.

An example of a miscarriage of poetic point is Hughes's controversial "Goodbye Christ," a poem which, in the 1930's and 1940's especially, attracted gusts of misinterpretation and calumny. Such repercussions bore upon the refusal of the Los Angeles Civic League in August, 1935, to let Hughes speak in a local YMCA building, and upon the picketing and circularizing by Gerald L. K. Smith's America First Party in April, 1943, at Wayne State University when the Student Council invited the poet to speak there. Hughes's defense of the tough-guy poem as not anti-Christ[2] but as "an ironic protest against racketeering in the churches" and as "anti-misuse of religion" implies that the gist of the poem is in these lines about the New Testament:

> But it's dead now.
> The popes and the preachers've
> Made too much money from it.
> They've sold you [Christ] to too many
> Kings, generals, robbers, and killers—
> Even to the Tzar and the Cossacks. . . .

The fact that the poem also excoriates "big black Saint Becton/Of the Consecrated Dime," the Harlem preacher shown as a charlatan in *The Big Sea*, has not redeemed features disliked by detractors. Redemption was not needed in the eyes of other readers, such as the Reverend Charles C. Hill, Chairman of the Citizens Committee of Detroit, who answered a letter from Gerald L. K. Smith by saying that Hughes "was expressing the feeling of most Negroes toward white Christianity as displayed every day." Emphasizing that a distortion of Christianity was the poet's point of attack, he added: "I can join Langston Hughes with teeming others in saying 'Goodbye Christ'—the Christ as held up by the white supremacists. . . ."[3]

Turning from this poem, which is the kind of pebble that can always be hurled at some open space in an author's reputation, one might consider two poems related to Hughes's literary humanizing of Jesus. The first, "Judgment Day," in *Selected Poems*, pictures a simple Negro who envisions Jesus as a kind man who speaks as he himself does. It opens thus: "They put ma body in the ground,/Ma soul went flyin' o' the town,/ Went flyin' to the stars an' moon/A-shoutin', God, I's comin' soon." The uplifted believer meets a Jesus who comforts him with "don't be 'fraid/ Cause you ain't dead."

The more anthropomorphic picture of Jesus in "Ma Lord" (in *The Crisis*, 1927) derives from a quaintly dressed old lady whom the author saw in church when he was a boy in Lawrence. Hughes explained to the moderator of the program "Viewpoint" how her reprimand to the youngsters giggling at her hung in his mind and grew into the poem. The first stanza reads:

> Ma Lord ain't no stuck-up man.
> Ma Lord he ain't proud.
> When he goes a-walkin'
> He gives me his hand
> "You ma friend," he 'lowed.

Hughes went on to say that this poem implies "that when religion places itself at the service of mankind, particularly the humble people, it can

. . . strengthen them and guide them. . . ." He added: "There's great beauty in the mysticism of much religious writing, and great help there— but I also think that we live in a world . . . of solid earth and vegetables and a need for jobs . . . and housing. . . ."

Brief as this introduction to his approach to religion is, it gives some personal meaning to the hard task undertaken in "On the Road," the genesis of which story he told in July, 1961, as follows: "I wrote this in Reno, about wandering Negro roustabouts who ran into prejudice in Relief. This was pure fantasy, but also growing out of my actions in Reno . . . and seeing troubled people who were really hungry, and seeing how churches are not equipped to handle a depression." In *I Wonder*, Hughes tells that many penniless Negroes stopped in Reno while hoboing across the nation. They found a hobo jungle, but no Negro section in Reno, then "a very prejudiced town with no public places where Negroes could eat other than two cheap Chinese restaurants."

Written first as "Two on the Road" and revised in Carmel in the fall of 1934,[4] "On the Road" was published by *Esquire* in January, 1935. Significantly illustrated by a picture of two figures, one more vague than the other, at the far end of a snowy street bearing only one set of foot-prints, it tells the end-of-the-line adventure of a Negro hobo.

Jumping from a freight train during the depression, Sargeant is too hungry, tired, and sleepy to notice the snow falling on the town. Finding himself on the porch of a parsonage, he is vaguely aware that the minister is shutting the door in his face and directing him brusquely to another relief shelter like the hundreds that have already drawn the color line against him. Moving to the adjoining church, he knocks at the door topped by a stone crucifix and stone Christ. By the time he must break the door open, whites are yelling at him from the street; and two club-swinging policemen have begun to pull and beat him. When Sargeant clings to the church pillars, the crowd helps the officers pull on him; and the church falls into the snow. Rising from the debris, he shoulders the stone pillar, walks away with it, then laughingly throws it six blocks up the street.

In an episode thus removed from reality, Sargeant sees walking be-side him the stone Christ, glad to have been broken off the cross. In a friendly, colloquial conversation, Christ says he is bound for Kansas City and recommends the doorless hospitality of the hobo jungle before they separate. At six the next morning, Sargeant tries to jump a freight train's coal car with other hoboes, but finds it full of policemen. One raps his knuckles with a night stick and says, "You ain't out in no jungle now. This ain't no train. You in jail."

These words, a plainer transition between fantasy and reality than the long toss of the pillar, accompany Sargeant's realization that he is in jail for breaking down the church door, that he has been yelling and shaking the bars. Fingers bruised and head bloodied and throbbing, he yells, "I'm gonna break down this door!" Suddenly his thoughts come back to Christ, to end the story: "I wonder if he's gone to Kansas City?"

Hughes told the writer Kay Boyle about this story in 1957:

> All I had in mind was cold, hunger, a strange town at night . . . and a black vagabond named Sargeant against white snow, cold people, hard doors, trying to go somewhere, but too tired and hungry to make it—hemmed in on the ground by the same people who hemmed Christ in by rigid rituals surrounding a man-made cross. It developed as a kind of visual picture-story out of night, snow, man, church, police, cross, doors becoming bars, then ending with a man shaking the bars, but Christ at least free on the precarious road—His destination Kansas City, being a half-way point across the country. . . .[5]

This, and other remarks made at the same time—that the story was "written completely at one sitting, like a poem," and was more intriguing to him in word music than in narrative—helps one to imagine Hughes at work. In the Negro boardinghouse to which Reno restricted him, after eating his supper of Home Relief supplies described in *I Wonder*, he sat before his typewriter and absorbed his mood of a tired, hungry wanderer, a situation not alien to his experience. Gathering up oppressive, wintry images to give substance to the racial texture of Reno, he launched his creating self against the doors he knew were there, responsive all the while to the music of phrases that came to him.

Because sense is more important than sound, one should first examine what the story means. Sargeant's odyssey, prolonged by discrimination and now limited to a search for food and rest before he succumbs to exhaustion, ends at the stone feet of Christ. At this point the purposes of Sargeant and of mankind join to enlarge the meaning. Once again Hughes's remarks to Kay Boyle help:

> I was writing of the little man. . . . I was writing, too, of Jesus as a human being whose meaning sometimes has been lost through the organization of the church. . . . The function of religion in daily life, as the Reverend [Martin Luther] King has made it function, is what I was talking about. . . . Sargeant had done as much for Jesus in getting Him down off the cross as Jesus had done for Sargeant in showing him that even the Saviour of men had nowhere to go except to push on. . . .

Before the violence on the steps of the church, involving symbolically all of society, Sargeant's purpose—survival—is blindly personal. Unlike blind Samson of the Bible, who invokes the aid of the Lord to pull down the two pillars for his own vengeance, Sargeant clings to church pillars to preserve himself before the people—the hostile law and the chain of Philistines—who never draw his thoughts away from himself.

Only after the church has crumbled and his fellow feeling has been aroused by another lone traveler does the hobo think of serving another. The comforting words exchanged by Christ and the vagabond suggests a triangular religion, connecting one's self, one's fellows, and the Lord.

Christ serves the hobo by his example of what might be called "Purity of Predicament," represented here by the ostracism with which society places its mark of infidelity on the brow of those too far removed, by excess either of lowliness or of sublimity, from its dead center. The hobo serves Christ by the destructive though liberating act of flesh mortified by travail. Then, though only in a dream born of pain, he offers the man-made Christ a man's pleasantries, a simple generosity.

This religious positivism agrees with the expressed views of the author. Surely the little man, the first excluded by the selfish rites that immobilize a living Christ, would most benefit from a religion of simple acts of human care. A Christ on the road, crossing half the nation on a single journey, although as humble in spirit and as deprived as a Negro vagabond, could light candles that could never be put out. Sargeant, in freeing Christ though incarcerating himself, unconsciously contributes to the idea of daily brotherhood, of a man-oriented religion.

Although a racial prejudice made more noxious by the depression is broadly reflected in this story, the religious strain is paramount. Systematized religion has failed. Christ is one of the dispossessed, impaled on a cross outside the church. He cannot free himself, yet must come down to the little man, down into the snow to become the companion of a lowly man who cannot enter the church that has petrified the Saviour. Thus the Negro identification with Christ develops. The new comradeship evokes a provocatively new religious image: a Christ who laughs aloud.

The complex style of "On the Road," told in the third person, can only be suggested in this discussion. In this "visual picture-story," a third of the passages characterizing the hobo show his appearance: he is all night, snow, cold, dampness; almost another third depict him bludgeoning or wrestling his way against door-like obstacles. All the images of the story comprise a remarkable pattern of sensations that support the action. The technique, which is like the heaping of sensory words in Hawthorne's "The Minister's Black Veil," can be glimpsed in this partial breakdown of the two hundred and ten patterned images in the six-page story, conveyed in fifty-four repeated words, listed by frequency of use: "door" (28); "snow" (21); "stone" (12); "black" (9); "pull" (8); "cold" (7); "white" (6); "sleepy" (6); "grab" (6); "fall" (6); "wet" (5); "hungry" (5); "tired" (5); "shut" (5); "push" (5); "cross" (5); "break" (5); "wham" (4); "cell" (4); and "jail" (4). Thus running the scale of images—visual, auditory, tactile, kinesthetic—Hughes mounts a total environment that is repellant, binding, crushing, wintry. Sargeant's world is closing doors, wet snow, cold stone.

Snow as illusion, the sidewalk and church steps as levels of Christianity, and the church edifice as dogma are symbols ably used. The author fuses dream and reality with artistic grace in the hobo's half-conscious montage of cell bars and the iron ladder of a coal car. On the other hand, the author's voice obtrudes unnecessarily at one point, and Christ's language is not perfectly consistent. In this story, included in Bernard Smith's *The Democratic Spirit* (1941) and Lillian Gilkes's *Short Story Craft* (1949), Hughes is master of his material, is poetically alive to every sensory nuance. His identification with Sargeant is complete.

Just as "Ma Lord" and Hughes's comments provide background for "On the Road," other poems and events illuminate "Big Meeting"—the other "Christ story" at the end of *Laughing to Keep from Crying*. "Ballad of Mary's Son" (*The Langston Hughes Reader* [1958]), applying the term "Mary's Boy" to a Negro lynched during Passover, and calling Christ "Mary's Son," merges the persons and deaths so that "This is my body/And this is my blood!" defines a spiritual bond between the crucified Christ and the lynched Negro.

"Christ in Alabama" concerns autobiographical events of a kind never far below the surface of Hughes's mind, events that influence stories like "Big Meeting," "Home" and "Father and Son." The poem caused excitement and threats of violence the night Hughes read it on November 21, 1931, at the University of North Carolina. On a poetry-reading tour of the South financed partly by a grant from the Rosenwald Fund, Hughes had been breathing the air of violence roused by the Scottsboro case in Alabama. And ten days or so earlier, he had felt the tragedy of two deaths caused by the peculiar inhumanity of the South. At Hampton Institute in Virginia, the poet had been approached by Dorothy Maynor, then "a chubby teen-age student choir singer," according to *I Wonder*. The students had selected her to tell him that a Hampton alumnus and new football coach had been beaten to death by an Alabama mob for accidentally parking his car in a "white" parking lot; and that Fisk University's Dean of Women, Juliette Derricotte, whom he had known in Paris and New York, had died the same weekend after an auto wreck in rural Georgia, upon being refused treatment in a nearby "white" hospital.

"Christ in Alabama," written about the Scottsboro Nine, was published with Hughes's satirical article, "Southern Gentlemen, White Prostitutes, Mill-Owners, and Negroes," on the front page of *Contempo*, an unofficial student newspaper at Chapel Hill, the day Hughes arrived. This ironic poem, he states in *I Wonder*, was inspired by the thought of "how Christ, with no human father, would be accepted were He born in the South of a Negro mother." It ends: "Most Holy Bastard/Of the bleeding mouth:/Nigger Christ/On the cross of the South!" Considering the original title of Hughes's rather sentimental "African Morning" ("Bastard of Gold") and his long, serious interest in the problems of mixed blood, the word "bastard" is as purely genetic as it can be.

And the phrase "Nigger Christ" penetrates beyond devotion to a sympathetic identification molded racially by sharing unmerited suffering and revilement. The literary father of this unfortunate Christ defended his paternity on December 18, 1931, in *The Atlanta World*, a month after its discovery in the South: ". . . anything which makes people think of existing evil conditions is worthwhile. Sometimes in order to attract attention somebody must embody these ideas in sensational forms. I meant my poem to be a protest against the domination of all stronger peoples over weaker ones." This poem induced shock, outrage, and serious thought. Varying proportions of each incited local groups to urge that Hughes be run out of town, hardened the university's resolve to withstand coercion, and enabled the author to shatter the peace further by dining with white students at a white restaurant and, in the words of local Negroes, to "come out, like Daniel, unscathed."

Hughes attitude toward the climactic events of "Big Meeting" can hardly be understood unless the reader can feel the grain of these events of the author's tour. The source of the narrative itself, he said in September, 1960, was "camp meetings and things I saw as a child." A letter of his specifies one, "held in Pinckney Woods in Lawrence—all Negroes inside the tent, lots of whites gathered outside in cars and otherwise to listen to the music."[6]

"Big Meeting," probably written in October, 1934, in Carmel or Reno,[7] and first published by *Scribner's Magazine* (July, 1935), details a revival in a lantern-lighted tent in the woods. The story is narrated by an unnamed Negro teen-ager who, with his friend Bud, stands under a tree smoking and laughing—somewhat like the whites in autos and buggies, including Mr. Parkes, a drugstore owner who refuses Negroes entry to his store. As the three-part service gets under way with testimonials and songs on this twelfth night of the Big Meeting, whites either variously repeat that they love "to hear darkies singing" or mock Negroes testifying to their troubles. The two teen-agers, amused and embarrassed, watch their own mothers' fervid part in the rocking, clapping, foot-patting, hopping, and handshaking.

The second part of the service begins suddenly as Reverend Duke Braswell strides forward; tall, black, strong, he sings with a voice "roaring like a cyclone." He vividly recounts the death of Christ. Then, with a histrionic style, moaning, gasping, and perspiring with gestic intensity, he grips the congregation with pictures of the crowd at the heels of the cross-bearing Christ, the transfer of the burden to black Simon of Cyrene, and the crucifixion itself. The narrator and Bud are entranced; the congregation moans and weeps. Striding back and forth across the platform, the minister evokes the cursing, spitting, stoning, and name-calling by the mob. "Then," he concludes, stretching his arms high, "they lynched Him on the cross." The narrator hears his mother sing "Were you there when they crucified my Lord?" and sees the nearby whites drive away suddenly and noisily in a cloud of dust. With unexpected tears, at the end, he yells after them: "They're about to call for sinners to come to the mourners' bench. Don't go!"

The boys' ability in this story to humanize their attitude as the suffering underlying the rituals becomes manifest makes the group posture of the whites all the more slack. The boys have exchanged early submission to religious ceremonies for cigarette puffs and street corner jokes, but they retain appreciative memories. The white adults, however, have firmly diked their sympathies inside the color line.

A variety of oblique remarks and phrases contour Southern race relations. During the congregational response to the prayer "guide those in other cities," mothers cry "Help him, Jesus!" as St. Louis, Memphis, and Chicago are named. They remember their faraway children who have fled their homes for a chance at happiness in less racist cities. Part of the pattern is the longing for rest, found only in Jesus, the helplessness amidst injustice and violence; four times the minister emphasizes that Christ's friends could not help him. Racial brutality is expressed as the sweating minister, imitating the sound of crucifying nails, shouts "Bam!" four times, whereupon a woman screams, "Don't drive them nails! For Christ's sake! Oh! Don't drive 'em!" This agony, obviously personal to these Southern Negroes, accentuates the literal and allied meanings of the deep wail of sorrow that has just accompanied the imagined raising of the Saviour to the cross.

The author controls spatially and strategically his theme of Negro identification with Christ. Worked slowly into the first part of the meeting by the unrehearsed expressions of worshipers, it continues unemphasized in the sermon that is divided into three parts that increase in length, importance, and intensity. Reverend Braswell first talks about the power of the lowly, represented by Christ, then about the ability of a man to stand alone, like Jesus, who knew that "all alone by Hisself He would go to His death" and therefore told His weakening friends to "sleep on." The listeners chant "sleep on, sleep on," feeling that each man, for heroic strength, needs only Christ.

Hughes, mindful of the minister's ability, does not voice the main theme when the second part of the sermon turns to images of violence. The minister recalls that Jesus "saw that garden alive with men carryin' lanterns and swords and staves, and the mob was everywhere." Once the word "mob" is used, the author need not even suggest that this congregation has been alerted to special images. The preacher supplies them in abundance, literally filling the tent with key words: "handcuffs," "prisoner," "mob," "chains," "trial," "lies." The reader sees the rituals of violence that these worshippers know too well: the people cry "crucify Him!" because they do not care; soldiers make sport of Jesus, strip Him naked and mock Him laughingly, calling Him "out o' His name." The minister reminds them that "nobody said, 'Stop! That's Jesus!'"—and the congregation adds its own analogy, that the good white Southerner does not face the mob to halt racial brutality in the name of Christianity.

Hughes now lets the minister close the gap between Christ and the Negroes. The preacher's pauses, before the third part, to recapitulate the roles of Peter, Judas, Pilate, and Christ's friends add suspense to his simulated climb, as he bears the heavy cross to Golgotha. "Then a black man named Simon," he continues, "blacker than me [a recurrent phrase in Hughes], come and took the cross"; and he pictures the taunting crowd. The dark minister, making Negro participation on the side of Christ visible by his own stance, and then making it biblical by reference to Simon of Cyrenaica, completes the identification begun before his arrival.

The picture of the crucified Jesus is finished:

> Mob cussin' and hootin' my Jesus! Umn!
> The spit of the mob in His face! Umn!
>
> .   .   .   .
>
> They stoned Him first, they stoned Him!
> Called Him everything but a child of God.
> Then they lynched Him on the cross.

Just as "mob" began the Negro verification of Christ's ordeal, the word "lynched" seals the listeners' absorption into the spirit of Christ, given symbolic sanction when the minister stretches his arms upward in the yellow light, his body making "a cross-like shadow on the canvas."

Picturesque scenes direct from life also give sensory zest to this story. The fancies of dreams come down from the testimonial platform, replete with moon-like haloes, silver wings, hoofs of gold. Songs rise humming from ever-moving bodies, swelling as the congregation steeps itself in real sorrows. Sometimes the songs are pulled spontaneously from individual bosoms struck resonantly by a phrase from the platform. Sometimes melody flows from the mass and rolls through the hot tent.

The minister is a man to stare at, "his green-black coat jim-swinging to his knees." Almost like the Reverend Becton scored in "Goodbye Christ," this minister slams the Bible shut and strides to the very edge of the platform before uttering a sermonizing word; but, unlike his wealthy Harlem prototype, he does not plan around the collection plate. His style of chants, half-moans, gasps, and indrawn "umn!" between rapid phrases still lingers, even in some metropolitan pulpits.

Thematically rich within its set limits, "Big Meeting" offers less that is purely literary than does "On the Road." Its view of Negro spirituals and old-time preaching is instructive. The narrative is realistic; the action complete and historically meaningful. The characters are not full, but they function adequately. The story primarily develops, not individuals, but the profound connection between a single holy martyrdom and a race-wide, centuries-old debasement.

II *The Killers*

In other poems and stories, the viciousness of racial violence, sometimes fatal, is not transformed by religious emphasis but by style. "Southern Mammy Sings" (*Poetry*, May, 1941) begins humorously ("Miss Gardner's in her garden./Miss Yardman's in her yard."), modulates the harshness of its meaning through the use of dialect, then ends:

> Last week they lynched a colored boy.
> They hung him to a tree.
> That colored boy ain't said a thing
> But we all should be free.
>   Yes, ma'am!
> We all should be free.
>
> Not meanin' to be sassy
> And not meanin' to be smart—
> But sometimes I think that white folks
> Just ain't got no heart.
>   No, m'am!
> Just ain't got no heart.

These words are a subtle play upon Southern custom and history. The Negro "mammy," mother to Negro youth and motherly nurse to whites who will likely grow up to abuse them, sings (a lovely sign of her contentment) about her travail. Her superficial apology for being so "sassy" as to pass judgment upon the murderous bent of whites accentuates the heroic silence of the boy who died like the victim in Vernon Loggins' story "Neber Said a Mumblin' Word."

It may be surprising that only about a score of the hundreds of poems written by Hughes strongly develop this theme of violence. Yet several of these are memorable. His "Roland Hayes Beaten," imbued with the slow fire of modern Negro spirit, supplied the motto and refrain for the pamphlet printed by the National Association for the Advancement of Colored People (February, 1962), *The Day They Changed Their Minds*, to commemorate the sit-in demonstrations that have brought historic upheaval to the South. The poem is brief:

> Negroes,
> Sweet and docile,
> Meek, humble, and kind:
> Beware the day
> They change their minds!

Wind
In the cotton fields,
Gentle breeze:
Beware the hour
It uproots trees!

The Negro Handbook for 1944 reads: "July 11 [1942]—Roland Hayes, internationally famous tenor, was beaten by three white policemen in Rome, Ga., where he lived with his family, following a brief argument that his wife had with a shoe store clerk." In the poem, Hughes elevates the gentle artist's ordeal into a tense warning. The repetition of *beware*, the contrast between *day* and *hour*, the analogy of the wind that brings both static sweetness and rushing holocaust—all are restrained prophecy. The physically precarious balance in the single-word lines carries much of the meaning. The poet's steadying irony insured artistic quality.

1. *"Home"*

Emotionally close to this poem is "Home," the first story written after Hughes's return from Yokohama. Composed in San Francisco in September, 1933, it appeared the following May in *Esquire* as "The Folks at Home," illustrated in color.[8] The narrative develops, said the author, various stories told by Negro performers back from Europe. He added, in July, 1961: "Louis Jones was studying and playing in Europe when I was over there. He achieved some concert note. I had in mind someone like him who might have come from a town in the Deep South. Roy is a real person in a sense."

The story opens with Hughes's narration of the return home to Hopkinsville, Missouri, of aiing Roy Williams, a violinist who has toured the world for several years. Weakened by a tubercular cough, he has made a sentimental journey home to die. Following a two-page flashback relating his pained closeness to poverty abroad, in Section II Roy moves through the racial insults of white loafers at the station. Section III contains a lyrical burst celebrating a Missouri summer, then pursues the contrast with Section II through a one-page flow of loving welcome, praise, and news from Roy's mother. An equally brief Section IV describes the colorful, perfumed filling up of the church where Roy is to give a home-coming concert. Section V opens with three pages of sustained lyricism in which Roy, standing fevered on the rostrum, muses nostalgically over his mother's sacrifices for his musical career. As it ends, he is praised by a cheaply dressed white woman, Miss Reese, who, his mother tells him, is "an old maid musicianer at the white high school."

In the final and longest section, the wasting artist plays for Miss Reese's sprawling students, who later tell their parents that "a dressed-up nigger had come to the school with a violin and played a lot of funny pieces," that the teacher had "grinned all over herself" and even bowed. One night Roy, hollow-cheeked and trembling, walks the street in spats and yellow gloves. Imagining Tauber singing, he does not hear the villagers cursing him; but he recognizes Miss Reese when she bows and speaks. He removes his hat and gloves and extends his hand. She screams when a fist strikes Roy's head, thus activating the hatred in a crowd emerging from a movie. Imaginations leap to the image of rape; they trample and pummel Roy and spit in his face. The screaming whites kick and drag him through town to the woods.

The final paragraph was unforgettable to book reviewers: "The little Negro . . . began to choke on the blood in his mouth. And the roar of their voices and the scuff of their feet were split by the moonlight into a thousand notes like a Beethoven sonata. And when the white folks left his brown body, stark naked, strung from a tree . . . it hung there all night, like a violin for the wind to play."

All violence can be misleading. It means little in itself, just as a striking fist means little in isolation from the mind directing it and the circumstances so narrowly stimulating that mind. Even the title "Home" gives texture to the brutality that is rather foreign to the basically sentimental main action. The reader must temporarily turn away from the savagery in order that other themes may fill the contours made for them. Roy, traveling in slowly disintegrating Europe, embodies the role of art in life. A sympathetic, humane man, he is the touchstone of sane good taste and decency by which one knows that Europe is in decay. He carried beauty, in the form of his music and his sensibilities, into the heart of adamant unconcern for the poor and helpless. He is grieved that young beauty must be debased by prostitution. Playing in happy cabarets, he images the destitute children slumped in doorways he must pass. Roy is man's wish for beauty and charity, crushed when European jackboots are fitted, or when home-town hatred is loosed.

Art, creating beauty, can thrive only when conditions approximate those of home—not the grossness Roy finds abroad where eaters of caviar take no thought of searchers for crumbs, but the care in his mother's greeting: "Son, I'm glad you's done come home. What can Ma cook for you?" Her several references to foods are more than realistic detail. Carefully contrasted with Europe's hunger and immorality, they are part of the home-like love that fosters art and beauty. Totally ignorant of classical music, Roy's mother can only vaguely express the bond between beauty and goodness: "Honey, when you plays that violin o' your'n it makes me right weak, it's so purty. . . . God's done give you a gift!"

The artist, finding the world "rotten," attempts the impossible: a return to the same home he left. Not only his cough is killing him; it is the *Zeitgeist* abroad, a spiritual decay inimical to his nature and to his beauty. His physical wasting at home is medically explainable, but it also accords with the malignant spirit he finds there: the native counterpart of Europe's hunger. What he yearns for, escape from decadence, not from death itself, is the fresh substance of the author's lyrical exuberance before Roy meets his mother: "Sing a song of Dixie, cotton bursting in the sun, shade of chinaberry trees, persimmons after frost has fallen. Hounds treeing possums October nights. O, sweet potatoes, hot, with butter in their yellow hearts."

The melding of life and art—seen in "The Blues I'm Playing," written the same month—occurs naturally in the fragmented thoughts of sick Roy, playing Massenet in the church (ellipses are Hughes's):

> This is the broken heart of a dream come true not true. This is music, and me, sitting on the doorstep of the world needing you. . . . O, body of life and love with black hands and brown limbs and white breasts and a golden face with lips like a violin bowed for singing. . . . Steady, Roy! It's hot. . . . This, the dream and the dreamer, wandering in the desert from Hopkinsville to Vienna in love with a streetwalker named Music. . . . Listen, you bitch, I want you to be beautiful as the moon in the night on the edge of the Missouri hills. I'll make you beautiful. . . .

This passage invites study never necessary for scenes of violence like those that end the story. Roy's diction itself, combining the colloquial with the formal in its description of art, merges two forms of experience, just as "wandering in the desert" links Missouri with Vienna, stretching the body of art in a synthesis of man's achievements. The "dream come true not true" joins the deeds of a musician who lived to be seventy, Massenet, with the abortive dreams of a violinist who died young and who needed art to help him briefly survive a poisonous environment. The subsequent impassioned salute to an art that gratefully employs rather than abuses racial differences is the heart of the passage. The final lines, showing the earthiness of Roy's love for his music, also reveal the ego that drives an artist to transcend the vulgar body of life in his reach for its spirit.

The motif of Southern racial habits almost coarsens the texture of the story, if one begins with esthetic considerations. The action, however, is grounded in those customs. Hughes merely alludes to some, like economic and educational discrimination; but he pointedly shows white resentment of good attire for Negroes. His most significant reflections of this kind are somewhat subtle. At the church concert, for example, Roy, instead of taking professional pleasure in Miss Reese's attention, wonders suspiciously, "What do you want from me?" Undergoing the perversions of racial prejudice, he distrusts the woman because of her color—in contrast to his gratitude to a Parisian girl who helped him regain his strength. Later, trampled and bleeding, he wonders why Miss Reese spoke to him on the street. The savagery of her townsmen had become the identifying mark of her race; she is no longer a music lover but just another treacherous white woman. The likelihood that Roy has been spat upon by a childhood playmate completes the wretched turnabout.

Commentary on racial violence as a psychological oddity—and on the author as a social observer—is implicit in the final scenes. The sincerity of Miss Reese is a bitter irony: her scream, caused by genuine fright, fatally ignites the ritual of group homicide. Hughes, by selecting young "ruffians" to be the killers, exempts the ordinarily humane citizens from material blame and suggests that the emotionalism and delusion that arouse brutality are typical only of the immature minority. The extent and nature of the blame deserved by other citizens, although morally impotent, are not made relevant to the action.

Hughes makes sure use of his repetitions. Carrying contrasts and interacting ironies, they usually hold to an axis between Missouri and Europe, between ugliness and beauty: the station loafers versus Roy's mother, Roy's sensitivity versus the barbarity of his attackers. Reflecting a similar pattern, Roy's mother believes her son honored by a request to play at the white school; she is unaware that a Carnegie Hall or a Salle Gaveau would be much more fitting.

The figurative language is usually vivid "the glittering curtains of Roy's jazz were lined with death." Some images are sharply effective: girls in church are "powdered bonbon faces . . . with red mouths pointed at Roy." Other techniques are questionable: the uninterrupted length of some dialogue, the usefulness in the plot of Roy's brothers and sister, the faltering point of view in Roy's soliloquy.

Realistic fiction exposing American racism has often been repressed, and "Home" provides an example. Speaking at the National Assembly of Authors and Dramatists Symposium on "The Writer's Position in America," at New York's Alvin Theatre on May 7, 1957, Hughes stated, without mentioning the name of the story, "Home": "I once sent one of my best known short stories . . . to one of our oldest and foremost American magazines. The story was about racial violence in the South. It came back to me with a very brief little note saying the editor did not believe his readers wished to read about such things."[9] The editors of *Atlantic Monthly* wrote his agent on January 8, 1934: "Why is it that authors think it is their function to lay the flesh bare and rub salt in the wound? ["Home"] is both powerful and delicate, but we cannot forget that most people read for pleasure and certainly there is no pleasure to be found here."[10]

"Home" does have a power whose delicacy throws it into vivid relief. Sometimes the style has the softness of Roy's yellow gloves or of his autumn reminiscences of Parisian evenings; sometimes it has the hardness of a swift blow to the head. Both music and discord are combined to reveal two civilizations. The passages of violence are extreme in meaning

rather than in style, the extremity of unwelcome truth rather than of
ungrounded exaggeration. A piece of art, this story discloses Hughes's
ability to transform revolting fact into tough beauty.

2. *"Father and Son": The Poems and the Story*

Racial brutality as a theme for an American writer explains itself,
especially when the writer is a Negro. Mention has been made of violence
that came early, both directly and vicariously, into Hughes's life, including instances in Mexico, Chicago, Virginia, and Alabama. One of his
earliest poems showing deep response to racial violence, "The South,"
first published in *The Crisis* (June, 1922) begins:

> The lazy, laughing South
> With blood on its mouth.
> The sunny-faced South,
> > Beast-strong,
> > Idiot-brained.
> The child-minded South
> Scratching in the dead fire's ashes
> For a Negro's bones.

The poet continues by picturing the South as "Seductive as a dark-eyed
whore," cruel, "Honey-lipped, syphilitic." The most extensive meaning
is captured in two lines: "And I, who am black, would love her/But she
spits in my face." This poem, written when Hughes was barely out of
his teens, ably employs the effects natural to the unpredictable mov-
ments half-anticipated in an adult idiot happened upon after the climax of
some brutal deed. The quoted lines further reflect some somber dementia
oddly mixed with confused self-pity. The stresses of juvenile, irrational
passion that supply energy to the unmoving images are played against
such unrevealing words as *sunny-faced* and *magnolia-scented*. The lines
are vigorous, economically sharp (except for lines 9–11, unquoted), and
they mix some biblical rhythm with short verses that seem to halt and
tersely revise complimentary phrases. The South, seen by a Negro
trapped in its dangers and desires, is painted with tense, brusque strokes
in Hughes's earliest period.

"Song for a Dark Girl" (*The Crisis*, May, 1927) employs a specific
instance of violence. The first two stanzas read:

> Way Down South in Dixie
> > (Break the heart of me)
> They hung my black young lover
> To a cross roads tree.

Way Down South in Dixie
(Bruised body high in air)
I asked the white Lord Jesus
What was the use of prayer.

The violence in this poem is subordinated to grief. The violence is an assumption, a strong one, based on the steady history of lynchings (averaging fifty a year in the early 1920's), the place of the killing, and the condition of the corpse. The conventionally pleasant South, ironically pictured in the nostalgic refrain borrowed from a thumping Dixieland tune, is juxtaposed with the heartbreak of a tortured girl. The severely simple technique, using only six different words longer than one syllable, matches the drained hopelessness. The separation of consciousness and bereaved flesh, made more anguished by the poet's "the heart of me" rather than "my heart," is of a piece with the girl's shriveled religious faith: she knows that Christianity is often the racial instrument of whites. This well-written poem, ending with a sterile concentration of feeling ("Love is a naked shadow/On a gnarled and naked tree"), shows Hughes's early ability to individualize images and events highly symbolic to Negroes without lessening social meaning.

Similar emphases are found in lesser poems like "Blue Bayou," "Silhouette," "Flight," and "Lynching Song," all concerned with lynchings. Racially motivated police brutality, North and South, is the subject of "Third Degree," "Who But the Lord?," and "The Ballad of Margie Polite." Connected also with racial customs, but only obliquely related to violence, are "Cross" and "Mulatto," inseparable from the final story to be treated in this chapter, "Father and Son."

These two poems and the story are representative of a substantial theme in Hughes's works: the problems of Negroes of mixed parentage.[11] In the chapter "Poetry" in *The Big Sea*, Hughes writes that his interest in such problems began in Lawrence, where he played with a blond boy "whose mother was colored and whose father, the old folks whispered, was white," a boy who later passed for white himself.

In *I Wonder* (in "Making Poetry Pay"), Hughes calls the poem "Cross" (*The Crisis*, December, 1925) his "ace in the hole" at poetry readings. His description of his reading technique—which reveals his custom of dispensing facts of Negro history from the lecture platform—has interest:

The first line—intended to awaken all sleepers—I would read in a loud voice:

My old man's a white old man. . . .

And this would usually arouse any who dozed. Then I would pause before continuing in a more subdued tone:

My old mother's black.

Then in a low, sad, thoughtful tragic vein:

> But if ever I cursed my white old man
> I take my curses back.

Hughes's poem then revokes possible maternal curses, and it ends:

> My old man died in a fine big house,
> My ma died in a shack.
> I wonder where I'm gonna die,
> Being neither white nor black.

The poem's description closes thus: "Here I would let my voice trail off into a lonely silence. Then I would stand quite still for a long time, because I knew I had the complete attention of my listeners again."

This poem written in 1925 and the author's testimony regarding its sure-fire effectiveness on the rostrum mark an important fact about Hughes's contemporary audience. Although "Cross" is a mediocre poem to the analytical-critical reader, it apparently serves many listeners as a complete, affecting experience because the protagonist's moral character is only vaguely, even ambiguously, related to his situation. The logic of the concluding two lines is poor, just as the protagonist's cursing of his "black old mother" weakens sympathy for him. Yet Hughes, in his unfailing platform delivery, has proved the emotional power in the lines. It is likely that "Cross," after its first two lines, loses its identity as a poem and becomes a dynamic creation in the imagination of an American audience caught up in its resentments and fears. The very unresolved nature of the topic of miscegenation in America, irrational as it is, makes the end of the poem emotionally acceptable. The allusions to slavery and modern economic discrimination (the big house versus the shack), the expression of Negro pride (the cursing of the white man), and subtle indications of white dereliction—all leaving the moral initiative in the hands of a Negro—place the poem in the spiritual mainstream of modern Negro thought.

The other poem, "Mulatto," related to Hughes's 1935 drama, is generally not emphasized by Hughes in the sequence of works leading to "Father and Son" and The Barrier. Yet "Mulatto" is more strictly faithful to the spirit of the story and the opera than "Cross" is. In the passage in The Big Sea preceding Hughes's recollection of the mulatto child in Lawrence, he writes of the former poem:

In New York in the summer of 1926, I wrote . . . "Mulatto" wich was published in the Saturday Review of Literature. I worked harder on that poem than on any other. . . . Almost every night that summer I would . . . change it. When I read it one night at a gathering at James Weldon Johnson's, Clarence Darrow said it was more moving than any other poem of mine he had read.

"Mulatto" opens as follows:

> *I am your son, white man!*
>
> Georgia dusk
> And the turpentine woods.
> One of the pillars of the temple fell.
>
> *You are my son!*
> *Like hell!*
>
> The moon over the turpentine woods.
> The Southern night
> Full of stars,
> Great big yellow stars.
>   What's a body but a toy?
>   Juicy bodies
>   Of nigger wenches
>   Blue black
>   Against black fences.
>   O, you little bastard boy,
>   What's a body but a toy?

This dramatic dialogue offers a tensely individualized conflict between father and son that is hardened by the vigor and scorn of the words and broadened by carefully placed, suggestive details from nature. The son's adamant voice opens the poem, but is transformed into a passive Negro feminine presence exuberantly recalled by the white father, who feels half-pleasurably nagged in his fancied return to the conception and infancy of his son. The poet, employing the past awakened in the white man, leaves him musing and moves the growing child swiftly through years of hostile rejection by his white half-brothers—implying virtual estrangement from his father, whom he no longer reminds of sexual freedom in the Negro quarter. *"Niggers ain't my brother"* is the rebuff so ungrammatically worded as to show the displacement of reason and truth by blind social restrictions. In the last third of the poem, the father's reminiscences of woods, stars, and exploitable black women are slightly rephrased, indistinctly merging the author's voice with the father's. At the end, *"I am your son, white man!"* is repeated as a challenging accusation, weaker now, yet taking precedence over the phrases enclosing it, the author-father's echoes of earlier sensuous memories. Oddly, this is the father's poem. The delicious memories, the unweakened sense of arbitrary power to take and to withhold, the expansive portents of nature, even though ironically misconstrued—all are his. The son is the catalyst, but the father glows. The author expands his profoundly racial material and so convincingly explores a white father's subconscious that the poet's own hovering irony becomes inseparable from the ambivalent remembrances of his subject.[12]

"Father and Son," thematically germinal, then, in other works, can hardly be traced to a time and place. Written in November, 1933, in Carmel,[13] the story closed *The Ways of White Folks*. The author remarked in September, 1960, that it came "from many common miscegenation stories. This was a build-up," he added, "of stories I have heard all my life." Almost twice as long as "Poor Little Black Fellow" but nearest it in length, "Father and Son" opens in the spring of 1931 at Colonel Thomas Norwood's Big House Plantation in Georgia. The Colonel, in his sixties, awaits with feigned casualness the homecoming of twenty-year-old Bert, his youngest son by his Negro mistress, Coralee Lewis, who has kept his house for thirty years and borne his five children. He recalls that Bert is like him: handsome, bright, bad, and now scholastic leader and football captain at the colored institute. Section I ends as the Colonel, surrounded by Negroes, speaks to Bert; but, sensing a "stiffness like steel nearing steel," the father ignores his son's extended hand.

Sections II and III are a flashback in Cora's memory. She recalls how the Colonel teased her as a boy, how his later affections were sealed one night by an oak tree in a conquest reminscent of "Mulatto," and how he moved her into the Big House after delicate Mrs. Norwood died. Section IV, containing two additional, smoothly introduced flashbacks, begins with one about Bert's ride home in a Ford with his oldest brother Willie, who calls his boldness "crazy." Bert's recollections reveal background: Cora's children had to live apart from her in a shack, but she influenced the Colonel to give them extra education. Young Sally is intelligent but bound to Georgia, and Bertha has clung to Chicago after one trip there. Bert also wants to live in the North, but knows his mother wants him to spend this last summer with her.

Section V lyrically salutes the transforming power of Bert's imported creed ("Let old knotty-headed Willie go on being a white-folk's nigger if he wants to, I won't!"), then returns to the handshaking scene. Sections VI and VII raise the tension by Bert's refusal to do field labor, by a nearly fatal beating the foreman Talbot gives a Negro, and by news of the Scottsboro trials. Bert inflames Junction whites on the final day of the story by demanding equal consideration in stores and by fighting off three men who assault him in the post office after he objects to receiving insufficient change.

In Section VIII, the furious Colonel commands Bert to "talk like a nigger should to a white man," excoriates him racially while holding a pistol, and orders him out of the county. Bert, with "the steel of the gun . . . between them," finally strangles his father. Told by his grief-stricken mother to run for the swamp, he takes the gun and leaves by the front door, that has always been forbidden him. The rest of Section VIII consists primarily of four scenes of harsh interrogation and violence on the part of whites, interspersed with four scenes of temporary derangement on the part of Cora. She urgently handles and addresses the body of the Colonel, berating the corpse alternately for not rising to help Bert and for joining the mob's pursuit of him. Amidst screams and bullets, Bert returns shooting and goes upstairs, one bullet left. Cora delays the mob until the shot is fired upstairs.

Section IX, the concluding page, opens the next morning, revealing "a bloody and unrecognizable body hanging in the public square at the Junction." Some onlookers, knowing Bert was taken dead, are unappeased. The story ends with this headlined article from an evening paper: "A large mob late this afternoon wrecked [sic] vengeance on the second of two Negro field hands, the murderers of Colonel Thomas Norwood. . . . Bert Lewis was lynched last night, and his brother, Willie Lewis, today. The sheriff of the county is unable to identify any members of the mob. . . . The dead man left no heirs."

This third-person story, stemming partly from Hughes's "poetic tragedy," forbidden to Philadelphians and almost banned in Chicago, has violent scenes that, again, might obscure the artistry. Certainly Hughes wants to show that racial violence is a way of life in the Deep South, perpetrated by low-class whites but openly sanctioned or actively tolerated by upper classes. Colonel Norwood was a member of a recent lynch mob. The story often mentioned the brutal beating he gave his son for calling him "papa" in front of whites. Cora's response to that ("I ain't bearin' him children for to beat 'em to death") defines an undercurrent of her emotional life. It joins her foreboding many years later as she brings Bert to his father for the fatal talk: "Son, you be careful. I didn't bear you for no white man to kill." The new term "white man" shows her long-borne realization of the barrier between father and son, between father and mother—one capable of swiftly destroying filial and domestic bonds.

Cora, not the author this time, blames the lower classes for most of the violence. To her, Bert is "runnin' from po' white trash what ain't worth de little finger o' nobody's got [Norwood] blood in 'em." The ritual of psychopathic attack signalled by a woman's scream, carried out in the post office, is ended by the lynching of servile Willie. Hughes, asked in July, 1961, whether he had any moral in mind when adding the lynching, replied: "Just to show how bad they could be; they go from bad to worse once they get on that savage rampage. Also to show there's no being a 'good nigger' in the South. They'll kill them too, if they feel like it."

Two passages near the end of the story picture the unequal forces at work in a racist environment. Bert, headed upstairs with his single bullet, looks back at "this little brown woman standing there waiting for the mob," which breaks inside but stops before her before running on.

Cora stands "looking down at them silently," unmoving. The diminutiveness and courage of Cora, the rush and cessation of movement, the pitting of mass against individual, and the superior physical placement of Cora (like that of Sargeant on the church steps) all have sure meaning in the context of racial deployment of forces in the South. The official lies and omissions in the newspaper further align on the Negro side the moral power which alone prevails over deep abuse.

Two other themes largely concern the actions of whites: interracial amours and Negro education. The liaison between the Colonel and Cora, the story goes, "like that of so many between Negro women and white men in the South, began without love." (Hughes's program note for *The Barrier*, mailed to the American Theatre Society in 1950, calls that related opera "a tragedy of love.")[14] Instead of exploiting this love—as Broadway producer Martin Jones was to do in 1935—Hughes strongly infuses Cora's romantic memories with references to overriding economic motives for Negro participation in such love affairs. Aunt Tobie Lewis, finding her daughter Cora pregnant, advises: "It's better'n slavin' in the cotton fields. I's known colored women what's worn silk dresses and lived like queens on plantations right here in Georgy." As for white management of Negro education, the author is directly critical. Bert's college, he qualifies, is "what they call a college in Negro terms in Georgia," and county educational policy is "to let Negroes remain unlettered" so that they will make better laborers.

Other motifs concern activities and attitudes of Negroes. Colonel Norwood orders an unsuccessful Baptist revival: "a useful outlet for sullen overworked darkies." Old Sam, a house servant, fearing rightly that he might end his days in a bonfire, cries out, "Lawd, is I sinned?"—and gives the lawless white mob the office of religious retribution. Besides these glances at religion, one sees intraracial color bias in light-skinned Bert's unopposed, sometimes scandalous, merrymaking in Atlanta society. Allusions to Negro emphases in the concept of death as rest recall the motif of weariness in "One Christmas Eve" and "Big Meeting."

The strongest theme hardly concerns race. Although race heightens the clash between father and son, the crucial issues (a son's feeling about his home and about his father's recognition of his whole being) could be just as formidable if color were replaced by another complication. The conflict is reflected in Hughes's techniques of characterization. The following breakdown [see page 194] reveals expanded meaning behind the two portraits. The numbers represent round percentages of the totals of characterizing phrases or passages (fifty-nine for Bert, and forty-nine for his father) devoted to various means of portraiture:

The remarkably close correlation between the frequencies of use of attitude to compare father and son shows the equal soundness with which Hughes conceives the two characters in terms of the general trait that

	Bert			Colonel Norwood	
Attitude:		44	Attitude:		43
Action:		17	Action:		20
Appearance:		14	Appearance:		2
Environment:		12	Environment:		10
Emotional reaction:		7	Emotional reaction:		16
Effect on others:		5	Effect on others:		6
Words:		2	Words:		2

most naturally and thoroughly searched out their mutual tragedy. The sharp differences in the use of appearance and emotional reaction confirm the importance to Bert of his looks, which bewildered him as a boy and emboldened him as a young man. The more than double attention given the Colonel's emotions, coupled with their nature, shows his disturbances to be not only personal and true to his temper, but broadly societal and expressing the resentment of the white townspeople.

The portrait of the Colonel appears more complete than that of Bert because his title raises an abundance of long-used details and because Hughes adds such humanizing touches. Within the rigid limitations of his society, which finally inflate his most intemperate and animal qualities, he is generous, faithful, and strong. He is enough of a father to feel pride and pain because of his son. He is enough of a husband to feel "something very like love," says the author, for the woman who has "supervised his life" and borne his children. His anguish derives from his race and religion, as does his ultimate callousness.

Bert is new to the experience and imagination of many readers: he is a hotheaded, proud Southerner—who happens to be colored. He comes to life through the rather narrow compass of his resentment, boldness, and pride—all concentrated in his attitude toward his father. For Bert is more son than Negro. Some readers who empathize with him as a frustrated son may not believe in him as a flesh-and-blood Negro, for want of more racially identifying marks. The author supports Bert's reality through the boy's weaknesses, not through the pedestrian use of clichés.

Bert is central in the symbolic approach to the story. The dust clouds in which he arrives and later careens in the Ford past his cane-waving father portend the catastrophic nature of his presence and his creed, "not to be a *white folks' nigger.*" Whatever the phrase itself does not achieve, the author supplies at once with winged lyricism: "Bow down and pray in fear and trembling, go way back in the dark afraid; or work harder . . . or stumble and learn; or raise up your fist and strike—but once the idea comes . . . you'll never be the same again. Oh, test tube of life! Crucible of the South, find the right powder and . . . the cotton will blaze and the cabins will burn and the chains will be broken and men, all of a sudden, will shake hands, black men and white men, like steel meeting steel!" Bert is symbolic of the author's hope: of his vision of some cataclysmic, healing change in the nation's body and spirit.

Other symbols and images are effective. Negro voices and laughter and the front porch are symbols employed to add tension, suspense, and historical meaning. Images perform an unusual function, moving from the ripple of brown backs in green cotton, through beguiling tableaux of Cora playing in the dust as a child, to the sunset as a "river of blood" and the lights of honking autos beaming through the woods. This painful change in imagery, Hughes suggests, as it shifts from nostalgia and innocent charm to animal brutality, is made imperative by the anomaly of Southern attitudes. Linking the beauty and ugliness of life, mainly limiting the former to the few years of youth, the contrast is faithful both to the essential condition of man and to modern racial variations of it.

Other techniques deserve analysis, among them the juxtaposition of the cruel and the tender—not consciously planned, the author said when asked about it in July, 1961. But the most skillful and subtle effect of all is produced when Hughes envelops and infuses Cora's "mad scenes" (which are mixed with and terminated by mob scenes—a total of eleven pages) with remarkable images of flight. Thirty-five are running footfalls, and three of the remaining four are vivid sense impressions.

These images of flight are ably patterned. Ten are concentrated in the two pages preceding the longest mad scene. Half are urgent terms (like "Run, chile!") that set in motion Bert's flight through the trees. The other half are images of running white men, a hurtling auto getting into high gear, the blood-like rush of sunset streaming after Bert. Ten of the next group of fourteen show Bert running; four, the Colonel. In the next group of seven, Sam and the cook Livonia join the flight, and the sound of "feet running, running, running" spreads through the woods. The last seven skillfully halt the running. The fugitive's feet seem still in motion when, back at the house, he tells his mother he has been fleeing seemingly "for hours." In a slowdown of motion after the mob breaks in, the running images reverse; and a leader of the unsteady mob almost induces stillness by saying, "Keep still, men. He's armed." Then comes the perfectly timed device that cuts off resurgent movement: the shot upstairs. Artfully, Cora's stepping aside intensifies the cessation. Thus Hughes gives almost a fourth of his story—the clusters of images having sustained their effect throughout intervening passages—a background of tension and excited motion, properly collapsed before the degradation of the final morning.

Although Hughes makes errors (the "hissing" of some nonsibilant words and the assignment of the same name, Jim, to the storekeeper and one undertaker), the story is admirably written. It is replete with individual and racial meaning, for the author as well as for the reader. It has no songs, no glee, no real romance. That befits the tragic story of a son who cannot be a son, of a father whose mortal debt to his own race is payable in that son's pride and blood. Father and son, white and black, in this story become forces that, in Hughes's own metaphor, are steel approaching steel. The author provides the collision; and the reader, left with the enormity of patricide and the bestiality of useless killing, must conclude why this grim reckoning had to be.

These poems and stories reveal the author's comprehension of Negro folk culture, his awareness of historical and individual forces at work in Southern life, and his implicit vision of a decisive moral encounter that will bring brotherhood to America. In his poems on racial exploitation and brutality, he reveals abomination as well as sensitivity to human weakness and valor. In his poems on religion, he shows the road not taken by the Negro folk in the wake of faltering Christianity (for "Good-bye Christ" and "Christ in Alabama" can be so understood); and he preserves authentic cameos of old-style Negro believers, bound to common people the world over by the simplicity and durability of their faith. From his related short stories, which powerfully condense and transform the central anguish of a whole race, one might say, remembering Yeats's contemplation of seemingly needless death, that "a terrible beauty is born."

Notes

1. Script of interview on Dec. 10, quoted with permission of Division of Radio and Television, Protestant Episcopal Church, New York.
2. *Vancouver Sun*, Dec. 3, 1958.
3. *Michigan Chronicle*, May 8, 1943.
4. 1934 list; autographed and variously inscribed drafts mailed from Visalia, Calif., by Mrs. Josephine DeWitt Rhodehamel, Jan. 1961.
5. Two-page script, "Revised Version of Remarks by Langston Hughes Concerning Analysis of 'On the Road,'" dated June 16, 1957, received by Emanuel from Hughes in 1961 with note on reading at Kay Boyle's house.
6. Letter to Emanuel, July 5, 1961.
7. 1934 list shows ms. mailed from Reno, Oct. 29, at a time when dates of composition and mailing were habitually close.
8. 1934 list; *Esquire* tear sheets in Schomburg Collection.
9. *The Langston Hughes Reader* (New York, 1958), p. 483.
10. Letter to Maxim Lieber.
11. See Arthur P. Davis, "The Tragic Mulatto Theme in Six Works of Langston Hughes," *Phylon* XVI (June 1955), 195–204.
12. Ibid., pp. 197–99, has a different interpretation.
13. 1934 list.
14. JWJMC has a copy of the note, signed by Hughes.

◆◆◆◆◆◆◆◆◆◆◆◆◆◆

"I've wrestled with them all my life": Langston Hughes's *Tambourines to Glory*

LESLIE CATHERINE SANDERS

Secular to the bone, as biographer Arnold Rampersad characterized him, Langston Hughes was notoriously reticent on matters of religion: "In an envelope marked: / *Personal* / God addressed me a letter. / In an envelope marked: / *Personal* / I have given my answer," he wrote enigmatically in 1935, in response to renewed attack over his infamous 1932 poem "Good-bye Christ." As a rule, Hughes stayed away from religious topics and themes, although he loved and respected the distinctive manifestations of black religious practice, and occasionally did draw on its forms and imagery. An early and notable poetic example is the "Glory! Halleluiah!" sequence in *Fine Clothes to the Jew* (1927), his second volume of poetry. Hughes's most extended use of religious material occurs in his plays, where his impulse to record the drama of black music and black religion found appropriate form.

Religious material first appears in Hughes's work for the theatre in *Don't You Want to Be Free?*, a "music-drama" written in 1937 expressly for his Harlem Suitcase Theater. In this chronicle of the black experience, Hughes uses spirituals to voice the sufferings of the slaves; for later sequences, he uses his own poetry. Religious sentiments, in this play, are positioned historically; the play moves its audience toward a secularly defined and self-reliant revolt, rather than a divinely inspired strength to endure.

Hughes's next dramatic exploration of religious material extends, and even corrects, this earlier effort. Arnold Rampersad suggests that Hughes's residence at the home of the devout Noel Sullivan encouraged "stirrings of religion in him," but Hughes may as well have been inspired by his tentative dramatic exploration, in the earlier work, of religious music as an articulation of black striving. Also written for a theatre he founded, the Skyloft Players, *The Sun Do Move* (1942) is the story of a slave named Rock, and his efforts to bring his family to freedom. In the original sermon from which the play takes its name, the preacher, John Jasper of Virginia, pitted his faith in God and the Biblical word, particularly Joshua 10:13, against science and "new discoveries" about the stationary Sun and revolving Earth. In Hughes's play, only Rock's faith and

197

imagination make his escape to freedom possible because, empirically, freedom does not exist. The reality of enslavement has robbed his fellow slaves of the ability to seek freedom, even to know in what direction it might lie.[1] *The Sun Do Move*, which begins in Africa and ends as Rock goes off to war with the Union army, exploits both the religious and secular meanings of the spirituals, for whether they are sung as an individual's or a group's response to events, or simply as a bridge between scenes, they continually draw upon both their levels of meaning—as songs of faith and as maps of the route to freedom. *The Sun Do Move* is, in part, a play about the meaning of the spirituals, and so not only a "music-play," as Hughes called it, but also a drama about the music itself.

There were few precedents for Hughes's foray into music plays about black music. Notably, his precursor was Hall Johnson's *Run Little Chillun'*, first produced on Broadway in 1933, which Johnson described to Doris Abramson as "what's behind the spirituals." But Johnson's play, a clear response to *The Green Pastures*, for which Hall Johnson's Choir provided the music, focused on the African roots of black Christianity in its portrait of the conflict between the Hope Baptist Church and the pantheistic New Day Pilgrims, not on the music itself.[2]

In bringing the black church, and black religious music, to the stage, Hughes was, in his characteristic fashion, not ony breaking new ground but also challenging white conventional depictions of black folk life. For example, presented frivolously in *The Prayer Meeting* and seriously in *Your Fiery Furnace*, both by the white playwright Paul Green, black religion and church service assume the shape of set responses, displays of characteristic behavior rather than serious explorations of the meaning of black belief. Just as Hall Johnson's *Run Little Chillun'* constituted a rebuke to *The Green Pastures*, Hughes undertook first to explore and then to reappropriate the dramatic presentation of black religion and its music.

Hughes's gospel plays, notably *Black Nativity*, but also its spinoffs, *The Prodigal Son* and *Gospel Glory*, comprise his most impressive success in this enterprise. Each play dramatizes a black church service during which exhorter and choir celebrate Biblical teachings, expressed in sermon and song. Hughes delighted in these plays, as well as in *Jericho-Jim Crow*, his "Song-Play" for the Civil Rights Movement, which also relied on gospel music to provide commentary and context for the narrative. Self-named "king of gospeleers in the American Theatre," Hughes gladly capitalized on the immense popularity of gospel music. But the gospel play that most engaged him was a more complex affair. Begun on July 14, 1956, *Tambourines to Glory: A Play with Spirituals, Jubilees, and Gospel Songs* was "an urban-folk-Harlem-*genre*-melodrama," and Hughes was elated by it. Finished in just ten days, *Tambourines to Glory*, for Hughes, achieved immediate dramatic life. He wrote Arna Bontemps:

If you're in a play reading mood, I'll send you a carbon of my new one just finished, Tambourines to Glory. It's short, mostly gospel songs, with a minimum of melodramatic script. If Mahalia Jackson won't go into the theatre, I'd like to have Juanita Hall and Sister Tharpe for the two leads, and pretty little Rari Gris (who was in *The Barrier*) for the daughter, Dots Johnson for the handsome villain, and the rest is up to the Tambourine Chorus and a little old lady drummer who turns the tables for the Lord, that could be played by Alberta Hunter. It's a singing, shouting, wailing drama of the old conflict between blatant Evil and quiet Good, with the Devil driving a Cadillac.

"What kind of car have you got?" (Present company excepted.)

A few days later, he continued:

The play slays me! It's got a nice slaying in it, too, to the tune of a gospel chorus above the robing room (Robe-ing Room), where evil is at work. I'm seeing Oscar Hamerstein Thursday and shall tell him about it. Maybe he could persuade Mahalia Jackson to play at the good woman, and Sister Tharpe the bad one. There would be shouting in the aisles at every performance. (Hughes to Arna Bontemps, 26 July 1956 and 31 July 1956)

Sadly, Hughes's high hopes for the play were never to be realized. It would take seven years to reach Broadway, where it would close after only a short run. A major difficulty for *Tambourines to Glory* was its venue, as one contemporary reviewer noted. Martin Gottfried called *Tambourines to Glory* a

warm, exuberant, modern Negro folk musical . . . deeply rooted in the ethnic patterns of the Harlem Negro. And in that may lie the drawback of this musical for many non-Negroes. The attitudes, humor and personal flavor of a particular group hold an enormous amount of warmth and affection for its members . . . [but] often become uninteresting and foolish to outsiders.

Predicting that black audiences would appreciate it more, Gottfried judged *Tambourines* a "very lively, very musical and very funny show." But he was virtually alone. Black and white audiences and critics alike were displeased by it, and commented on what seems to have been an altogether shoddy production. The Westport tryouts in 1960 also raised controversy. That production, directed by Herbert Machiz, had been variously praised and panned, but the Theatre Guild had backed off taking it to Broadway because, according to Rampersad, some judged it in appalling taste on "religious, moral, and political grounds."

Understanding Hughes's great attachment to *Tambourines to Glory* is critical to understanding an aspect of his artistic intent. Loften Mitchell's comments to Arnold Rampersad begin to provide insight into the play's difficulties:

The attack on the black storefront churches was not only justifiable, it badly needed to be made. But I'm not sure that whites were interested in such a matter, so the theater patrons stayed away. But there wasn't anything superficial about the play. Religion meant a lot to Langston. He and Richard Wright had been victims of the same kind of religious fundamentalism in their childhood, so they had expectations about religion that religion could not deliver, and they hated dishonesty in the church. In so many of Langston's productions, I don't know if the audience knew half the time what they were looking at. *Tambourines to Glory* was like that.

George Bass, secretary to Hughes during the time *Tambourines to Glory* was in production, blames its failure on director Nikos Psacharopoulos, who, he feels, did not understand the play at all.[3] Clearly *Tambourines to Glory*'s depths were not plumbed in either production.

The genesis of *Tambourines to Glory* lies in Hughes's urban comedies of the 1930s, *Little Ham* and *Joy to My Soul*, as much as it does in personal history or in his exploration of the dramatic possibilities of black religion. In those earlier plays, written for the black Gilpin Players of Karamu Theatre in Cleveland, Hughes recorded the fabric of Northern urban life, in both plays embedding a comic love story in settings through which he parades an assortment of the little people of the black ghetto. Both plays are also about surviving: In *Little Ham*, everyone tries by playing the numbers, and some labor as well—as numbers runners, as hairdressers, as entertainers, as shoeshiners. In *Joy to My Soul*, shysters vie with those who labor: The hero, whose father owns oil wells, is just plain lucky; his romantic interest sells cigarettes in the hotel lobby, where doormen, elevator operators, and desk clerks watch an assortment of frauds and petty crooks attempt to con the hero—and each other.

Both plays aim at entertaining black audiences with representations of themselves, and by making light of misfortune. Neither digs as deeply as a blues: Individual troubles, in these plays, are temporary and resolved by good fortune or kindness. Yet underlying both plays is an insistent irony: They are, after all, set in the Depression, which compounded the already hopeless economic condition of the black masses. Animating these plays is Hughes's unabashed delight in depicting what he called, in a program note about *Little Ham*, the "comic contrasts and humorous moves" of the black belts of Northern cities. As do his poems and Simple columns, the plays particularly express his often noted love of the black masses, who were the true subject of and preferred audience for his art (Program for *Little Ham*).

Hughes began *Tambourines to Glory* while the script for *Simply Heavenly*, his play based on Simple, was making the rounds. Transformed into a musical only at the request of sponsor Arnold Perl, *Simply Heavenly* had been written as "Simple Takes a Wife," a translation onto stage of the book of the same name. Thus, although fourteen years, and many other theatrical projects, had intervened, the last play Hughes had expressly conceived and written for the theatre was *The Sun Do Move*, a "music-play" about black religious music.

Rampersad notes that as early as 1947 Hughes had devoted an entire column to the arrival of a highly paid gospel singer in black entertainment, and in 1953 had made gospel singers the topic of a Simple column. Speaking of the churches that were moving into movie theatres, Simple comments: "But old-time store-front churches are going out of style. From now on, it looks like you will have to call them *movie-front* churches—except that the box office has turned into a collection plate, and the choir is swinging gospel songs. Money is being made, just one collection after another. . . . I am not opposed," he adds, "not when they put on a good show." As long as he is moved, Simple is untroubled by singers who "invest most of [their money] in automobiles," feeling that "good singers deserve their just rewards, both in this world and in the other one."

Simple is not, of course, simply being ironic. C. Eric Lincoln writes of the preacher:

> Perhaps the peculiar genius of the black preacher derives from the fact that he has never been far from the people. He rose up among them as someone they knew and trusted—someone God raised up in their midst. He did not have to come from far off. . . . When he made good as a preacher, the community shared in his accomplishment[,] and when they rewarded him for his faithfulness, it was a vicarious expression of the satisfaction the people felt with their own attainments. He was more than leader and pastor, he was the projection of the people themselves, coping with adversity, symbolizing their success, denouncing their oppressors in clever metaphor and scriptural selection, and moving them on toward the day of Jubilee which would be their liberation.

It is, in part, this generosity in dispensing the spirit, if not generosity of spirit, that Simple acknowledges; similarly, in the novel version of *Tambourines to Glory*, Laura responds to comments about the quality of her mink coat: "Since prostitutes dress good, and call girls and madams, there's no reason why saints shouldn't." "Saints should look the best," Sister Mattie replies.[4] Of course, Laura is the sinful Reed sister, but that is not the only import of the comment. In the economy of the ghetto, few women have access to wealth: The sex trade, particularly if controlled by women, has always represented opportunity of a kind. The church, the female preacher, has always been another.

Tambourines to Glory explores black religion and certain of its institutions, and celebrates the music through which faith is expressed. A small note, however, suggests the complex nature of Hughes's investment in the play: "We'll call ourselves sisters," says Laura, "—use my name—the Reed Sisters—even if we ain't no relation—sisters in God." The name is an allusion, for Reed is also the surname of the couple with whom Hughes lived as a child after the death of his grandmother, and whom he loved dearly.

In his autobiography *The Big Sea*, in a chapter titled "Salvation," Hughes recounts the first of only two episodes in his life that brought him to tears. Seated on the mourners' bench at a church revival, the twelve-year-old Hughes kept waiting to "see Jesus." When no vision emerged, and only he remained on the bench, he decided "that maybe to save further trouble . . . he['d] better lie . . . and say that Jesus had come, and get up and be saved." Later that night he wept bitterly, "because I couldn't bear to tell [my aunt] that I had lied, that I had deceived everybody in the church, that I hadn't seen Jesus, and that now I didn't believe there was a Jesus any more, since he didn't come to help me."

According to this account, Hughes trusts implicitly that Jesus will make himself visible and does not doubt the ecstatic expression of those around him. When no vision occurs, it is Jesus who has failed him. Rampersad argues that the love Hughes invested in the Reeds became later the love he invested in the race, making his lifelong project to please and appease the black masses.

Tambourines to Glory is the play Hughes wrote for Aunt Reed, who had protected and nourished him through much of his childhood, and for the black congregation into which Mary Reed had brought him "as a shining star". It recognizes, too, Uncle Reed, who, Hughes remarks in *The Big Sea*, "was a sinner and never went to church as long as he lived, nor cared anything about it. . . . both of them were very good and kind— the one who went to church and the one who didn't. And no doubt from them I learned to like both Christians and sinners equally well."

In *Tambourines to Glory*, the real sinners are those who pervert the church, not those simply outside it. Religion constitutes a valid response to human belonging; the church can exploit those who bring their burdens to the Lord. In *Tambourines to Glory*, Essie and Laura, saint and sinner, begin their church in order to pay the rent. Essie, the good woman, soon finds her own salvation in her ministry; Laura, the sinner, delights in the wealth the ministry brings and links up with the well-connected, no-good Buddy, who suggests such lucrative scams as selling tap water as being from the River Jordan and giving out numbers in church. The entertainment side of the gospel music phenomenon emerges under Buddy's auspices. Through Buddy the church moves from storefront to theatre; he arranges radio broadcasts and helps an attractive choir member to a record contract and the choir to a TV special. In the final stage version, Buddy *is* the Devil, who even pretends to be saved to increase the church's credibility.

The Laura and Buddy story is also a ballad and a blues, the tale of a woman done wrong by her man, exploited and abandoned for a younger woman. In revenge, she murders him. Her secular response to the pain of life is, in a sense, beyond good and evil; Laura's sin, for which she later repents and is saved, is not the murder of Buddy, who is, after all, the Devil, and who had just threatened to kill her, but rather her lie, her attempt to pin the deed on Essie.

The lie, of course, has a complex resonance. Essie also repents, "Me, I let our church become a devil's playground. Religion's got no business being made into a gyp game. That part of God that is in anybody is not to be played with—and everybody's got a part of God in them" (250), Exploiting faith, misusing the word of God, pretending to salvation—these are the real sins in *Tambourines to Glory.*

The church is a powerful force and presence in black society, and the church of *Tambourines to Glory* is a recognizable "black *cult*" with a "black ethos":

> Black cults which sprang up in the first third of this century tied their religious excitement to improving the basic concerns of blacks for food and shelter. Even more important was the drive that stemmed from the black cults for unity and self-sufficiency and pride and advancement, a general concern with secular advancement. . . . black leaders of cults came with the answer to secular advance in religious garb—[which] may mark them as sagacious and their adherents as gullible. It may also be that leaders coming forth in the name of the black *cult* and followers responding to the vibrations of the black *cult* are witnesses to the common tie that binds, the power of the black cult.

When the church moves from street corner to storefront, Laura orders a Garden of Eden mural with a white Devil, an Adam like Joe Louis, and an Eve like Sarah Vaughan. When Essie proposes Sunday School cards with black angels, Laura exclaims, "I second everything black." Essie's plans for the church include playgrounds as well as day care and employment centers; Laura plans only personal gain, but, as she points out, "everything people are talking about around here was my idea!" and if Marty is "the devil—and Buddy his shadow in the form of a snake[,] well, I'm not afraid of devils myself. I've wrestled with them all my life" (208). Her boast is, eventually, prophetic.

In the novel *Tambourines to Glory,* Laura is betrayed by Birdie Lee, who witnessed the killing; the play ends with her in jail and Essie in control of the church. At the play's conclusion, Laura returns on bail, having confessed of her own accord, turned state's evidence, and thus reduced her charge to manslaughter. In both play and novel, it is the church that triumphs, not simply as a symbol of faith, but also as an institution for community. In the novel, Essie rejoices: "Oh, friends, so many nice things we're gonna do for this Harlem of ours with His help!"

Washington writes further about black cults:

> It is this fundamental power of a people that black sects and black cults can contribute out of their long experience to the vitality, imaginative reinterpretations, and confident unity of the black community. With it, black secularists can engage in giving shape and direction. Without it, black secularists are powerless, for black people are impotent without their power station, the black *cult.* . . . Only a black folk religion which issues power to the people and leads them to act as a people can be faithful to itself, its heritage, its people, and its purpose. Black folk religion is not an intellectual analysis, it is the

calling forth of the meaning of the black experience. The black *cult* in the black experience is power, an imperative for union and action: a whole people, seeking through their whole way of life, their natural destiny.[5]

It is this vision of the black church that Hughes assumed; it is this manifestation of the church that he criticized as well as celebrated in *Tambourines to Glory*. Perhaps that is the reason that he so resisted people who were embarrassed by the play, who wanted him to write into it more "contemporary" attitudes, who saw it as, if not the new *Porgy and Bess* the Theatre Guild had hoped it would be, or an updated *The Green Pastures*, a playing to stereotype and ignoring of the critical issues of the day.

"An entertaining slice of dramatic Negro life in Harlem that makes for great theatre. No messages, no lectures, just theatre and good fun," Hughes said of *Tambourines to Glory* in an interview ("Fulfillment"). Perhaps. Perhaps not.

Notes

1. For an elaboration of the relation between play and sermon, see my book *The Development of Black Theater in America* (109).
2. See chapter nine of E. Quita Craig's *Black Drama of the Federal Theatre Era* for an excellent extended discussion of the play's central philosophic conflict.
3. Private communication, Mar. 1990.
4. The novel was written from the original playscript and provides evidence of the shape of the original script and Hughes's original intentions.
5. Washington defines *cult* as follows: "The dynamic center of every ethnic social formulation or culture (in the beginning) is this religious formation *(cult)* which seeks to bring about the will of the community in public action or worship. The purpose of the cult is to gain through community involvement and worship the power necessary for social order, the protection and advancement of the goals of the ethnic group. Thus, the *cult* or central act of the community is worship. What is worshipped or sought is the power of God as it is understood to be extended in mind, body, and spirit of beings and things. In this context, Africans and Afro-Americans share the *cult* of power worship. They are at bottom power worshippers. Power means life (from God) and ability to do all things necessary to meet the needs and will of the community" (158).

◆◆◆◆◆◆◆◆◆◆◆◆◆◆

Old John in Harlem: The Urban Folktales of Langston Hughes

SUSAN L. BLAKE

"If you want to know about life," says Simple in the story that introduces him to readers of *Simple Speaks His Mind* and *The Best of Simple*, "don't look at my face, don't look at my hands. Look at my feet and see if you can tell how long I been standing on them." In the well-known catalogue of things Simple's feet have done—the miles they've walked; the lines they've stood in; the shoes, summer sandals, loafers, tennis shoes, and socks they've worn out; and the corns and bunions they've grown—Langston Hughes characterizes Jesse B. Semple, Harlem roomer, as the personification of the accumulated black experience. But what is especially significant about Simple is that he not only acknowledges his past, but uses it to shape his present. When his bar-buddy Boyd challenges him to name one thing his feet have done that makes them different from any other feet in the world, Simple points to the window in the white man's store across the street and replies that his right foot broke out that window in the Harlem riots and his left foot carried him off running, because his personal experience with his history had taught him, as he says, "to look at that window and say, 'It ain't mine! Bam-mmm-mm-m' and kick it out."

In creating the and Simple stories, Hughes has done the same thing with the black folk tradition that his character does with black history—made it live and work in the present. It is easily recognized that Hughes has a relationship to the folk tradition. He wrote poetry in vernacular language and blues form. He edited *The Book of Negro Humor* and, with Arna Bontemps, *The Book of Negro Folklore*, which includes several of his own poems and Simple stories as literature "in the folk manner." Simple himself has been called a "folk character" on the basis of half a dozen different definitions of the term: sociological average, composite of Southern folk types, epic hero, ordinary man, wise fool, blues artist. But Simple is more than vaguely "folk," and Hughes's relationship to the folk tradition is direct and dynamic. Simple is the migrant descendant of John, the militant slave of black folklore, and the fictional editorials that Hughes wrote for the *Chicago Defender* from 1943 to 1966 function as real folktales in the political story-telling tradition of the John-and-Old-Marster cycle. Not only do they follow the pattern of the John tales in characterization and conflict, not only do they include traditional motifs, they also recreate on the editorial page of a newspaper the dramatic relationship between storyteller and audience that characterizes an oral storytelling situation.

The principal difference between folk and self-conscious literature is in the relationship between the work and the audience. Generally speaking, self-conscious literature, usually written, isolates the experience of individuals; is addressed to individuals, who may or may not share either personal or social experience with either the author or the characters; and is experienced by the individual as an individual. Folk literature, usually oral, isolates the experience of a socially defined group; is addressed to all members of the group; and is experienced by a group, even if it consists of only two members, as a group. The self-conscious artist tells a story to suit himself, and the audience takes it or leaves it. The folk storyteller chooses and adapts a traditional text according to the occasion and the audience. The folk audience, therefore, participates in the storytelling and, in a sense, is also part of the story told. The story is told by, to, and for the people it is about; it is part of their lives as they are part of it. The Simple stories close the gap between story and audience created by the medium of print in several ways. They, too, adapt traditional materials from black folk-lore, the Bible, U.S. history, and popular culture. They, too, are occasional, as they deal with current events and social conditions. Their consistent subject, race, is the one experience that unites and defines the folk group to which they are addressed. Their principal character is an avid reader of the very publication in which the audience encounters him. Their story-within-a-story structure creates a dialogue between characters and audience. And their purpose is to function in the social conflict in which both characters and audience are engaged.

The typical Simple story is narrated by Boyd, who reports an encounter with Simple in which Simple has narrated an experience of his own. Each story contains two conflicts—one expressed in Simple's confrontation with an outside antagonist, the other in the conversation with Boyd in which he narrates it. Both conflicts are based on the consequences of race, which Simple defines in this exchange:

> "The social scientists say there is *no* difference between colored and white," I said. "You are advancing a very unscientific theory."
> "Do I look like Van Johnson?" asked Simple.
> "No, but otherwise—"
> "It's the *otherwise* that gets it," said Simple. "There is no difference between me and Van Johnson, except *otherwise*. I am black and he is white, I am in Harlem and he is in Beverly Hills, I am broke and he is rich, I am known from here around the corner, and he is known from Hollywood around the world. There is as much difference between Van Johnson and me as there is between day and night. And don't tell me day and night is the same. If you do, I will think you have lost your mind."

The *otherwise* that Simple is talking about—the social, political, and economic disparity between blacks and whites—generates other disparities: between Christianity and racism, legislation and application, "race leaders" and black folks, "say-ola" and "do-ola," *ought* and *is*, the American Dream and the American Dilemma. These in turn produce the psychological disparity, the twoness that Du Bois classically defined, between being black and being American. In general, the story Simple narrates addresses the social disparity; his dialogue with Boyd addresses the psychological. The dual structure of the stories makes Simple both actor and storyteller; it makes Boyd actor, teller, and audience. It enables Hughes to explore all the implications of American race discrimination and to bring them home to the audience that experiences them.

In the inside story, Simple follows the model of John, the insubordinate slave in the cycle of folktales about the perpetual contest between John and Old Marster. John is Old Marster's favorite slave, his foreman, his valet, his confidant, his fortune-teller, his alter ego. When Old Marster throws a party, John plays the fiddle; when he gambles with his neighbors, he bets on John; when he goes on a trip, he leaves John in charge. John is as close to Old Marster as a slave can be, but he is still a slave. He spends his life trying to close the gap between himself and Old Marster, between slavery and manhood. In the words of Julius Lester, John does "as much living and as little slaving" as he can.

He does so by effectually swapping places with Old Marster. At every opportunity, he puts himself in Old Marster's shoes: throws a party in the big house when Old Marster takes a trip, appropriates Old Marster's hams and chickens, "borrows" his clothes and his best horse, copies his manners, kisses his wife, and generally assumes the prerogatives of manhood that Old Marster takes for granted. He also shows Old Marster what it is like to go barefoot. When Old Marster and Old Miss sneak back from their trip in ragged disguise to spy on his party, John sends them to the kitchen like white trash. When Old Marster sends John out at night to guard his cornfield from a bear, John ends up holding the gun while Old Marster plays ring-around-the-rosy with the bear.

John is neither big nor strong, and he is more than clever. He is a political analyst. When he wins a round with Old Marster, his victory is the result of an objective understanding of the political and psychological principles of slavery that enables him to turn those principles back upon the institution. In one version of a popular tale called "The Fight," for example, John bluffs his opponent into forfeiting a fight on which Old Marster has staked his entire plantation by slapping Old Miss across the face. Since John has saved the plantation, Old Marster is reduced to diffidence when he inquires why John has violated the rock-bottom rules of slavery. When John explains, "Jim knowed if I slapped a white woman I'd a killed him, so he run," there is nothing further Old Marster can say. Even when John himself loses, the tale contains the analysis of slavery that represents the teller's and audience's intellectual control over their situation. Whether he wins or loses, John is the personification of this control.

Simple, the character in his own stories, like John, has the circumstances of a slave and the psychology of a free man. Although he works for a wage instead of for life, it's a subsistence wage, as evidenced by his chronic inability to save the One Hundred and Thirty-Three Dollars and Thirty-Four Cents to pay for his share of his divorce from Isabel so he can marry Joyce. Although he doesn't need a pass to leave Harlem, as John needs a pass to leave the plantation, Simple knows that there are barber shops, beaches, and bars outside Harlem where he would be unwelcome or in danger. Although his antagonists are as various as newspaper reporters, hotel clerks, Emily Post, and Governor Faubus, they all represent institutions of a society that excludes him, just as Old Marster represents slavery. But just as John refuses to behave like a slave, Simple refuses to be restricted by race: "What makes you think I'm colored?" he demands when told a factory is not taking on any "colored boys." "They done took such words off of jobs in New York State by law."

As a storyteller, Simple points out the same kinds of disparities that concerned the tellers of John tales. First, there are the practical disparities between life uptown and life downtown. The folk storyteller points out that John sees chicken on Old Marster's table and fat bacon on his own. Simple observes that Joyce buys her groceries downtown because "everything is two-three-four cents a pound higher in Harlem"; that he could get a hotel room if he asked for it in Spanish, but not if he asked for it in English; that white folks Jim Crow and lynch him "anytime they want to," but "suppose I was to lynch and Jim Crow white folks, where would I be?" Second, there is the disparity between stated and practiced values. Two of the themes that Simple returns to most frequently are also common themes in folk literature: the difference between Christian doctrine and Christians' doing, and the reversed status of people and animals when the people are black. In "Cracker Prayer," a variant of a traditional type of satiric prayer of which there is an example in Hurston's folklore collection *Mules and Men*, Simple impersonates a pious bigot who prays to the "Great Lord God, Jehovah, Father . . . to straighten out this world and put Nigras back in their places." In "Golden Gate," he dreams a dream based on the traditional tale of The Colored Man Barred From Heaven, in which he arrives at the gate of Heaven and finds "Old Governor of Mississippi, Alabama, or Georgia, or wherever he is from," telling him to go around the back. Black folklore compares the lot of the black man, often disadvantageously, to that of the mule. Simple does the same thing with dogs. "Even a black dog gets along better than me," says Simple. "White folks socialize with dogs—yet they don't socialize with me." The army "Jim Crows me, but it don't Jim Crow dogs." In slavery days, Simple recalls, "a good bloodhound was worth more than a good Negro, because a bloodhound were trained to keep the Negroes in line." And dogs are still, he observes, more carefully counted than Negroes, better fed, sometimes even better clothed.

As an actor, Simple, like John, endeavors to resolve the disparities he has pointed out. His most common method is the folktale expedient of swapping places. He dreams that he is the one "setting on the wide veranda of my big old mansion with its white pillars, the living room just full of chandeliers, and a whole slew of white servants to wait on me, master of all I surveys, and black as I can be!" He turns himself into a general in charge of white troops from Mississippi: "They had white officers from Mississippi in charge of Negroes—so why shouldn't I be in charge of whites?" He sets himself up in the Supreme Court, where he uses the principle of swapping places to enforce the laws he promulgates: "For instant, 'Love thy neighbor as thyself.' The first man I caught who did not love his neighbor as hisself, I would make him change places with his neighbor—the rich with the poor, the white trash with the black and Governor Faubus with me."

Just as John not only seats himself at the head of Old Marster's table, but uses the opportunity to treat Old Marster as Old Marster has treated him, Simple insists not simply on integration, but on "reintegration": "Meaning by that, what?" asks his white boss. "That you be integrated with *me*," replied Simple, "not me with you." If a white reporter from one of the downtown newspapers were to interview him about life in Harlem, for example, Simple would suggest that they swap apartments for thirty days: "'By that time, you will have found out how much the difference is in the price of a pound of potatoes uptown and a pound of potatoes downtown, how much the difference is for what you pay for rent downtown and what I pay for rent uptown, how different cops look downtown from how cops look uptown, how much more often streets is cleaned downtown than they is uptown. All kinds of things you will see in Harlem, and not have to be told. After we swap pads, you would not need to interview me,' I would say, 'so let's change first and interview later.'"

The circumstance that makes Simple act as John acts is the same one that makes Simple experience what John experiences. Slavery and Jim Crow are both manifestations of the idea that race determines place. The society dictates the theme of swapping places by creating places:

> "You talk just like a Negro nationalist," I said.
> "What's that?"
> "Someone who wants Negroes to be on top."
> "When everybody else keeps me on the *bottom*, I don't see why I shouldn't be on top. I will, too, someday."

What Simple really wants is not for top and bottom to be inverted but
for there to be no top or bottom, no "place," to swap:

> "Anyhow," said Simple, "if we lived back in fairy tale days and a good
> fairy was to come walking up to me and offer me three wishes, the very first
> thing I would wish would be:
>
> THAT ALL WHITE FOLKS WAS BLACK
>
> then nobody would have to bother with white blood and black blood any
> more."

But Simple does not live back in fairy-tale days, so he tries to combat
racism by showing how unfair it would look if the tables were turned.
The principle of swapping places is literally the principle of revolution.
But the elimination of places is equally revolutionary. Hughes's purpose
in Simple's stories is to make revolution look simple.

To the extent that inside and outside plots can be separated, the
inside plot of a Simple story is addressed to the problem of Jim Crow
and the outside plot to the people who suffer from it. The narrator of
the Simple stories, identified in the later stories as Boyd (though "Boyd"
in the earlier stories is the name of another roomer in Simple's house),
is both the immediate audience of Simple's narrative—and, thus, a stand-
in for the newspaper audience—and one of Simple's antagonists. For
although Simple and Boyd are both black, and in full agreement on what
should be, they disagree about what *is*. Because Boyd views reality in
terms of American ideals and Simple views it in terms of black experience, their friendly disagreements focus on the psychological disparity
between being black and being American.

Boyd talks American. He is a romantic, an idealist, one of the two
hundred ninety-nine out of a thousand people, as George Bernard Shaw
figured it, who recognize the conventional organization of society as a
failure but, being in a minority, conform to it nevertheless and try to
convince themselves that it is just and right. Simple talks black. He is
Shaw's realist, the one man in a thousand "strong enough to face the
truth the idealists are shirking." The truth he faces and Boyd shirks is
the importance of race. Though Boyd is black, rooms in Harlem, listens
to Simple nightly, sees the evidence of race discrimination all around
him, he keeps trying to believe that what ought to be is. The police are
there to "keep you from being robbed and mugged"; "violence never
solved anything"; "bomb shelters will be for everybody"; "Negroes today
are . . . advancing, advancing!" "I have not advanced one step," counters
Simple, getting down to cases, "still the same old job, same old salary,
same old kitchenette, same old Harlem and the same old color." "You
bring race into everything" complains Boyd. "It is in everything," replies
Simple.

Boyd considers Simple's race-consciousness provincial, chauvinistic,
and un-American. He repeatedly encourages Simple to "take the long

view," "extend a friendly hand," get to know more white people, try some foreign foods. But Simple insists on his Americanness as much as his blackness. In his imaginary encounters with representatives of all the institutions that exclude him because he is black, he replies, "I am American." The difference between Simple's and Boyd's assumptions about what it means to be American is dramatized by their response to a folk joke Simple tells about an old lady who enters a recently integrated restaurant, orders various soul-food specialties, is politely but repeatedly told "we don't have that," and finally sighs, "I knowed you-all wasn't ready for integration":

> "Most ethnic groups have their own special dishes," I said. "If you want French food, you go to a French restaurant. For Hungarian, you go to Hungarian places."
> "But this was an American place," said Simple, "and they did not have soul food."

To Boyd, as to the hotel clerks and employers Simple encounters, "Negro" and "American" are mutually exclusive; "American" identity is an achievement upon which "Negro" identity may be put aside. To Simple, they are mutually necessary. America is not American *unless* it has room for him, "black as I can be," "without one plea." From Simple's point of view, Boyd's is not American at all, but white. Though Boyd voices the ideals of freedom, he represents the influence of racist conventions in his interpretation of them. The repartee between Simple and Boyd puts a contemporary conflict of attitudes into the context of the historical conflict between John and Old Marster. Through Boyd, Hughes shows that to deny the reality of racial oppression is actually to support it.

Since Boyd, as Simple's audience, also represents the reading audience, Simple's argument with him becomes an argument with his audience as well. The framework conversation with Boyd applies the meaning of Simple's narrative to the audience and anticipates their objections. Through it Simple the folk narrator confronts the legacy of Old Marster in the audience as Simple the folk hero confronts Jim Crow. Folktales could not free the slaves who told them, but they could keep the slaves from being tricked into believing they were meant to be slaves; the tales could keep the distinction between living and slaving clear. The Simple stories do the same for the distinction between American ideals and black reality. The principle of the Simple stories is that the way to overcome race discrimination is to confront it, and they keep their audience confronted not only with the principle of confrontation but also with the evidence of discrimination. In the words of Ellison's definition of the blues, they keep alive the painful details and episodes of black experience and transcend them—keep them alive in order to transcend them—just as Simple remembers his past in order to free his future.

The similarity between Simple's conflict and John's make the Simple stories resemble folktales, but the active engagement in the audience's social and psychological experience makes them be to an urban newspaper-reading folk what the John tales must have been to a rural story-telling folk: a communal affirmation of the group's own sense of reality. Like the folk storyteller, Hughes speaks of and to the group. He speaks of their immediate experience, by commenting on current events, and puts it into the context of their historical experience and the fundamental fact of their group identity, race. He uses the medium, the newspaper, that draws the largest audience, and a narrative form that not only simulates narrator-audience exchange in the dialogue between Simple and Boyd, but stimulates it by making Simple and Boyd personify conflicting attitudes he knows his audience—individually as well as collectively—holds. The Simple stories seek to show that, though the forms of life in mid-twentieth-century Harlem are different from those on the ante-bellum plantation, the fundamentals are the same. The stories themselves are written and published on this same principle; and the adaptation of their form to the realities of an urban, literate, mass society is what in fact allows them to function as folktales.

Implicitly in the Simple stories, Hughes has redefined the notion of black folk tradition. Most of the writers who consciously used black folk materials in the first half of the twentieth century located "the folk tradition" in the South, in the past, in a pastoral landscape. They either employed it—as did Toomer, Hurston, O'Neill in *The Emperor Jones*, Heyward in *Porgy*—or rejected it, as did Wright, as a retreat from the social complexities of modern life into either pastoral simplicity or the individual psyche. But Hughes's definition of black folk tradition is dynamic. Limited by no time, place, or landscape, it is simply the continuity of black experience—an experience that is "folk" in that it is collective and a "tradition" in that it defines the past, dominates the present, and makes demands on the future.

Hughes asks his audience to recognize their place in this tradition and use it as Simple uses the history stored up in his feet. The force and purpose of his writing is to project his understanding of the folk tradition out among the folk, to bind black people together in a real community, united by their recognition of common experience into a force to control it. Modestly, like a relay runner, Langston Hughes picks up the folk tradition and carries it on toward the goal of social change in the real world.

◆◆◆◆◆◆◆◆◆◆◆◆◆◆

The Practice of a Social Art

MARYEMMA GRAHAM

I am both a Negro and poor. And that combination of color and of poverty gives me the right then to speak for the most oppressed group in America, that group that has known so little of American democracy, the fifteen million Negroes who dwell within our borders.

—LANGSTON HUGHES
Second International Writers
Congress, 1937

Unlike Richard Wright, Langston Hughes was caught in the transition between a flourishing literary and aesthetic rebellion and a political and ideological movement. He responded by assuming the task of redefining the artistic function in new social and political terms. Writing as a young poet virtually nourished by the Renaissance, Hughes brought to the literary art of the 1930s an artistic expertise and a progressive view which helped to define him as an early radical.

According to Hugh Gloster, Hughes' poetry, rather than his prose, manifested a strong proletarian element. The volumes published during the 1930's—*Scottsboro Limited: Four Poems and a Play in Verse* (1932), *Don't You Want to Be Free* (1938) and *A New Song* (1938) have the same ideological content as one story in *Ways of White Folks* (1934), "Father and Son." This is the only one of the fourteen stories in the volume, says Gloster, "which aggressively voices proletarian ideology . . . wherein Hughes states:

> Crucible of the South, find the right powder and you'll never be the same again—the cotton will blaze and the cabins will burn and the chains will be broken and men, all of a sudden will shake hands, black men and white men, like steel meeting steel![1]

In this study, the choice of Hughes' fiction over his poetry has been made because of the assumption that there is in fiction a more complete depiction of man's life in society. The choice, too is more appropriate for a comparative study of the two authors, Wright and Hughes. Furthermore, I would maintain that Hughes' fiction in the 1930's, much less frequently discussed than his poetry of the same period, pulsates with the themes and sentiments of the radical movement. More importantly, a substantial number of Hughes' short stories indicate a working out of the contradictions between the concepts of revolutionary literature and national literature, contradictions posed in the polemical essays in *New Challenge*. The controversial ideological issues which occupied most

213

Marxists of that period—the issues of bourgeois and proletarian literature, and of artistic individualism and collective responsibility—are also
a part of the author's general concerns. At the same time, Hughes represented a challenge to many orthodox Marxists who did not look kindly
upon traditional folk culture and the non-realistic elements it incorpo-
rated.[2] For Langston Hughes was not merely a folklorist; he successfully
fused the black folk heritage with what was considered a revolutionary
consciousness. It is not surprising, therefore, that echoes of Hughes
were especially frequent in the 1960s, during the emergence of the Black
Arts Movement, a black nationalist-oriented popular arts movement. All
of these facts make Hughes particularly significant in any study of the
development of American literature.

Wright himself was aware of Hughes' particular importance as an
artist. In a review of *The Big Sea*, entitled "Forerunner and Ambassador," Wright says:

> The double role that Langston Hughes has played in the rise of realistic
> literature among Negro people resembled in one phase the role that Theodore
> Dresier played in freeing American literary expression from the restrictions
> of Puritanism. . . [the] realistic position taken by Hughes has become the
> dominant outlook of all those Negro writers who have something to say.[3]

The other aspect of Hughes' contribution, according to Wright, is that
he serves as cultural ambassador: he takes the American Negroes' condition to the court of world opinion through his writings and brings the
experiences of other national writers to the American Negro through his
work as a translator.

Langston Hughes seemed clear about his role as an artist. He told
an interviewer:

> I have often been termed a propaganda or protest writer. That designation
> has probably grown out of the fact that I write about what I know best, and
> being a Negro in this country is tied up with difficulties that cause one to
> protest naturally. I am writing about human beings and situations that I know
> and experience and, therefore, it is only incidently [sic] protest—protest in
> that it grows out of a live situation.[4]

The view that is proposed here is one that regards Hughes as having
advanced, more than any other black artist, a concept of social art. Generally, this has come to mean an art that uses a popular literary style,
derived from vernacular language and other forms of oral folk (national)
expression, for conveying social content. It is in this sense that Hughes
is regarded as a revolutionary or, more precisely, a proletarian author.
The concept of social art is at the crux of Hughes's writings on aesthetics,
indicated most clearly in his early essay in *The Nation*. Written in 1926,
"The Negro Artist and the Racial Mountain" expresses a radical view of
black art and the black artist. Although the most often quoted section
of the essay has been frequently used as a testament to artistic individu-

alism and cultural nationalism, the underlying ideas are those very similar to ones expresses in Wright's "Blueprint": the contradictions between
the role and the experience of the black artist, and how one might go
about resolving these contradictions. In other words, in "The Negro Artist . . .", Hughes shows himself to have been a pioneer in exploring the
revolutionary heritage of the black masses and in fusing both traditional
and revolutionary elements in black expression.

From the very beginning of the essay, Hughes emphasizes the effects
of the class contradictions in society on the black artist. He quotes an
example of a "Negro poet" from a middle-class family who said, "I want
to be a poet, not a Negro poet."[5] Such "nordicization" of the black artist
is the real temptation, according to the author, the "mountain" for the
black artist "who works against the undertow of sharp criticism and
misundertanding from his own group and unintentional bribes from
whites."

> "Oh, be respectable, write about nice people, show how good we are," say
> the Negroes. "Be stereotyped, don't go too far. Don't shatter our illusions
> about you, don't amuse us too seriously. We will pay you," say the whites.[6]

Implicit in these words is a criticism of the Harlem Renaissance and
of the artists who collaborated—as Hughes did himself in *The Weary
Blues* (1926) and in a dozen or so individual poems—in the perpetuation
of a popular image of the black masses that bore little relationship to the
real conditions as they existed. Gilbert Osofsky talks about this point
with regard to Harlem:

> The Negro community was discovered in the twenties, and its reputation was
> not that of a tragic slum, but a place of laughing, swaying, and dancing; and
> this image spread not only throughout the nation but throughout the world. . .
> It would be difficult to find a better example of the confusions, distortions,
> half-truths, and quarter truths that are the foundations of racial and ethnic
> stereotypes than the white world's image of Harlem in the 1920s.[7]

Undoubtedly in agreement with Osofsky, Hughes, nevertheless, recognized the over-all importance of the Harlem Renaissance:

> The present vogue in things Negro, although it may do as much harm as good
> for the budding colored artist, has at least done this: it has brought him
> forcibly to the attention of his own people among whom for so long, unless
> the other race had noticed him beforehand, he was a prophet with little honor.[8]

The major portion of "The Negro Artist . . ." challenges the view
that the black artist must plead for recognition through white channels,
conforming to the standards of the black middle class, "among whom
there will be perhaps more aping of things white than in a less cultured
or less wealthy home."[9] Hence, the class question is raised alongside the
question of race.

The challenge to middle-class respectability is presented in two parts.

First Hughes explains that the serious black artist is the one who recognizes the inherent value and cultural richness of the black masses:

> But there are the low-down folks, the so-called common element, and they are the majority—may the Lord be praised—They live on Seventh Street in Washington or State Street in Chicago and they do not particularly care whether they are like white folks or anybody else. . . These common people are not afraid of spirituals, as for a long time their more intellectual brethren were, and jazz is their child. . . And perhaps these common people will give to the world its truly great Negro artist, the one who is not afraid of himself.[10]

Secondly, Hughes suggests how the artist should reconcile his social commitment and artistic impulses. He uses his own poetry as an example:

> Most of my own poems are racial in theme and treatment, derived from the life I know. In many of them I try to grasp and hold some of the meanings and rhythms of jazz. I am as sincere as I know how to be in these poems and yet, after every reading, I answer questions like these from my own people: Do you think Negroes should always write about Negroes? . . . Why do you write about black people? You aren't black. What makes you do so much jazz poems?[11]

In short, "The Negro Artist. . ." is not so much a declaration as it is a statement about social commitment, and about solidarity between the artist and the masses of people, in the form and through the process of social art. That is, the artist must strive to create an art which serves the interests of the working masses by making them the subject and object—their language and culture, the means—of artistic representation. Rather than provide an explicit analysis on revolutionary commitment, Hughes states that the artist must first reject the elitism and escapism of the middle-class way of life and reestablish his relationship with the struggling masses. By implication, then, the artist will realize his critical revolutionary task: a responsibility to that social class which has the greatest interest in putting an end to exploitation and oppression, the proletariat.

For Hughes, art derived from the cultural forms and the historical consciousness represented in the popular expressions of black people. But Hughes was equally aware of the fact that the rich cultural heritage of black people did not necessarily imply a revolutionary consciousness.[12] One explanation of this fact, which Hughes accepted, was the class differences in art, which were expressed as differences between "high" or formal art and folk art. Bernard Bell explores the historical relationship between formal and folk art in his study of black poetry. A number of Bell's observations are pertinent here. For example, Bell observes that the leading scholars in black intellectual and cultural movements, W. E. B. Du Bois, Alain Locke, James Weldon Johnson (and we add Benjamin Brawley) were nurtured in the tradition of high art, but that they had an affinity for the Afro-American folk tradition.[13] We can conclude from Bell that when this tradition merged into the liberal and pluralistic notion associated with American progressivism, the idea was advanced that high art, identified with the cultivated classes, rested on the basis of folk art, especially music and the oral tradition, identified as products of the less sophisticated masses. Du Bois, Locke, Johnson and Brawley acknowledged the distinctive racial character of black folk art and viewed it as an essential ingredient in the development of a formal American literary and cultural expression. Prompted by the optimism of the 1920s, together with the characteristic idealism of Black Americans, these intellectuals predicted that social equality would result from the recognition of the cultural uniqueness and greatness of black people.[14] The faith in the inevitability of social equality was undoubtedly reinforced by the popular notions of cultural pluralism.

The pluralistic concept of society and the cultural solutions posed by intellectuals in the 1920s did not take into account the class contradictions in society, a basic tenet of Marxism. In the Marxist view, folk and oral forms of expression—the work song, the spiritual, the field holler, the sermon, the narrative, the gospel, the blues, and jazz—were a part of the Afro-American folk tradition, yes; but rather than become the means through which the masses of black people achieved social equality, they become commercial commodities to be exploited. Marxists, therefore, noted the inadequacy of cultural nationalism as a solution to the problems of black people, first because it lacked an understanding of the nature of exploitation and oppression in a capitalist society, and secondly because it facilitated exploitation.

The concept of class struggle in the material world together with its various cultural manifestations was articulated by Gordon, Holmes, and Wright; a class analysis of literature and art in relation to society became the accepted approach for radical thinkers. A most succinct expression of this approach came from Hughes himself at the American Writers' Congress. His address there, "To Negro Writers," admonished the black artist to be "practical" in his creative work:

> To expose duplicity and discrimination; and to criticize reactionary religion, false black leadership and the "O-Lovely-Negroes" school of American fiction, which makes an ignorant black face and a Carolina head filled with superstition appear more desirable than a crown of gold; the jazz-band; and the o-so-gay writers who make of the Negroes' poverty and misery a dusky funny paper.[15]

Hughes also realized that cultural solutions were not sufficient for coping with such a complex economic problem that black people's relationship to American society represented. He makes this point later in *The Big Sea* (1940) when he says of his Harlem contemporaries, "They thought the race problem had at last been solved through art . . ."[16] For

Hughes, although a people's artistic expression might have derived from a peculiarly racial experience, all the perimeters of this experience had to be subject to the most careful scrutiny. Hughes found that, based on the reality of the "low down folks," the working masses, the artist could struggle to find what Mao Tse Tung called "the unity of political content and the highest possible perfection of artistic form."[17] The essence of Hughes' work is that it strives to transform this vision of reality into individual expression. The most significant fact about Hughes the artist is that he was able to do this more consistently and more sucessfully than any of his contemporaries.

An essential harmony, therefore, characterized the aesthetic and political views of Hughes. His work suggested that elitist concepts of art and culture could be broken down if the artist kept before him the interests and aspirations of the masses of working-class people and an understanding of social and economic history. By producing an art about the people for the people—a people who as a class are "definitively the force which ensures a continuous affirmation of what is human"; a people who are "the creative ferment of the historical process"—the artist could be certain that his work maintained a necessary political content.[18] For Hughes, because the indigenous culture of black people was charged with the strength and humanity of a particular national minority primarily and fundamentally working class, black popular expression would continue to be a profound source of social and revolutionary art.

It is Hughes' ability to discern and translate popular working class culture that have caused most critics to interpret his art as more consistent than that of Richard Wright. Hughes had more than a literary interest in the working class. Although there is no clear evidence that he joined the Communist Party, Hughes was an early and an active member of the League of Struggle for Negro Rights, a united front organization which struggled for black liberation. No doubt, he understood capitalism and the necessity of extirpating its abuses.

That Hughes recognized the broader social function of art as opposed to a traditional approach to literature and art is eminently clear from his comments on his poetry recorded in an essay written for *Phylon* in 1947. "My Adventures as a Social Poet" reflects the artist's attitude about the relationship of art and society.

> Some of my earliest poems were social poems in that they were about people's problems—whole groups of people's problems—rather than my own personal difficulties. Sometimes, though, certain aspects of my personal problems happened to be also common to many other people. And certainly, racially speaking, my own problems of adjustment to American life were the same as those of millions of other segregated Negroes. The moon belongs to everybody, but not this American earth of ours. That is perhaps why poems about the moon perturb no one, but poems about color and poverty do perturb many citizens. Social forces pull backwards or forwards, right or left, and social poems get

caught in the pulling and hauling. Sometimes the poet himself gets pulled and hauled—even hauled off to jail . . . I have never known the police of any country to show an interest in lyric poetry as such. But when poems stop talking about the moon and begin to mention poverty, trade unions, color lines, and colonies, somebody tells the police.[19]

This essay also reports Hughes' attitudes toward popular culture. Included in the discussion is the author's first adventure in a black church, where he was commanded by the minister to stop reading blues poems from the pulpit. Another experience recorded by Hughes sheds light on his evaluation of the patronage system operating in the Renaissance and his own move to a more intense form of social commitment. Speaking of the "generous woman" who helped him through college and who sponsored him for a period of years, he says:

Perhaps had it not been in the midst of the great depression of the late '20's and early '30's, the kind of poems that I am afraid helped to end her patronage might not have been written. But it was impossible for me to travel from hungry Harlem to the lovely homes on Park Avenue without feeling in my soul the great gulf between the very poor and the very rich in our society. In those days, on the way to visit this kind lady, I would see the homeless sleeping in subways and the hungry begging in doorways on sleet-stung winter days. It was then that I wrote a poem called "Advertisement for the Waldorf-Astoria," satirizing the slick-paper magazine advertisements of the opening of that deluxe hotel.[20]

In describing his various political interests and experiences, Hughes relates his detention in Cuba, his relationship to the Scottsboro boys, the confrontations at the University of North Carolina after reading the line "Christ is a Nigger" (From "Christ in Alabama"), his travel to the Soviet Union, a journey which brought the reward of being labelled a Communist. After his return from Russia, his speaking engagements were often cancelled, or he was met with picket lines and denounced as as "atheistic red." One such boycott was conducted by the Detroit Mothers of America. Hughes concludes this essay with a characteristic irony:

So goes the life of a social poet. I am sure none of these things would even have happened to me had I limited the subject matter of my poems to roses and moonlight, but, unfortunately, I was born poor—and colored and almost all the prettiest roses I have seen have been in rich white people's yards—not mine. That is why I cannot write exclusively about roses and moonlight—for sometimes in the moonlight my brothers see a fiery cross and a circle of Klansmen's hoods. Sometimes in the moonlight a dark body sways from a lynching tree—but for his funeral there are no roses.[21]

For "poets [or critics] who write mostly about love, roses, moonlight, sunsets and snow," Hughes does appear quite an ordinary writer, indulging a great deal in "dish water," to quote from a statement by Alain Locke.[22]

In examining the fiction of Hughes, I have chosen two of his collections, *Ways of White Folks* (1934), and a later volume, *Something in Common* (1963), containing a number of short stories written by Hughes throughout the 1930s. One story, "The Sailor and the Steward," appears in the volume edited by Faith Berry, *Good Morning Revolution* (1973). These stories demonstrate the major point being made about Hughes: that he used simple popular styles to convey social content. Hughes' fiction represents a special kind of fusion of traditional artistic expression and radical social and political ideas. Using these stories to illustrate, I suggest that Hughes' compositional tendency is to deal in antithesis and contradiction. In other words, Hughes' familiarity with the cultural and historical experiences of black people and his efforts to socialist art formed the basis for two related considerations: first, the continuous resistance to oppression expressed in black cultural expression; and secondly, the contradiction between the promise and practice of America. For the first consideration, Hughes looks for internal values to extol within the black community; for the second, his arena is the exploitative nature of American society.

Hughes' novel, *Not Without Laughter* (1930), combines both of these features and it is unique in that it carries over some of the popular characterization from the novels of the Renaissance into what is clearly a more realistic depiction of black life than most Harlem novels provided. According to Eugene Gordon, the novel is unique for another reason:

> Thus far, Langston Hughes, in *Not Without Laughter,* has written the only novel in which the Negro worker is pictured as seeing the way out through the class struggle; it is the only novel by a Negro which is at the same time a critique of fiction. *Not Without Laughter* is lacking in many important elements, the reason being chiefly that Hughes at that time was lacking wholly almost in political development; but his political development since the novel was written indicates a fulfillment of the promise it contained.[23]

No doubt, Gordon, like Gloster, could see a more fully developed proletarian line in those works written by Hughes in the context of more conscious political activity such as the 1930s represented.

Not Without Laughter presents a black working-class family, one generation removed from the rural South. Aunt Hager, the dominant character in the novel, represents both continuity and change and is a point of departure for each person within the novel. Living with Hager is Anjee, her middle daughter, who is visited too frequently by her husband, Jimboy. The focus of Hager's attention is Sandy, the grandson.

Each of Hager's daughters has responded to her oppression in a different way. Each gives Sandy a different orientation and a vision of the working class. Harriet, the youngest, and a talented singer, is subject to the advances of lustful men at the country club where she works. She becomes a prostitute on her way to stardom. Tempy, the oldest, whose maturity was supervised by a condescending white patron for whom she served as traveling companion, has been told by this grand lady, "You're so smart and such a good, clean, quick little worker, Tempy, that it's too bad you aren't white. And Tempy took this to heart, not as an insult, but as a compliment."[24] It is not surprising that she has adopted a middle-class elitist attitude and resents the few encounters she must necessarily have with her black family and black life in general. She is aloof from black culture—in fact, she hates blackness—as Harriet and Jimboy are entrenched in black culture—they hate whiteness. Annjee, disappointed with an unsuccessful marriage and saddled with child, takes advantage of Hager's emotionally secure home.

There is a foreshadowing in this novel of the simple plot narrative that Hughes preferred in all of his prose fiction. The descriptive characterization suggests that the people in the novel are meant to contrast with one another rather than to attract our interest in their individual complex development. In fact, the entire novel moves through a series of descriptive contrasts: Hager's strength is contrasted with daughter Annjee's weakness; Tempy's escapism and disdain are contrasted with Harriet's desire for involvement as an artist; Sandy's increasing sense of responsibility is contrasted with his father Jimboy's irresponsibility. The uncomplicated plot gives us some glimpse of each character's world, emphasizing the tensions in the relationships between individual characters. Finally, upon Hager's death, there is the knowledge that a powerful legacy will help Sandy combat, though not necessarily change, the world. This is the legacy of working-class struggle, handed down to him through the life experiences of his grandmother, his mother, and Harriet.

The short stories, too, give us simplistic, vividly drawn social contrasts, but Hughes substitutes much more aggressive characters in most cases. By restricting his focus in the short stories to working-class characters, Hughes shows how this particular class must struggle against all forms of oppression. The kinds of concerns represented in most of the stories move from the mythical prosperity (for Blacks) of the Renaissance to the background of the Depression. The real social truths are told by those characters who appear to have gained little and, therefore, have very little to lose. A close examination of these stories reveals a typical Hughes' character whose life is bound by an extremely obvious set of oppressive and exploitative socio-economic conditions but whose consciousness, moral or otherwise, is aroused, causing the character to act positively in directing his own personal liberation. An understanding of the forces operating in society is implicit. Hughes, like Wright, indicates a pattern of individual character development. Additionally, the stories can be grouped according to the extent to which they reflect a proletarian ideology.

One large group of stories, written during the Depression, discusses a variety of themes pertaining to black oppression as traditional racial oppression. It is to be expected that Hughes would depict the cultural legacy of racism and its inherent features, interracial hypocrisy, sexual exploitation, and psychological repression. These are the themes of most of the stories in *Ways of White Folks:* "Home," "Red-Headed Baby," "Mother and Child," "Passing," and "Little Dog," which has a white woman as the central character. "Father and Son," a violent (for Hughes) and dramatic response to the racism theme, also makes an explicit reference to class struggle, as Gloster indicated. Yet the racism theme is effective as Hughes shows, for example, in "A Good Job Gone," how facile and non-productive relationships between blacks and whites can be, even under the most propitious circumstances. The spurious liberalism for which Americans possess a great talent is subject to careful scrutiny in "Slave on the Block" and "Poor Little Black Fellow." And the more humorous side of Hughes mixes with his critical side as he attacks the commercial exploitation of black culture in "Colony of Joy," "Slice Him Down," and "Tain't So."

There is present in all of these stories the influence of the stereotypes common to earlier black literature[25] and a number of them use the Harlem exoticism and primitivism as a setting, although Hughes makes a point of criticizing these trends. Hughes presents characters as new "slaves" who are not "contented," but who are instead aggressive and rebellious (the New Negro?). The subject of racial mixing (sexual and social) in many of these stories evokes the typical violence of white reaction and black rebellion in one form or another. On the whole, then, these stories reveal Hughes' relationship more to the tradition of black writing than to any real consciousness of class struggle.

On the other hand, one might say that Hughes' treatment of the black *and* white characters who appear in all of these stories suggests that he is moving more toward social, and away from exclusively racial, protest. In a comment made almost thirty years after some of the stories were written, he confirmed his belief in the common humanity of men, implying a criticism of society:

> Through at least one (maybe only one) white character in each story, I try to indicate that they are human, too. The young girl in "Cora Unshamed," the artist in "Slave on the Block," the white woman in the red hat in "Home," the rich lover in "A Good Job Gone," helping the boy through college, the parents-by-adoption in "Poor Little Black Fellow," the white kids in "Berry," the plantation owner in "Father and Son," who wants to love his son, but there's a barrier of color between them. What I try to indicate is that circumstances and conditions make it very hard for whites, in interracial relationships, each to his 'own self to be true.'[26]

In a second large group of stories, however, there is a sharper focus on the economic exploitation of the black working class. In this group can be found the broad range of social and political views advanced by the deepening crisis of the 1930s. One can also detect Hughes' increasing adherence to the view that if people can be identified on the basis of a common humanity, they can also be identified and united on the basis of a common exploitation and oppression.

For Hughes, a line of distinction can be drawn between the middle class and a more politically conscious working class, the proletariat. The first fictional treatment of this theme was perhaps *Not Without Laughter*, where Hughes criticized the black middle class (Tempy) for its selfishness and its aloofness from the masses. The culmination of this theme might be said to have been reached in the *Simple* stories, recorded dialogues of a fictitious working-class hero, Jesse B. Semple. In the group of stories written between the novel and *Simple*, Hughes shows us the life and experiences of the black masses as the more positive proletarian element in society actively engaged in struggle against oppression and exploitation, but who need not become middle class to improve their lot. This is clear, for example, in "The Blues I'm Playing," where a talented black pianist, Oceola of Harlem, is discovered and trained by a wealthy white widow, Mrs. Dora Ellsworth. At the same time, Oceola continues a loyal commitment to Pete Williams, the Southern boyfriend who is struggling through Meharry Medical School. Both have planned to return to the South where medical services are sorely needed. Oceola's musical career blossoms in the United States and in Europe, but her acceptance of the lifestyle offered by Mrs. Ellsworth is clearly temporary. When Oceola includes one of her own variations on the spirituals in her concert of classical music, the kindly patron is startled. Marriage to the young doctor signals her departure from her classical musical career. As Oceola goes to play for Mrs. Ellsworth for the final time, the following dialogue between the pianist and her patron illuminates the theme:

'You could shake the stars with your music, Oceola. Depression or no Depression, I could make you great. And yet you propose to dig a grave for yourself. Art is bigger than love.'

'I believe you, Mrs. Ellsworth,' said Oceola, not turning away from the piano, 'But being married won't keep me from making tours, or being an artist.'

'Yes, it will,' said Mrs. Ellsworth. 'He'll take all the music out of you.'

'No, he won't, said Oceola.

'You don't know, child,' said Mrs. Ellsworth, 'what men are like.'

'Yes, I do,' said Oceola simply. And her fingers began to wander slowly up and down the keyboard, flowing into the soft and lazy syncopation of a Negro blues, a blues that deepened and grew into rollicking jazz, then into an earth-throbbing rhythm that shook the lilies in the Persian vases of Mrs. Ellsworth's music room. Louder than the voice of the white woman who cried that Oceola was deserting beauty, deserting her real self, deserting her hope in life, the flood of wild syncopation filled the house, then sank into the slow and singing blues with which it had begun.

The girl at the piano heard the white woman saying, 'Is this what I spent thousands of dollars to teach you?'

'No,' said Oceola simply. 'This is mine. . . Listen! . . . How sad and gay it is. Blue and happy—laughing and crying. How white like you and black like me . . . How much like a man. And how like a woman. Warm as Pete's mouth . . . These are the blues . . . I'm playing.'

Mrs. Ellsworth sat very still . . . looking at the lilies trembling delicately in the priceless Persian vases.

'And I,' said Mrs. Ellsworth, 'would stand looking at the stars.'[27]

The passage, very reminiscent of sections in *Not Without Laughter*, reminds us that the extremities of isolation and despair, joy and humor sounded in the blues bespeak the ultimate limits of man's ability to endure loneliness, oppression, and pain, transforming them into an unresolved but affirmative song. In a sense, it is this spiritual reinforcement which accompanies Oceola as she chooses to return to her people as a poor doctor's wife, realizing the immense difficulties ahead of her. She might well have chosen another route, that of the deceitful and decadent middle class, whom Hughes criticizes in the "The Professor." The story makes it clear that the contrast between middle-class and popular working-class culture does not necessarily parallel racial distinctions in society. In its emphasis upon the complicity of "petty bourgeois nationalism," "The Professor" keynotes one of the most important issues among radicals. Allyn Keith's essay in *New Challenge*, for example, detailed the various forms of nationalism and insisted that

> . . . the Negro writer returning to the soil folk and the industrial masses as creative sources must be intellectually and emotionally alert. He must know the true difference between nationalism as a limiting concept and nationalism as a phase which is difficult but rich in the materials for progress into wider channels.[28]

Published in *Anvil* magazine before it was collected in *Something in Common*, "The Professor" is Dr. T. Walton Brown (suggesting a parody of Booker T. Washington, according to James Emmanuel), who is invited to have dinner with a white philanthropic family which is considering the establishment of a chair of sociology for Brown at a small black university in the South. The thought which continues to flow through Brown's mind as he talks with the Chandlers is, "How on ten thousand dollars a year he might take his family to South America in the summer where for three months they wouldn't feel like Negroes."[29] Since Brown is representative of the accomodationist and opportunistic leadership among black intellectuals, his book, *The Sociology of Prejudice*, "appeals to the old standards of Christian morality and the simple concepts of justice by which America function,"[30] and in a "sane and conservative way" presents the needs of the struggling college in such a diplomatic and non-demanding way, that, "The white people were delighted with Dr. Brown. He could see it in their faces, just as in the past he could always tell a waiter when he had pleased a table full of whites by tender steaks and good service."[31] Thus the professor, who

> had to study two years in Boston before he could enter a white college, when he had worked nights as redcap in the station and then as a waiter for seven years until he got his Ph.D. and then couldn't get a job in the North but had to go back down South to the work where he was now—convinced the family not to build a junior college in their own town, but to donate the money and encourage Black students in their town to go down South to this small college and be taught by committed Blacks of their own race like Dr. Brown.[32]

Hughes' exposure of the duplicitous behavior of the black middle class ends on a sharp note of criticism. The Professor has earned his success by "dancing properly to the tune of Jim Crow education."[33] It is difficult to be in the least sympathetic with Professor Brown for this self-seeking role he plays with rich and influential whites.

The relationship of the black middle class to the black masses is the crucial factor in determining the progress and the direction of the struggle for freedom. The Professor serves as a deterrent in the struggle for quality education. A true story gave Hughes an opportunity to extend the meaning of this idea even further. The opportunity was the Washington premier of *Green Pastures*, "that famous white play about black life in a scenic heaven. . . . Songs as only Negroes can sing them. Uncle Tom come back as God."[34]

The story is called "Trouble with the Angels" and appeared in *New Theatre* in 1935. A typical situation emerged at the opening of the performance: blacks were not allowed to attend because there was no Jim Crow section of the theatre. The action involves Johnny Logan, one of the "angels," who, in his dismay, attempted to get the cast to strike. "God"—played by Richard B. Harrison—discouraged the protest, fearing that such an action would jeopardize future bookings. In this story and in "The Professor," previously discussed, black intellectuals allow their desire for personal success to govern their political judgments, judgments which ultimately affect the masses of black people.

Hughes' most sharply stated argument against working-class exploitation is presented in those stories where race is important, but secondary in the face of economic exploitation. Ironically, the principal spiritual and material values of the exploited worker, values which he gains through his work and activity, shape the nature of his struggle. This theme is dominant in "Cora Unashamed," a story of a poor black domestic who criticizes the values of and rebels against a middle-class white family. Cora has worked for the Studevants since childhood:

> The Studevants thought they owned her, and they were perfectly right: they did. There was something about the teeth in the trap of economic circumstance

that kept her in their power practically all her life—in the Studevant kitchen, cooking; in the Studevant parlor, sweeping; in the Studevant backyard, hanging clothes.[35]

The circumstances of Cora's life cause in her a budding militancy. When her own illegitimate child dies with the whooping cough, she curses God for taking away the child: "My baby! God Damn it! My baby! I bear her and you take her away!"[36] When Cora transfers her love and affection to Jessie, the last Studevant child, she and the girl become extremely close, so close in fact, that when Jessie becomes pregnant at 19, it is Cora in whom she confides and Cora who informs Mrs. Studevant. Cora's attitude toward Jessie's pregnancy is quite unlike the moral pretentiousness of the Studevants, who, after confining Jessie, plan her abortion in order to prevent her marriage to the Greek boy who has fathered the child. It is Cora and Jessie, of course, who share a common exploitation at the hands of the Studevants.

Throughout the story, Cora's attitude is contrasted with the values and attitudes of the Studevants. Cora encourages Jessie to marry the boy she loves, for example, while the Studevants whisk Jessie off before the public gets a chance to discover the "awful crime." Soon after the abortion, however, Jessie dies and the Greek boy's father loses his ice cream store license; a campaign is also started to rid the town of "objectionables," especially Greeks. At the funeral, Cora's militancy wells up again and she exposes the Studevant's crime:

'They killed you! And for nothin' . . . They killed your child . . . They took you away from here in the springtime of your life and now you'se gone, gone, gone!'

Cora went on: 'They preaches you a pretty sermon and they don't say nothin'. They sings you a song, and they don't say nothin'; But Cora's here, honey, and she's gone tell 'em what they done to you. She's gonna tell . . . They killed you, honey. They killed you and your child. I told 'em you loved it, but they didn't care. They killed it before it was . . .'[37]

Before she is able to finish she is dragged away from the scene of the funeral. Her outburst nonetheless gives her the strength to leave the Studevants. Cora, in the end, returns to her family, an ailing mother and a drunken father, and they "somehow manage to get along."[38]

More typical of Langston Hughes is the story, "Berry," which serves to link one form of exploitation with that of another segment in the society. Told in the same simple manner as "Cora Unashamed," the story of Berry's oppression and exploitation by the Summer Home for Crippled Children parallels that of the crippled and deformed children of wealthy parents who are under the staff's care. Having been sent by the "High Class Help Agency," Berry is, to the surprise of the staff, black. The staff of the Home must quickly decide where he will stay and what he will be paid.

". . . You say he can do the work? How about the attic in this building? It's not in use . . . And by the way, how much did we pay the other fellow?"

"Ten dollars a week," said Mrs. Osborn, raising her eyes.

"Well, pay the darkie eight,' said Dr. Renfield. 'and keep him".[39]

Thus, this uneducated boy, a recent migrant accepted a job for eight dollars a week where he served as cook, butler, dishwasher, and general houseboy. "Milberry knew they took him for a work horse, a fool—and a nigger. Still he did everything, and didn't look mad—jobs were too hard to get, and he had been hungry too long in town."[40] The description of Berry's destitute state is as important as Berry's recognition of the exploitation of the children.

> The Summer Home was run for the profits from the care of permanently deformed children of middle class parents who couldn't afford to pay too much, but who still paid well—too well for what their children got in return . . . he thought he wouldn't even stay there and work if it wasn't for the kids.[41]

Berry's relationship with the children develops in the context of their common exploitation; the children seem to recognize his honest affection for them.

Despite the very obvious affection, an accident occurs and is quickly blamed on Berry. When a crippled child falls from a wheelchair to the ground, Berry is accused of "criminal carelessness." Looking for an excuse and fearing that the parents might bring a damage suit against the home, the doctor fires Berry, deducting his wages to pay for the broken wheelchair. The Home, a microcosm of society, is guilty in two fundamental ways: Their treatment of Berry is racially oppressive at the same time that it is economically exploitative. In other words, he is underpaid in comparison to the amount of work he does and he is paid less because he is black. The Home's treatment of the children raises the issue of exploitation which cuts across race. Berry's affinity for the children is logical since they, in this particular setting, belong to the same class.

The final short story to be discussed is perhaps Hughes' most clever demonstration of how individual freedom and personal development are subject to the negative impact of oppression and exploitation. "One Christmas Eve" reflects the apparent contradiction in the promise and practice of America. The character and the setting are familiar to a Hughes reader: Arcie is the maid in a white, middle-class home. On Christmas Eve, Arcie is given only five of her usual seven dollars, four of which must go for rent. With the rest, she hopes to purchase mittens and some necessary clothes, including a surprise, for her five-year old's Christmas present. At ten o'clock she sets out with Little Joe to do her shopping.

Joe's passion to see the mysterious "Santa Claus" results in his wandering into a theatre, where he is made fun of by the customers. When the frightened child is found by Arcie, he tearfully tells about the "moving picture show," and the Santa Claus who "didn't give me nuthin. He made a big noise at me and I runned out."

> "Serves you right," said Arcie, trudging through the snow. "You had no business in there. I told you to stay where I left you."
>
> "But I seed Santa Claus in there," Little Joe said, "so I went in."
>
> "Huh! That wasn't no Santa Claus in there," Arcie explained. "If it was, he wouldn't a treated you like that. That's a theatre for white folks—I told you once—and he's just a old white man."
>
> "Oh . . . !" said Little Joe.[42]

In this second large group of stories, racial oppression and class exploitation are two parts of the total theme of economic exploitation. Although all of Hughes' stories can be said to be about the working class, it is in these latter stories that the proletarian ideology is strongest. While only one story, "The Sailor and the Steward," argues for united radical action, all the stories impart a class outlook, even if it is subtly comprehended. By having the black characters involved in situations which can not be explained exclusively by a theory of racial oppression, and by contrasting the middle class with the working class, Hughes points the reader to class exploitation as the important factor which offers the most concrete explanation for the condition of the masses. Hughes took advantage of the analysis offered by Marxism, but unlike Wright, he did not move to a position of consistently advocating revolutionary solutions to oppression and exploitation, i.e. the violent overthrow of the bourgeoisie by the proletariat. Remaining independent organizationally, but accepting the Marxist analytical method, Hughes shaped his own brand of "socialist realism" apart from the "cult of proletarianism." Hughes, it should be remembered, called for a social aesthetic in his essay in the *Nation* and in his speech before the American Writers Congress: the artist should commit himself to solving the problems of elitism and escapism, two major aspects of the "racial mountain"; and the artist should be guided by the expression and the experience of the working masses in society. Hughes' practice of socialist realism integrated the classic Marxist view of class struggle and national identity without falling victim to propagandistic phrase-mongering. It was in this way that he met the challenges of radicalism in black writing as they were presented throughout the 1930s.

As an independent radical, Hughes' thinking about literature and society did not constitute a formal ideology. He rejected the view that the writer's world view could be prescribed by the Communist Party during the 1930s. On a number of occasions Hughes was asked why he had not joined the party. His response to Arthur Koestler, whom he met in his travels in Soviet Russia, was typical:

I told him that what I had heard concerning the party indicated that it was based on strict discipline and the acceptance of directives that I, as a writer, did not wish to accept. I did not believe political directives could be successfully applied to creative writing. They might well apply to the preparation of tracts and pamphlets, yes, but not to poetry or fiction, which to be valid, I felt, had to express as truthfully as possible the individual emotions and reactions of the writer, rather than mass directives issued to achieve practical and often temporary political objectives.[43]

Hughes' rejection of the Communist Party was not a rejection of the view that the struggle for socialism was a struggle for a better society. The determination of the *specific* relation between politics and literature which the majority of American proletarian writers accepted in the form of commandments, borrowed from the Soviet example, did not take into consideration the particularities of the Black American experience; this fact Hughes realized. Thus, Hughes could actively support the socialist/Communist philosophy but would work out his own particular approach to a socialized art. His point of departure was the black experience.

It is clear that Hughes consistently appealed for a black national expression in literature. For him, the relationship between the artistic and the political had to be defined in terms of the artist's relationship to black life. The work of the artist assumes political significance as the artist perceives his importance in estabishing the priorities of black life. Hughes himself was extraordinarily perceptive in this regard. By reaching into the rich empirical evidence of the life and culture of black people, he was continuously updating an authentic national expression, that is, the musical forms, vernacular language, and other peculiarly oral forms of expression, and the social (secular and religous) customs associated with the black working class, partly rural but increasingly urban. It was Langston Hughes, more than any other black artist during the 30's, who realized the political implications of the cultural manifestations of the national oppression of the black masses. He proposed cultural nationalism—the overt physical, emotional, and psychological manifestations of the struggle of black people. It was, however, the collective and, by implication, communal nature of the black experience, emobodied in the wealth of folkloric material, that made cultural nationalism, not alien to, but the base upon which any consciousness of economic exploitation within the class structure of the American capitalist society would have to depend. Moreover, Hughes realized that the majority of black people saw themselves as an element of the American population who were defined racially; their history and culture attested to this fact. It was, however, this particular fact that made the general functions of capitalist society more operational. Hughes' works are a real indication of the necessity and the possibility of using the *particular* facts of the experience of black people to reach a broader understanding of the *general* nature of society.

Thus, while Wright struggled to *create* an identity for what he designated as an urban, industrial phenomenon and what he feared might become an American norm (the alienated and isolated Bigger Thomas), Hughes *confirmed the existence* of a transforming national identity, influenced by social and economic (class) factors and by cultural (racial) factors. Therefore, Wright and Hughes represent two different views on two essential problems which came to haunt black writers: identity and alienation. Wright was unable to understand and was highly suspicious of the socializing function of the black cultural experience (the church, Wright said, had ceased to be effective); he was therefore unable to make a connection between the Marxian concept of the alienated worker, be he rural or urban proletariat, and the concept of cultural identity and cohesion—the means through which black people transformed their wretchedness into tolerable forms, and made a dehumanizing experience humanizing.

For Wright, Western man was finally and ultimately isolated from any kind of human community. Hughes, on the other hand, with a full understanding of the collectivizing, socializing process implicit in the cultural experience of the oppressed, sought an analysis which could explain the alienation and dispossession of black people, but one which would also recognize the heritage of resistance to oppression embodied in the most authentic forms of black expression. He found such an analysis in a materialist conception of society, an analysis that was able to contain his own view of black folk culture as resistance to social, political, and cultural domination, from which a revolutionary cultural consciousness could emerge. If alienation and marginality resulted from oppressive living conditions and the exploitation of the unskilled in urban societies as the Marxist materialist analysis insisted, Hughes would find in the cultural and historical experience of black people a form of reconciliation, although clearly not a total solution. He demonstrates this resistance and reconciliation in his fiction. In "Blues I'm Playing," for example, Oceola, who moves between two worlds, as a talented black musician and a black worker, chooses the latter. "The Professor," however, allies himself with the duplicity and accommodation of the black middle class as Hughes sets an attack against the false directions of racial chauvinism.

It is this consciousness of national oppression, one that could be extended to a consciousness of exploitation and oppression in its national and international contexts, that characterized the thinking of Hughes and found its most effective expression in his work and radical writing. In a speech before the Second International Writers Congress in Paris, July 1937, Hughes left no doubt about his commitment and his materialist vision:

> We Negroes of America are tired of a world divided superficially on the basis of blood and color, but in reality on the basis of poverty and power—the rich over the poor, no matter what their color. We Negroes of America are tired

of a world in which it is impossible for any group of people to say to another: 'You have no right to happiness, or freedom, or the joy of life.' We are tired of a world where forever we work for someone else and the profits are not ours. We are tired of a world where, when we raise our voices against oppression, we are lynched. Nicholas Guillen has been in prison in Cuba, Jacques Romain, in Haiti, Angelo Herndon in the United States. Today a letter comes from the great Indian writer, Raj Anand, saying that he cannot be with us here in Paris because the British police have taken his passport from him. I say, we darker peoples of the Earth are tired of a world in which things like that can happen.[44]

While we cannot ascribe a consistent theory of art to Hughes, the ideology behind his artistic preoccupations is far more coherent than is generally recognized by his critics. There is, of course, his series of poems on revolutionary heroes and on class struggle, as well as the poems on the popular themes of radical protest, many of which have been collected in Faith Berry's *Good Morning Revolution* (1973). The series of articles appearing in the *Chicago Defender*, the *Crisis* and *International Literature* in the '30's and '40's, and the autobiographical travelogue *I Wonder as I Wander* (1956) especially reveal that it was his stay in Russia in 1932–33 that expanded his consciousness of the positive aspects of socialism. Hughes reflects a definite enthusiasm for the Soviet Union and the socialist system:

> There is ONE country in the world that has no JIM CROW of any sort, no UNEMPLOYMENT of any sort no PROSTITUTION or demeaning of the human personality through poverty, NO LACK OF EDUCATIONAL FACILITIES for all of its young people; and NO LACK OF SICK CARE or DENTAL CARE for everybody. That country is the Soviet Union.[45]

Seeing a relationship between minorities and dominant racial groups in Central Asia and black and whites in the U.S., Hughes was particularly impressed by the fact that in only a few years the Soviets had succeeded in removing the color line throughout Soviet Asia. But he did not foster an idealism in this regard. He says in "Faults of the Soviet Union,"

> The Soviet Union is far from being a communist country in a theoretical or practical sense. At the moment socialism is what they have achieved. Salaries and living conditions are still unequal. But nobody can profit from or exploit the labor of another. What one makes must be made from one's own labor, initiative, and intelligence.[46]

Likewise, seventeen years later, Hughes viewed China's importance in the international struggle against oppression and exploitation. In a 1949 *Chicago Defender* article, Hughes commented:

> What is happening in China is important to Negroes, in fact, to people of color all around the world, because each time an old bastion of white supremacy crumbles[,] its falling weakens the whole Jim Crow system everywhere. Under the Nationalist government in China with its white western backers, there was a great deal of Jim Crow . . . Being colored, I felt it . . . I do not like Jim Crow in either Chicago or China . . . Chiang Kai-Shek was a Chinese Uncle Tom.[47]

In Soviet Russia and China, Hughes saw the models of a world united, at least theoretically, in its ideal of a classless society. It was no doubt his experience in these countries undergoing dramatic social and economic transformations that made it possible for him to merge the aesthetic and ideological, the artistic and political aspects of society.

The black cultural heritage provided an appropriate framework for Hughes' approach to literature. The search for an appropriate ideological method, such as Wright attempted, has continued to prove difficult for the black artist. Seldom are historical and socio-political perspectives considered adequate requirements for determining aesthetic theory.

The question as it has been posed here and as it is posed for radical black writing, however, is the working out of a revolutionary method that takes cognizance of the historical experience of black people, the experience of racial oppression and resistance to that oppression as represented through cultural forms. Aesthetically, this is interpreted as the relationship between *folk forms* and *formal literary expression*. Ideologically this involves an understanding of the contradiction between an increasingly revolutionary consciousness of the masses (proletariat) who evolved from the rural folk and the increasing conservatism of the black middle class, whose relationship to the dominant class in society must be preserved in order to insure its own survival. At the same time, it is this class who has the skills and resources to develop a literature, whether based upon the folk heritage or upon the upwardly mobile bourgeoisie. Hughes examines these very questions in the course of his fiction. A strong optimism, ever present in his fiction, appears to rest in the indomitable qualities of the common man, rather than upon the inevitability of revolution. But these two concepts were identified characteristically in the popular thinking of the 1930s. By representing the interests of the working masses, Hughes' fiction was implicitly radical in content.

Black writers in general owe to Hughes a great debt for recognizing the immense creative potential in the black folk heritage. And although the use of folklore continues to create ideological disparities for the black artist's formal expression, its real importance lies in its fundamentally dialectical nature. Sterling Brown, no doubt, shares Hughes' thinking in his materialist analysis of black folk culture and the development of society:

> It is evident that Negro folk culture is breaking up. Where Negro met only with Negro in the Black belt the old beliefs strengthened. The migration of the folk to the cities, started by the hope for better living and schooling and greater self-respect, quickened by the industrial demands of two world wars, is sure to be increased by man-displacing machines. In the city the folk become a submerged proletariat. Leisurely yarn-spinning, slowpaced aphoristic conversation become lost arts; jazzed up gospel hymns provide a different sort of release from the old spirituals; the blues reflect the distortions of the new

way of life. Folk arts are no longer by the folk; smart businessmen now put them up for sale. And yet in spite of the commercializing, the folk roots often show a stubborn vitality. Just as the transplanted folk may show the old credulity, so the folk for all their disorganization may keep something of the fine quality of their old tales and song. Finally, it should be pointed out that even in the transplanting, a certain kind of isolation—class and racial—remains.[48]

Sterling Brown, himself a leading folk scholar, has given us a clear sense of the dialectical transformation from a feudal to a proletarian culture, shaped by the forces of social and economic development. Hughes was both a part and a visionary in this process.

Notes

1. Hughes, quoted in Gloster, pp. 219–220.
2. A popularly held view among Marxists was that myths and folklore, including religion, tended toward idealism and abstractness, and represented a flight from revolutionary reality. Granville Hicks touches on this in his four-part article, "Revolution and the Novel." See also Wright's criticism of Zora Hurston's and Waters Turpin's novels, "Between Laughter and Tears," *New Masses* (5 October 1937), pp. 22–25.
3. Richard Wright, "Forerunner and Ambassador," *The New Republic* 103 (28 Oct. 1940), p. 69.
4. Rochelle Gibson, "This Week's Personality," *Saturday Review* 35 (19 April 1952), p. 63.
5. Langston Hughes, "The Negro Artist and the Racial Mountain," *The Nation*, 1926, rpt. in *The Black Aesthetic*, ed. Addison Gayle, Jr. (New York: Doubleday, 1971), p. 175. Hereafter cited as "Negro Artist."
6. "Negro Artist," p. 176.
7. Gilbert Osofsky, *Harlem: The Making of a Ghetto* (New York: Harper, 1963), pp. 179–180.
8. "Negro Artist," p. 178.
9. "Negro Artist," p. 176.
10. "Negro Artist," pp. 176–177.
11. "Negro Artist," p. 179.
12. Most black artists agreed that the real tradition of the black masses embraced a revolutionary consciousness that was not understood or consistently indicated by black writers, most of whom were middle class or wanted to be identified as such. See Eugene Gordon's "Negro Artist and the Negro Masses"; Eugene Clay Holmes speech, "The Negro in Recent American Literature," in *American Writers' Congress*, ed. Henry Hart (New York: International Publishers, 1935), pp. 145–153.
13. Bernard Bell, *The Folk Roots of Contemporary Afro-American* Poetry (Detroit: Broadsides, 1974), p. 24.
14. Bell, pp. 32–32.

15. Langston Hughes, "To Negro Writers," in Hart, *American Writers' Congress*, p. 140.
16. Langston Hughes, *The Big Sea* (1940; rpt. New York: Hill and Wang, 1963), p. 228.
17. Mao Tse Tung, "Talks at the Yenan Forum on Literature and Art," in *Selected Readings from the Works of Mao Tse Tung* (Peking: Foreign Languages Press, 1967), p. 225.
18. Adolfo Sanchez Vazquez, *Art and Society: Essays in Marxist Aesthetics*, trans. Mario Riofrancos (New York: Monthly Review, 1973), p. 272. I am indebted to Vazquez's discussions in this important text, especially Chapters 20–24.
19. Langston Hughes, "My Adventures as a Social Poet," in *Good Morning Revolution*, ed. Faith Berry (New York: Lawrence Hill, 1973), pp. 135–136. Edition hereafter cited as *Revolution*.
20. Hughes, "Adventures," p. 137.
21. Hughes, "Adventures," p. 143.
22. Alain Locke's criticism of Hughes reads: "*Laughing to Keep from Crying* is typical Langston Hughes. That means many things, among them uneven writing, flashes of genius, epigrammatic insight, tantalizing lack of follow-through, dish-water—and then suddenly crystal springs." Alain Locke, "From Native Son to Invisible Man," *Phylon* 14 (1953), p. 38.
23. Gordon, "The Negro Artist," p. 20.
24. Langston Hughes, *Not Without Laughter* (1930; rpt. New York: Collier-Macmillan, 1969), p. 254.
25. See Sterling Brown, "Negro Character as Seen by White Authors," *Journal of Negro Education* 2 (January 1933), rpt. in *Dark Symphony*, ed. James Emanuel and Theodore Gross (New York: Free Press, 1968), pp. 139–171.
26. Langston Hughes, quoted in James A. Emanuel, "The Short Stories of Langston Hughes," Diss. Columbia University, 1962, p. 406.
27. Langston Hughes, "The Blues I'm Playing," in *Ways of White Folks* (1934; rpt. New York: Random House, 1971), pp. 119–120. Edition hereafter cited as *Ways*.
28. Allyn Keith, "A Note on Negro Nationalism," *New Challenge* 2 (Fall 1937), p. 69.
29. Langston Hughes, "The Professor," in *Something in Common and Other Stories* (New York: Hill and Wang, 1963), p. 141. Edition hereafter cited as *Something*. Short story hereafter cited as "Professor."
30. "Professor," p. 141.
31. "Professor," p. 142.
32. "Professor," p. 142.
33. "Professor," p. 143.
34. "Trouble with the Angels," in *Something*, p. 205.
35. Hughes, "Cora Unashamed," in *Ways*, p. 4. Hereafter cited as "Cora."
36. "Cora," p. 8.
37. "Cora," p. 17.
38. "Cora," p. 18.
39. Hughes, "Berry," in *Ways*, p. 173. Hereafter cited as "Berry."
40. "Berry," p. 175.
41. "Berry," p. 177.
42. Hughes, "One Christmas Eve," in *Ways*, p. 199.
43. Langston Hughes, *I Wonder as I Wonder*, First American Century Series ed. (1956; rpt. New York: Hill and Wang, 1964), p. 122.

44. Hughes, "Too Much of Race," in *Revolution*, p. 98.
45. Hughes, "The Soviet Union," in *Revolution*, p. 80.
46. Hughes, "Faults of the Soviet Union," in *Revolution*, p. 91.
47. Hughes, "The Revolutionary Armies in China—1949," in *Revolution*, p. 11.
48. Sterling Brown, "Negro Folk Expression," *Phylon* 14 (1953), p. 60–61.

Essayists

RICHARD K. BARKSDALE is professor emeritus of English at the University of Illinois at Urbana. He is the author of *Langston Hughes* and *Praisesong of Survival: Lectures and Essays, 1957–89* and is the editor of *Black Writers of America: A Comprehensive Anthology*.

SUSAN L. BLAKE is an associate professor of English at LaFayette College, Easton.

JAMES A. EMANUEL is the author of *Black Man Abroad: The Toulouse Poems, Panther Man, Langston Hughes*, and the editor of *Dark Symphony: Negro Literature in America*.

MARYEMMA GRAHAM is an associate professor of English and Afro-American Studies at Northeastern University. She is the author of *The Afro-American Novel* and editor of *How I Wrote Jubilee and Other Essays on Life and Literature* and *Complete Poems of Francis E. W. Harper*.

ONWUCHEKWA JEMIE is the author of *Langston Hughes: An Introduction to the Poetry* and the coauthor of *Toward the Decolonization of African Literature*.

R. BAXTER MILLER is a professor of English at the University of Tennessee at Knoxville. His books include *The Art and Imagination of Langston Hughes, Black American Literature and Humanism*, and *Langston Hughes and Gwendolyn Brooks: A Reference Guide*.

ARNOLD RAMPERSAD is a professor of English and American Studies at Princeton University. He is the author of *The Life of Langston Hughes*, a two-volume biography; *Melville's Israel Potter: A Pilgrimage and Process;* and *The Art and Imagination of W. E. B. Du Bois*, as well as the coeditor, with Deborah McDowell, of *Slavery and The Literary Imagination*.

LESLIE CATHERINE SANDERS is Associate Professor of Humanities and English and Coordinator of Writing Programs at Atkinson College, York University, Ontario. Her book *The Development of Black Theater in America* was published by Louisiana State University Press in 1988. She is currently editing the plays of Langston Hughes.

STEVEN TRACY lives and works in Cincinnati. He is the author of *Langston Hughes and the Blues* and *Going to Cincinnati: A History of the Blues in the Queen City*.

Chronology

1902   February 1: Born James Mercer Langston Hughes in Joplin, Missouri, to James Hughes and Carrie (Langston) Hughes.

1903–14   Lives in New York State; Cleveland, Ohio; Lawrence and Topeka, Kansas; and Mexico, with his parents and then grandmother.

1920   Graduates from high school in Cleveland, Ohio.

1921   Moves to New York City; enters Columbia University. Publishes "The Negro Speaks of Rivers" in *The Crisis*, as well as poems for the juvenile magazine *Brownie's Book*.

1922–23   Drops out of Columbia. Explores Harlem and begins working at various menial jobs. A cooking job on a steamer takes him to Africa, Holland, and Paris.

1925   Wins several prizes in poetry contests, including first place in the *Opportunity* contest.

1926   Wins a scholarship to Lincoln University. Receives Witter Bynner undergraduate poetry award. Publishes a collection of poems, *The Weary Blues*, with the publishing house Alfred Knopf.

1927   Publishes *Fine Clothes to the Jew* (the title refers to pawnshops and their owners). Tours the American South with Zora Neale Hurston.

1929   Receives BA from Lincoln University, Pennsylvania.

1930   Publishes *Not Without Laughter*, a novel. Collaborates with Hurston on *Mule Bone*, a play. Travels to Haiti.

1931   Privately publishes two volumes of poetry, *Dear Lovely Death* and *The Negro Mother and Other Dramatic Recitations*.

1932   Publishes *The Dream Keeper and Other Poems* and *Scottsboro Limited: Four Poems and a Play*. Travels to Russia.

1934   Publishes a short story collection, *The Ways of White Folks*.

1935   Receives Guggenheim Fellowship. *Mullatto*, a play, staged on Broadway. Also writes *Little Ham*, another play.

1936   Writes three plays: *When the Jack Hollers*, *Troubled Island*, and *Emperor of Haiti*.

1937   Covers the Spanish Civil War for the *Baltimore Afro-American*. Writes *Front Porch*, *Joy to My Soul*, and *Soul Gone Home* (plays).

1938   Publishes *A New Song*, a volume of poetry. Writes *Little Eva's End, Limitations of Life, The Em-Fuehrer Jones*, and *Don't You Want to Be Free* (plays). Founds the Harlem Suitcase Theater.

1939   Founds the New Negro Theater in Los Angeles, California. Writes a play, *The Organizer*.

1940   Publishes *The Big Sea*, an autobiography covering his life to age twenty-eight.

1941   Receives Rosenwald Fund Fellowship.

1942   Publishes a volume of poetry, *Shakespeare in Harlem*, with Robert Glenn. Writes *The Sun Do Move* (play) and *Way Down South* (screenplay). Moves to Harlem and founds Skyloft Players.

1943   Publishes *Jim Crow's Last Stand* and *Freedom's Plow*, (books of poetry). Writes *For This We Fight* (play). Begins writing columns for the *Chicago Defender*.

1944   Publishes *Lament for Dark Peoples and Other Poems* in Holland.

1947   Publishes *Fields of Wonder* (poetry). Visiting professor of creative writing at Atlanta University.

1948   Writes lyrics for *Street Scene*, an opera by Kurt Weill.

1949   Publishes *One-Way Ticket* (poetry). Edits and publishes *The Poetry of the Negro, 1746–1949* with Arna Bontemps. Teaches at the University of Chicago's Lab School.

1950   Publishes *Simple Speaks His Mind* (short fiction). Writes the libretto for *The Barrier*.

1951   Publishes *Montage of a Dream Deferred* (poetry). Translation of Federico Garcia Lorca's *Gypsy Ballads* published.

1952   Publishes *Laughing to Keep From Crying* (short fiction).

1953   Publishes *Simple Takes a Wife* (short fiction). Writes *The Glory Around His Head* (play).

1955   Publishes a number of short works for children, including *The First Book of Jazz*.

1956   Publishes *I Wonder as I Wander*, his second autobiography.

1957   Publishes *Simple Stakes a Claim* (short fiction) and a translation, *Selected Poems of Gabriela Mistral*. Writes *Esther* and *Simply Heavenly* (plays).

1958   Publishes *Tambourines to Glory*, his second novel.

1960   Writes *The Ballad of the Brown King* (play). Receives the Springarn Medal from the NAACP.

1961   Publishes *Ask Your Mama: Twelve Moods for Jazz* (poetry). Writes *Black Nativity* (play).

1962   Publishes *Fight for Freedom: The Story of the NAACP*. Writes *Gospel Glow* (play).

1963   Publishes *Something in Common and Other Stories*. Writes *Tambou-*

rines to Glory and *Jericho-Jim Crow* (plays). Receives honorary doctorate from Howard University.

1965   Publishes *Simple's Uncle Sam* (short fiction). Writes *The Prodigal Son* (play).

1966   Edits *The Book of Negro Humor.*

1967   May 22: Dies in New York City. *The Panther and the Lash* (poetry) published posthumously.

Bibliography

Ako, Edward O. "Langston Hughes and the Négritude Movement: A Study in Literary Influence." *CLA Journal* 28 (1983–84): 46–56.

Barksdale, Richard K. *Langston Hughes: The Poet and His Critics*. Chicago: American Library Association, 1977.

———. "Comic Relief in Langston Hughes' Poetry." *Black American Literature Forum* 15 (Fall 1981): 108–111.

Berry, Faith. *Langston Hughes: Before and Beyond Harlem*. Westport, Conn.: Lawrence Hill, 1983.

Beyer, William C. "A Certain Kind of Aesthete: Langston Hughes' Shakespeare in Harlem." In *A Humanist's Legacy: Essays in Honor of John Christian Bale*, edited by Dennis M. Jones. Decorah, Iowa: Luther College, 1990.

———. "Langston Hughes and Common Ground in the 1940's." *American Studies in Scandinavia* 23 (1991): 29–43.

Blake, Susan L. "The American Dream and the Legacy of Revolution in the Poetry of Langston Hughes." *Black American Literature Forum* 14 (1980): 100–4.

Bloom, Harold, ed. *Langston Hughes*. New York: Chelsea House, 1989.

Bogumil, Mary L., and Moliao, Michael R. "Pretext, Context, Subtext: Textual Power in the Writing of Langston Hughes, Richard Wright, and Martin Luther King, Jr." *College English* 52 (Nov. 1990): 800–12.

Bonner, Patricia E. "Cryin' the Jazzy Blues and Livin' Blue Jazz: Analyzing the Blues and Jazz Poetry of Langston Hughes." *West Georgia College Review* 20 (May 1990): 15–28.

Brown, Lloyd W. "The Portrait of the Artist as a Black American in the Poetry of Langston Hughes." *Studies in Black Literature* (1974): 24–27.

Bruck, Peter. "Langston Hughes: 'The Blues I'm Playing' (1934)" In *The Black American Short Story in the 20th Century: A Collection of Critical Essays*, edited by Peter Bruck. Amsterdam: B. R. Gruner, 1977.

Caputi, Jane, "Specifying Fannie Hurst: Langston Hughes's 'Limitations of Life,' Zora Neale Hurston's *Their Eyes Were Watching God* and Toni Morrison's *The Bluest Eye* as 'answers' to Hurst's 'Imitation of Life.'" *Black American Literature Forum* 24 (Winter 1990): 697–717.

Carey, Julian C. "Jesse B. Semple Revisited and Revised." *Phylon* 32 (1971): 158–63.

Clark, VeVe. "Restaging Langston Hughes' *Scottsboro Limited:* An Interview with Amiri Baraka." *Black Scholar* 10 (1979): 62–69.

Clarke, John Henrik. "The Neglected Dimensions of the Harlem Renaissance." *Black World* 20 (November 1970): 118–29.

Cobb, Martha K. "Concepts of Blackness in the Poetry of Nicholás Guillén, Jacques Romain and Langston Hughes." *CLA Journal* 18 (1974–75): 262–72.

Cullen, Countee. "Poet on Poet." *Opportunity* 4 (March 1926): 73.

Davis, Arthur P. "The Harlem of Langston Hughes' Poetry." *Phylon* 13 (Winter 1952): 276–83.
———. "The Tragic Mulatto Theme in Six Works of Langston Hughes." *Phylon* 16 (Spring 1955): 195–204.
———. "Langston Hughes." In *From the Dark Tower.* Washington, D.C.: Howard University Press, 1974.
Dixon, Melvin. "Rivers Remembering Their Source: Comparative Studies in Black Literary History—Langston Hughes, Jacques Romain, and Negritude." In *Afro-American Literature: The Reconstruction of Instruction,* edited by Dexter Fisher and Robert B. Stepto. New York: Modern Language Association, 1979.
Emanuel, James A. *Langston Hughes.* New York: Twayne, 1967.
Franke, Thomas L. "The Art of Verbal Performance: A Stylistic Analysis of Langston Hughe's 'Feet Live Their Own Life.'" *Language and Style: An International Journal* 19 (Fall 1986): 377–87.
Garber, Earlene D. "Form as a Complement to Content in Three of Langston Hughes' Poems." *Negro American Literature Forum* 5 (1971): 137–39.
Garner, Thomas, and Carolyn Calloway-Thomas. "Langston Hughes's Message for the Black Masses." *Communication Quarterly* 39 (Spring 1991): 164–78.
Gates, Henry Louis, Jr. "The Hungry Icon: Langston Hughes Rides a Blue Note." *Village Voice Literary Supplement* (July 1989): 8–13.
———. "Why the 'Mule Bone' Debate Goes On." *New York Times*, Arts and Leisure (Feb. 10, 1991): 5, 8
Gomes, E. "The Crackerbox Tradition and the Race Problem in Lowell's *The Bigelow Papers* and Hughes' *Sketches of Simple.*" *CLA Journal* 27 (1983–84): 254–69.
Hansell, William H. "Black Music in the Poetry of Langston Hughes: Roots, Race, Release." *Obsidian* 4 (Winter 1978): 16–38.
Hathaway, Heather. "'Maybe Freedom Lies in Hating': Miscegenation and the Oedipal Conflict." In *Refiguring the Father: New Feminist Readings of Patriarchy,* edited by Patricia Yaeger and Beth Kowaleski-Wallace, with an afterword by Nancy Miller. Carbondale, Ill.: University of Illinois Press, 1989.
Hudson, Theodore R. "Technical Aspects of the Poetry of Langston Hughes." *Black World* 22 (September 1973): 24–25.
Jackson, Blyden. "A Word About Simple." *CLA Journal* 11 (1967–68): 310–18.
———. "From One 'New Negro' to Another." In *Black Poetry in America: Two Essays on Historical Interpretation.* Baton Rouge, La.: Louisiana State University Press, 1974.
———. "Claude McKay and Langston Hughes: The Harlem Renaissance and More." *Pembroke Magazine* 6 (1975): 43–48.
———. "Renaissance in the Twenties." In *The Twenties: Fiction, Poetry, Drama,* edited by Warren French. Deland, Fla.: Everett/Edwards, 1975.
Jemie, Onwuchekwa. *Langston Hughes: An Introduction to the Poetry.* New York: Columbia University Press, 1976.
Johnson, Patricia A., and Walter C. Farrell. "How Langston Hughes Used the Blues." *Melus* 6 (Spring 1979): 55–63.
Kent, George E. "Langston Hughes and Afro-American Folk and Cultural Tradition." In *Blackness and the Adventure of Western Culture.* Chicago: Third World Press, 1972.
Klotman, Phyllis R. "Jesse B. Semple and the Narrative Art of Langston Hughes." *Journal of Narrative Technique* 3 (1973): 66–75.

———. "Langston Hughes's Jesse B. Semple and the Blues." *Phylon* 36 (1975): 68–72.

Martin, Dellite L. "Langston Hughes' Use of the Blues." *CLA Journal* 22 (1978–79): 151–59.

———. "The 'Madame Poems' as Dramatic Monologue." *Black American Literature Forum* 15 (Fall 1981): 97–99.

Mikolyzk, Thomas A. *Langston Hughes: A Bio-Bibliography.* New York: Greenwood Press, 1990.

Miller, R. Baxter. "'Even after I was Dead': *The Big Sea*—Paradox, Preservation and Holistic Time." *Black American Literature Forum* 11 (1977): 39–45.

———. "For a Moment I Wondered': Theory and Symbolic Form in the Autobiographies of Langston Hughes." *The Langston Hughes Review* 3 (Fall 1984): 1–6.

———. *The Art and Imagination of Langston Hughes.* Lexington, Ky.: University Press of Kentucky, 1989.

Mullen, Edward J. *Langston Hughes in the Hispanic World and Haiti.* Hamden, Conn.: Arcon, 1977.

Nichols, Charles H., ed. *Arna Bontemps and Langston Hughes: Letters 1925–1967.* New York: Dodd, Mead, 1980.

Nifong, David Michael. "Narrative Technique and Theory in *The Ways of White Folks.*" *Black American Literature Forum* 15 (Fall 1981): 93–96.

O'Daniel, Therman B. "Lincoln's Man of Letters." *Lincoln University Bulletin* (July 1964): 9–12.

———. ed. *Langston Hughes, Black Genius: A Critical Evaluation.* New York: William Morrow, 1971.

Peidra, Jose. "Through Blues." In *Do the Americas Have a Common Literature?* edited by Gustavo Perez Firmat. Durham, N.C.: Duke University Press, 1990.

Presley, James. "Langston Hughes: A Personal Farewell." *Southwest Review* 54 (1969): 79–84.

———. "The Birth of Jesse B. Semple." *The Southern Review* 38 (1973): 219–25.

Prowle, Allen D. "Langston Hughes." In *The Black American Writer.* Vol. 2, *Poetry and Drama.* Edited by C. W. E. Bigsby. Deland, Fla.: Everett/Edwards, 1969.

Rampersad, Arnold. "The Origins of Poetry in Langston Hughes." *The Southern Review* 21 (Summer 1985): 695–705.

———. *The Life of Lanston Hughes, 1902–1967* 2 volumes. New York: Oxford University Press, 1986–88.

Randall, Dudley. "The Black Aesthetic in the Thirties, Forties, and Fifties." In *The Black Aesthetic,* edited by Addison Gayle, Jr. Garden City, N.Y.: Doubleday-Anchor, 1972.

Redding, Saunders J. *To Make a Poet Black.* Chapel Hill, N.C.: University of North Carolina Press, 1939.

Singh, Amritjit. "Beyond the Mountain: Langston Hughes on Race/Class and Art." *The Langston Hughes Review* 6 (Spring 1987): 37–43.

Story, Ralph D. "Patronage and the Harlem Renaissance: You Get What You Pay For." *CLA Journal* 32 (March 1989): 284–95.

Tracy, Steven C. "Simple's Great African-American Joke." *College Language Association Journal* 27 (March 1984): 239–53.

———. "'Midnight Ruffles of Cat-Gut Lace': The Boogie Poems of Langston Hughes." *College Language Association Journal* 32 (Sept. 1988): 55–68.

————. *Langston Hughes and the Blues.* Chicago: University of Illinois Press, 1988.

Turner, Darwin T. "Langston Hughes as Playwright." *CLA Journal* 11 (1967–68): 297–309.

Wagner, Jean. "Langston Hughes." In *Black Poets of the United States from Paul Lawrence Dunbar to Langston Hughes.* Urbana, Ill.: University of Illinois Press, 1973.

Waldron, Edward E. "The Blues Poetry of Langston Hughes." *Negro American Literature Forum* 5 (1971): 140–49.

Walker, Alice. "Turning Into Love: Some Thoughts on Surviving and Meeting Langston Hughes." *Callaloo* 12 (Fall 1989): 663–66.

Winz, Cary D. "Langston Hughes: A Kansas Poet in the Harlem Renaissance." *Kansas Quarterly* 7 (Summer 1975): 58–71.

Yestadt, Sister Marie. "Two American Poets: Their Influence on the Contemporary Art-Song." *Xavier University Studies* 10 (Spring 1971): 33–43.

Acknowledgments

Untitled review of *The Weary Blues* by Countee Cullen from *Opportunity* 4 (March 1926), ©1926 by the National Urban League, Inc. Reprinted with permission.

Untitled review of *The Weary Blues* by Jessie Fausset from *The Crisis* (March 1926), ©1926 by the National Association for the Advancement of Colored People. Reprinted with permission.

"A Poet for the People." Review of *Fine Clothes to the Jew* by Margaret Larkin from *Opportunity* 5 (March 1927), ©1927 by the National Urban League, Inc. Reprinted with permission.

"Sing a Soothin' Song." Review of *Fine Clothes to the Jew* by DuBose Heyward from the *New York Herald Tribune Book Review* (February 20, 1927), © 1927 the New York Herald Tribune Co. Reprinted with permission.

"This Negro." Review of *Not Without Laughter* by V. F. Calverton from *The Nation* 31 (August 6, 1930), ©1930 by Nation Associates, Inc. Reprinted with permission.

Untitled review of *Not Without Laughter* by Sterling A. Brown from *Opportunity* 15 (September 1930), ©1930 by the National Urban League, Inc. Reprinted with permission.

"Paying for Old Sins." Review of *The Ways of White Folks* by Sherwood Anderson from *The Nation* 139 (July 11, 1934), ©1934 by Nation Associates, Inc. Reprinted with permission.

"Forerunner and Ambassador." Review of *The Big Sea* by Richard Wright from *The New Republic* 103 (October 18, 1940).

"A Negro Intellectual Tells His Life Story." Review of *The Big Sea* by Katherine Woods from *The New York Times Book Review* (August 25, 1940), ©1940 by the New York Times Co. Reprinted with permission.

"Hughes's *Fine Clothes to the Jew*" (originally entitled "Langston Hughes's *Fine Clothes to the Jew*") by Arnold Rampersad from *Callaloo* 9 (1986), ©by The John Hopkins University Press. Reprinted with permission.

"To the Tune of Those Weary Blues" (originally entitled "To the Tune of those Weary Blues: The Influence of the Blues Tradition in Langston Hughes's Blues Poems") by Steven C. Tracy from *MELUS* 8 (Fall 1981), ©1981 by MELUS, The Society for the Study of Multi-Ethnic Literature in the United States. Reprinted with permission.

"Hughes: His Times and His Humanistic Techniques" (originally entitled "Langston Hughes: His Times and His Humanistic Techniques") by Richard K. Barksdale from *Black American Literature and Humanism*, edited by R. Baxter Miller, ©1981 by the University Press of Kentucky. Reprinted with permission.

"'Some Mark to Make': The Lyrical Imagination of Langston Hughes" from *The Art and Imagination of Langston Hughes* by R. Baxter Miller, ©1986 the University Press of Kentucky. Reprinted with permission.

"The Evolution of the Poetic Persona" (originally entitled "Langston Hughes: Evolution of the Poetic Persona") by Raymond Smith from *The Harlem Renaissance Re-examined*, edited by Victor A. Kramer, ©1987 by AMS Press, Inc. Reprinted with permission.

"Or Does It Explode?" from *Langston Hughes: An Introduction to the Poetry* by Onwuchekwa Jemie, ©1976 by Columbia University Press. Reprinted with permission.

"The Christ and the Killers" (originally published as chapter 4 of *Langston Hughes*) by James A. Emanuel, ©1967 by Twayne Publishers, Inc., an imprint of Macmillan Publishing Co. Reprinted with permission.

"'I've wrestled with them all my life': Hughes's *Tambourines to Glory*" (originally published as "'I've wrestled with them all my life': Langston Hughes's *Tambourines to Glory*") by Leslie Catherine Sanders from *Black American Literature Forum* 25 (Spring 1991), ©1991 Leslie Catherine Sanders. Reprinted with permission.

"Old John in Harlem: The Urban Folktales of Langston Hughes" by Susan L. Blake from *Black American Literature Forum* 14 (Fall 1980), ©1980 by Indiana State University. Reprinted with permission.

"The Practice of a Social Art" by Maryemma Graham, ©1990 Maryemma Graham. Printed with permission.

Index

This is one of six volumes of literary
criticism launching the
AMISTAD LITERARY SERIES
which is devoted to literary fiction
and criticism by and about African Americans.

◆

The typeface "AMISTAD" is based
on wood and stone symbols
and geometric patterns seen throughout
sixteenth-century Africa. These hand-carved
motifs were used to convey the diverse
cultural aspects evident among
the many African peoples.

◆

Amistad typeface was designed
by Maryam "Marne" Zafar.

◆

This book was published with the
assistance of March Tenth, Inc.
Printed and bound by Haddon Craftsmen, Inc.

◆

The paper is acid-free
55-pound Cross Pointe Odyssey Book.